Jacques Rose at his arraignment.

Beverage room at the Nelson Hotel — Robert Lemieux' residence — during Lemieux' appearance on T.V.

Paul Rose, Bernard Lortie, Francis Simard and Jacques Rose entering the Palais de Justice to set the trial date.

Lortie and M. Viger, who rented the hideout house.

Francis Simard.

Paul Rose in court.

Robert Lemieux (twice) and his father, applying for bail at the Palais de Justice.

Paul Rose arraigned in the Provincial Police Building.

Gaby

Pierre Laporte, Quebec Minister of Labour.

James Cross, after his release by the FLQ, in London with his daughter Susan, left, and his wife Barbara, right.

RUMOURS OF WAR

Ron Haggart and Aubrey E. Golden

new press Toronto

1971

Design/ Peter Maher

Illustrations/ Duncan Macpherson

Jacket photograph/ Toronto Star

Published simultaneously in the USA by Follett of Chicago

Parts of this book have previously appeared in Maclean's magazine.

Manufactured in Canada
ISBN 0-88770-037-3

To
Judith Golden
Laura & Kelly Haggart

Contents

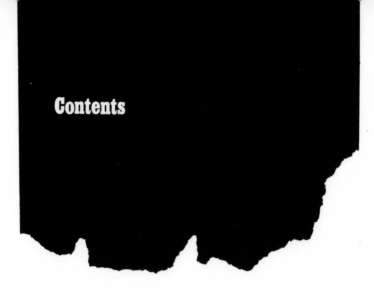

*"And ye shall hear of wars and
rumours of wars: see that ye be not
troubled: for all these things must
come to pass, but the end is not yet."*

St. Matthew, Chapter 24, Verse 6.

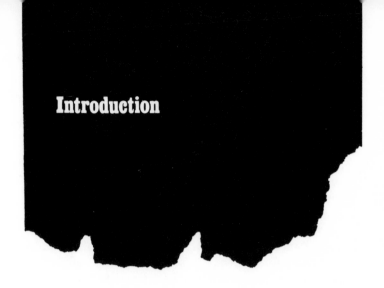

Introduction

There is a distinction, not always easy to see, between the settled majority view of a usually diverse nation and the emotional surge of the mob. In October of 1970, we felt a sense of unease, both of us, at the unprecedented waves of popular support in all parts of Canada which followed the suspension of civil rights in the Province of Quebec. Two men had been kidnapped and one of them subsequently murdered by two tiny bands of terrorists from the outer fringes of the much larger Quebec independence movement. In the few days between the kidnappings and the murder, hundreds of Quebec citizens found themselves in jail, the number eventually reached more than 450, although the vast majority was charged with no crime. Procedural guarantees such as the right to appear immediately in court were swept aside; membership was outlawed in an organization which had no rolls.

Each of us, one as a lawyer, one as a newspaper columnist, knew that the diminution of personal liberty, the abuse of individual rights by agencies both public and private, is always done in the name of a noble cause, always under the protective mantle of apparent legality and, most times, at the hands of honest men. Civil liberties are always most popular as a cause, we realized, when no threat exists to their exercise. Inevitably, the right of personal liberty is most severely tried in times of national emergency—real, apprehended or imagined.

Normally, everyone is in favor of a fair trial and all that jazz. The heat which tests the steel of our resolve is always more intense than that in which it is fashioned. We legislate, usually, in times of calm and enforce, too often, in times of passion.

We realized, too, that those who defend the beleagured must often share their fate. Those few who spoke out after Pearl Harbour against the confiscation of property owned by native-born Canadian citizens of Japanese ancestry (a number which lamentably included but one member of the House of Commons) often were catalogued as being in favor of enemy invasion. Those who believed that a Communist is perfectly capable of teaching mathematics in a state-supported school were made to answer for every excess of the Soviet system. Those who wondered why laws against obstructing the sidewalk were enforced against long-haired youths but not against window-shopping adults were thereby in favor of dirty feet and dangerous drugs.

Both of us had observed the "law and order" issue in the United States, particularly the "no knock" provisions of the 1970 District of Columbia Crime Bill, as well as the proposals advanced by Attorney-General John Mitchell (as amendments to the 1966 Bail Reform Act) which would keep many accused persons in jail pending trial and, in addition, impose a system of preventive detention. If Americans cared to look, they could see, just north of the St. Lawrence, a model demonstration of their attorney-general's repressive proposals. They might be interested to discover that those accused of substantive crimes in the wake of the Cross-Laporte kidnappings were not apprehended by the use of any new-found legal gimmickry but, rather, by ordinarily competent and diligent police work under the authority of the long-existing criminal law. That is not to say that the use of emergency powers in Canada was not effective. It was. It put eight times as many people in jail as were eventually charged with anything.

Neither of us is an absolutist. There are situations

which demand the breaching of our normal standards. The choice of time, and the sure identification of the victim, constitute the problem. We are not opposed to strength; we are opposed to strong-arm methods. We are uncertain whether there are absolute answers to the use of absolute power. There may, perhaps, be an acceptable historical rationalization for the expulsion of the Japanese from the West Coast of Canada. Perhaps the other citizens of the area needed the assurance, in time of stress, that their Government was doing *something*. We set for ourselves, therefore, this problem: Was the invocation of the War Measures Act and the regulations proclaimed thereunder an effective response consistent with the danger of the times, or was it the government giving reassurance by doing *something?*

We admit to our bias. Neither of us believes that civil liberties are the frosting on the cake, to be pushed aside frivolously. Neither of us believes that the rules of the courtroom are only the playthings of lawyers. Just as the internal combustion engine needs the cam shaft to exercise its power, so the liberty of the subject in a democratic state requires the fine mechanisms of the law to find effect.

The decision to undertake this project was made almost contemporaneously with the event which prompted it. In the days that followed, we were blessed, on the one hand, with an understanding editor in Arnold Agnew, vice-president of *The Toronto Telegram*, and, on the other hand, with understanding clients. Our task was materially assisted by Pamela Sigurdson, who initiated a number of sound expositions of Canadian law; by Maurice Green, who brought us a diligence in research and a background as an English law student; by Dr. Anne Golden, assistant professor of American History at the University of Toronto, who spent considerable time and effort on research into the use of emergency powers in the United States; by Anne Bogina, who typed her way through many tens of thousands of words of tape-recorded interviews, and then through the manuscript; by Maxine Crook, without whose organizational, research and interviewing skills too many of the facts would have remained obscure and too many people in jail would have remained anonymous.

Toronto   *Ron Haggart*
February, 1971   *Aubrey E. Golden*

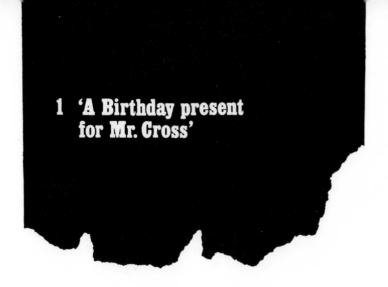

1 'A Birthday present for Mr. Cross'

Montreal, among its other delights, is a city whose streets are thick with taxicabs. With 2.4 million persons, it has 4,500 cabs and 1,300 of them bear the roof light of LaSalle. They are black, undistinguished cars, anonymous by their very familiarity; thus no one gave it much attention when yet another LaSalle cab stopped in front of the handsome stone house on Redpath Crescent which happens to be owned by the British Ministry of Public Works.

In his dressing room inside the house, Jasper Cross was puttering about in his bathrobe, his dog nearby; his wife, Barbara, was also getting ready for the day. As British Trade Commissioner in Montreal, a rank equivalent to consul-general, Cross planned later that day to meet David Nicholson who was arriving in Montreal as chairman of the Canadian committee of the British National Export Council. A reception for him had been arranged for the next day, all routine work for Cross, who had had five overseas postings as a career officer with the British Board of Trade, three of them in Canada.

He had left Kuala Lumpur in 1966 with some friendly apologies about leaving troubled Malaysia for a job at home running his department's trade fairs. Two years later he was sent to Montreal, and to the big stone house half-way up the side of Mount Royal. The house possessed a commanding view of the lights of downtown

Montreal, a view sweeping from McGill University down past the great tower of Place Ville Marie to the river bank and Terre des Hommes, the site of Expo 67.

Four men were in the LaSalle taxicab as it wound its way up the side of Mount Royal. They had stolen it that morning, but LaSalle has so many taxicabs nobody noticed. When they stopped in front of 1297 Redpath Crescent they were at the highest point the streets go on that side of Mount Royal. Behind the home of Jasper Cross was the woodland park where pheasants roam undisturbed, and here they had found the symbol they were looking for, the local representative of "English economic Imperialism."

A skillful driver was behind the wheel, 37-year-old, pencil-moustached Marc Carbonneau, a former taxi driver and a militant of the Taxi Liberation Movement, a group of perhaps 150 cab drivers dedicated to exploiting the legitimate grievances of Montreal's thousands of full and part-time drivers. A year before, almost to the day, a line of 75 cabs had paraded through the streets of Montreal to the garage of the bus company which had the monopoly to take passengers from the Montreal airport. A bus was sent rolling through the doors of the Murray Hill garage; other buses and the garage itself were set on fire. Pierre Vallières, the philosopher of armed revolution in Quebec, had written two years before of the need for "radicalization of social protest" and although most of Montreal's cab drivers rejected such notions, nowhere had the idea been more successful than with the Taxi Liberation Movement.

With Carbonneau in the taxi were three other men. One of them was Jacques Lanctôt and for him, at least, this was a third attempt at political kidnapping. His brother, François, was already in jail, charged with participating in two plans which went awry: one to kidnap the U.S. consul-general, Harrison W. Burgess, the other to kidnap Moshe Golan, the Israeli trade commissioner in Montreal. Three months before, in a raid on a cottage in the Laurentian mountains north of Montreal, the police had found pamphlets announcing the kidnapping of "the disgusting representative of the U.S.A. in Quebec", and demanding a ransom of half-a-million dollars in gold bars and the release of 13 convicted bombers and bandits they referred to as "political prisoners". Not without their own cutting humour, the planners of the kidnapping referred to the half-million dollars as a "voluntary tax", the same phrase Montreal's Mayor Jean Drapeau had used to describe the civic lottery he conducted (and later stopped when the courts ruled it illegal) to help bail out Montreal from its $28 million deficit after Expo. As a result of that discovery in the Laurentian cottage, François Lanctôt and some others were in jail, and a police guard was posted at the home of Harrison Burgess, not far away from the home of Jasper Cross. But Cross had no police guard. He was soon to become a name known in headlines around the world, the first kidnap victim of the Front de Libération du Québec. Dozens of the friends Jasper Cross had made in a lifetime of amiable diplomatic service were to remark how curious it was to learn for the first time, in such a bizarre way, that his full and proper name was James Richard Cross.

Cross had turned 49 six days before the Monday morning in October, 1970, when the front doorbell rang and two men announced to the Portuguese maid Analia Santos, who had her baby in her arms, "Birthday present for Mr. Cross." They displayed a long, brightly wrapped gift-package and Mrs. Santos said she did not have a pen to sign for it. "Here's one," said one of the men, pulling a revolver from his inside pocket. Pushing the maid into the house, the two men opened their gift, and withdrew a sub-machine gun. "It's the FLQ," they said.

Upstairs in his bedroom, Cross encountered the invader with the revolver. He told Cross to lie face down on the rug, then he called for his companion with the submachine gun, who escorted Cross into the dressing room where the gun-wielder put Cross' clothes on for him.

Within a few minutes Cross was downstairs, where a third man with yet another submachine gun had appeared, and with a raincoat thrown over his shoulders, Cross was escorted to the cab and told to lie on the floor. Across the street, gardener Domenico Lasource had paused at raking the fall leaves when he saw a woman on the front porch at the top of the high stone steps; she was convulsed in tears. His first thought was that she was a lady who had been beaten up by her husband.

The taxi drove for about five minutes and Cross was transferred into another car, this time with a gas mask over his face, paint obscuring the eye-pieces. The LaSalle taxi was taken back to its garage and nobody ever missed it. In a beaten-up old Chrysler, Cross was taken to a small house in the suburb of Montreal North, and there Cross was to spend the next 59 days—the 12th diplomat to be kidnapped in the Western Hemisphere in 13 months, but the first in North America.

René Lévesque was in his office across the street from a littered roofing company storage yard; he was preparing to leave for a three-week vacation to think over whether he should continue as leader of the Parti Québecois. The party, a successful amalgamation of several separatist groups, had fought its first election campaign six months before on a platform of democratic socialism. It also promised, if elected, a referendum to decide if the people of Quebec desired a separate country. When he heard of the kidnapping, that afternoon, he knew there could be no holiday for him. In the weeks ahead, he would have to fight off the compromising embraces of those far to his left who had brought political terrorism to Quebec and who scattered their communiqués with embarrassing tributes to Lévesque. Fighting back, he was to call them "sewer rats".

In Ottawa, Robert Stanfield began to take a few precautions for his own safety. He began to confine his walks to the well-travelled roads near his official residence in Rockcliffe. It occurred to him that as Leader of the Opposition in Parliament, he could be a prime target for political kidnapping. The test of whether the Government was being fair and judicious would be particularly grave if the victim was a Government adversary.

Because Cross was a foreign diplomat, the Federal Government's share of responsibility was assigned to the Department of External Affairs. Within a day, telephone and telecommunications equipment was moved into its East Block headquarters on Parliament Hill, where a command headquarters was quickly established. In Quebec, the responsibility fell to Jérôme Choquette, to whom the irony must have been apparent that when he came into office in April he had said he wanted to be known as Quebec's most liberal Minister of Justice in a decade. Almost his first official act had been to instruct Crown attorneys to no longer oppose bail for Pierre Vallières, whose conviction for manslaughter had been overturned in scathing language by the Quebec court of appeal. After four years in jail, all of it while awaiting trials and appeals, Vallières was released on bail in early May.

For Premier Robert Bourassa, still untried in office, a major decision to be made at once was whether to continue with a trip to New York to convince bankers and brokers that Quebec was a sound place to invest. On Tuesday, the day after the Cross kidnapping, he made up his mind to go, as planned, to New York on Thursday. The Quebec cabinet met for hours on end with a leader many of them hardly knew. They were more familiar with Bourassa's deputy, Pierre Laporte, who had been his rival for the leadership. Laporte was an old hand around Quebec City, both as muck-raking journalist for *Le Devoir* in the days of Duplessis and now as Minister of Labor. "There is a wind of madness blowing across the province," Laporte said, going into the first cabinet meeting after the Cross kidnapping, "I hope it won't last long."

The Montreal police, called to the home of Jasper Cross that morning, somehow got the wrong address and ended up at the home of the Greek consul. They were

20 minutes in straightening out the confusion and by the time they got to Redpath Crescent, so far as Jasper Cross could reconstruct it afterwards, he was already inside the bare, ground-floor flat in Montreal North which his kidnappers had rented the month before. The little house was the only investment its owner had, so that police checks with rental and real estate agents would never find him. And if the rent was paid on time, which it always was, he seldom went near the house. From that direction at least, privacy and anonymity were assured.

At noon on Monday, the kidnappers tried the first of what was to become their routine method of communication: a phone call to radio station CKLM directing it to a hidden communiqué. Most of the later ones were to be found in trash cans and phone booths in or near the Montreal subway, but the first one was found in a locker in the Lafontaine Pavilion of the University of Quebec. It bore a striking, in fact an almost word-for-word, similarity to the communiqué which had already been discovered in the thwarted plan to kidnap the U.S. consul. "Here," the Cross communiqué began, "are the conditions that the ruling authorities must fulfill in order to preserve the life of the representative of the ancient, racist and colonialist British system . . . "

There were seven demands which, in summary, were: 1. An end to police investigation. 2. Wide publicity by press and radio for the FLQ political manifesto. 3. The release of 20 "political prisoners" either serving time or awaiting trial, plus the discharge of three others awaiting trial on bail. (The list included Jacques Lanctôt's brother François but not, curiously enough, Pierre Vallières, then free on bail, and the man whose writings had supposedly inspired Quebec's escalating reign of terror.) 4. Air transportation for the "political prisoners" to Algeria or Cuba. 5. The rehiring of postal truck drivers in Montreal who had been unceremoniously thrown out of work when the government changed contractors. 6. The same $500,000 in gold bars as would have been demanded in the Burgess plot. 7. Public disclosure of the informer ("this low scoundrel") who led police to the Laurentian cottage.

By the evening of the second day, the federal and Quebec cabinets had agreed on the answer to be given and the hot line had exchanged their consensus. Mitchell Sharp, the Minister of External Affairs, told the leaders of the opposition parties, and then rose at 8 p.m. in a House of Commons which, preparing to discuss the Canada Grain Act, contained a bare 17 of its 265 members; most of the rest were at the Prime Minister's official residence for a reception for MPs and their wives.

Sharp's reply to the kidnappers was, on the one hand, a flat refusal of their demands, but on the other hand, the offer of negotiations in some form. He was careful to reject "this *set* of demands", indicating that there were other demands the two Governments might well consider.

"Clearly, these are wholly unreasonable demands," Sharp told the near-empty chamber, "and their authors could not have expected them to be accepted. I need hardly say that this set of demands will not be met.

"I continue, however, to hope that some basis can be found for Mr. Cross' safe return. Indeed, I hope the abductors will find a way to establish communication to achieve this.

"All the authorities concerned are dealing with this case on the basis that we have the double responsibility to do our best to safeguard Mr. Cross and at the same time to preserve the rule of law in our country.

"The House can be sure that everything possible is being done. I trust that honorable members will not ask me to go into this delicate matter further at this moment." The few members there were those interested in the Grain Act and they respected the Minister's request.

The "tough line" was undoubtedly popular in Canada although it was difficult to determine precisely what it meant. Stanfield's understanding was that: "They weren't going to make any concessions excepting possibly minor ones and, as I recall it, their purpose was to keep the discussions going." A minority, but influential view was that the government should negotiate on the basis of the FLQ statement.

Claude Ryan, the editor-in-chief of *Le Devoir*, asked the question: "How far do we have to go to save a human life?" In answering his own question, Ryan wrote: "The Canadian authorities should consider seriously the possibility of releasing a number of prisoners for Mr. Cross' life . . . It appears that his life could be saved by considering the release of a few of the prisoners at least. The number of prisoners to be freed can be a matter of discussion." Ryan's view was that the prisoners would be carrying on the same political agitation whether they were inside a Canadian jail or in some foreign land, a point he blunted by adding: "In financial terms, the cost of their trip will be compensated for by the money, that the Government will save in not keeping them in prison."

Ryan had not been a supporter of Pierre Trudeau for the Liberal leadership in 1968, nor of the Liberal party in the national election which followed. But *The Toronto Star* had supported both and its first reaction was to urge a considerably softer line than Mitchell Sharp's first statement. The "ransom must be paid," *The Star* declared on the day after the Cross kidnapping. Despite the objection that success in one kidnapping might encourage others, said *The Star*, "We believe that the government should—after bargaining for a reduced ransom—meet the kidnappers' demands. Diplomats like Mr. Cross are in a very special sense under Canada's protection. Securing the trade commissioner's release, unharmed, must take precedence over everything else; it is an obligation of honor."

Thus, the two most influential liberal newspapers in the country, speaking in both official languages, saw the problem in the first week, at least in part, as a problem of money. Claude Ryan was going to save the Government prison expenses; *The Toronto Star* thought the ransom was too high, and should be reduced, but paid. While these were minority views, they were symptomatic of a general view in the first week after the Cross kidnapping that the country faced a serious and new type of crime, but certainly no crisis. Bourassa went off to New York as planned. The MPs went to their party as planned. Arrangements went ahead for Trudeau's forthcoming trip to Russia.

Immediately after the kidnapping, the first reports began to appear in the press of the huge amounts of dynamite believed to be in the hands of the FLQ. *The Toronto Telegram* on Wednesday gave modest display to the statement that: "Police say the FLQ is believed to have 9,000 pounds of dynamite in its possession as the result of thefts throughout Quebec. It also has machine guns, recoil-less rifles, and mortars, stolen from armouries." The next day, The Canadian Press improved on these figures by reporting that: "Nearly 10,000 sticks of dynamite have been stolen (in Quebec) so far this year . . . . . "

The dynamite figures were to become a major consideration in the days ahead. Some dynamite had fallen into the hands of Quebec terrorists, but it could not possibly have been as much as the exaggerated figures which found their way into the press and, eventually, into the minds of the federal cabinet ministers who were making the crucial decisions during the crisis. In 1969, all thefts of dynamite throughout Quebec amounted to 4,117 sticks, according to figures kept by the Quebec Police Forces. In the first 10 months of 1970, up to the time Jasper Cross was kidnapped, another 2,576 sticks were stolen, for a total of 6,693. It went completely unnoticed at the time that the rate of thefts had fallen drastically in 1970.

Still, 6,693 sticks of dynamite is a lot of dynamite, but several factors made the facts less ominous than they seemed. Dynamite is stolen for any number of reasons, the chief one being that it is a product with value that is there to be stolen. (Similarly, a theft of rifles from a ship at Three Rivers during the height of the FLQ crisis turned out to be without significance: the guns were stolen by longshoremen with an eye to profit, not politics.) Farmers and others use dynamite to clear their fields and to blast out beaver dams; they do not always come by it legally. Some of the "stolen" dynamite was undoubtedly simply abandoned by road gangs and other legal users who did not fancy transporting it back to storage. Dynamite is stolen everywhere, but only Quebec keeps figures.

Unless dynamite is stored in a cool, dry, well-ventilated location, it deteriorates quickly and becomes either useless or highly dangerous. It freezes at a temperature warmer than the freezing point for water and becomes useless. Its optimum storage temperature is 65 degrees; its sensitivity to shocks rises rapidly with an increase in temperature. It disintegrates in conditions of moisture or humidity. Dynamite storage is a considerable problem in the continental climate of Montreal, with its hot, humid summers and freezing winters. Indeed, it was known at the time of the FLQ crisis that at least one cache of dynamite had been buried in the Laurentian mountains north of the city by a terrorist group. No one with any knowledge of dynamite would bury it in the ground, and when found the dynamite was, of course, useless.

In any event, the report that "nearly 10,000 sticks have been stolen so far this year" was false. About 6,700 sticks had been stolen in 22 months, but by the fall of 1970 much of that dynamite had disintegrated. The report that the FLQ had 9,000 *pounds* of dynamite was simply ludicrous. Since the common half-pound sticks were the most likely to fall into FLQ hands, this presumed 18,000 sticks, or almost three times as much as had been purportedly stolen throughout the vast terrain of Quebec in almost two years. Like all legends, the notion of huge FLQ storehouses of dynamite had a foundation in fact: the FLQ did have dynamite. The kidnappers of James Cross, for example, had dynamite in their house in Montreal North, an amount totalling 40 sticks.

On the first day after Cross' kidnapping, the police kept under observation as many members of the FLQ as they knew. At dawn on the second day, they raided a number of houses and took into custody 27 men and three women. By Friday, the fourth day after the kidnapping, the police had made by their own count 1,001 raids and had detained overnight or for other brief periods, some 44 persons. A week later, the police were to complain that the normal requirement of obtaining arrest and search warrants was hampering their work.

On Thursday, October 8, the complex meaning of Mitchell Sharp's statement in rejecting "this *set* of demands" became more clear: the Government acceded to one of the demands. Over Radio-Canada, the French language arm of the nationally-owned Canadian Broadcasting Corp., announcer Gaetan Montreuil sat in front of a television camera and for 13 minutes read in a dull, flat monotone the manifesto of the Front de Libération du Québec.

It was not a pleasant task. The manifesto referred to "Trudeau the queer", and "Drapeau the dog", and "Bourassa the hypocrite" and the sidekick of the Simards (the wealthy shipbuilding family of Bourassa's wife—the name was spelled $imard in the original.) Since the broadcast was not carried in English, and not many English-language newspapers carried the full text (an expurgated version was carried on the wires of The Canadian Press) few English-speaking Canadians appreciated the enormity of the Government's concession.

The FLQ manifesto was full of the most outrageous slanders against private citizens, to say nothing of calling the Prime Minister of the country *la tapette.* An appreciation of the Government's concession was further diminished by euphemistic translations in the press. The Montreal *Gazette* said the Prime Minister had been called Trudeau the chatterbox; *The Montreal Star* admitted the word was slang for homosexual. Some reports merely said "effeminate"; *The Toronto Star* went all the way and said the phrase meant "Trudeau the queer".

Rémi Paul, the former Quebec Minister of Justice, was referred to as a whore and the owners of Murray Hill Limousine Service were called murderers. Others who got off more lightly, such as the Bronfmans (Distillers Corp.—Seagram's Ltd.) and the Steinbergs (a super-market chain) were called simply the employers of terrorized slaves. Several officials of both French and English-language universities in Montreal were identified by name and referred to as monkeys and sub-monkeys.

While these slanders were being broadcast in the French language, English-language viewers in Canada were watching the evening re-runs of that afternoon's Speech from the Throne, which is written by the Government and handed to Governor-General Roland Michener to read. The Government, on the afternoon of October 8, did not feel inclined to alter the Governor-General's script, which said of Canada's internal problems: "None takes the form of those dilemmas or irreconcilable issues which elsewhere fire the violence of despair. Notwithstanding its difficulties, Canada continues to enjoy social stability to an exceptional degree."

The Governor-General's script contained, rather uncharacteristically for such occasions, a long and pious passage of Canadian self-congratulation:

"This stability is not simply a matter of luck. Good fortune is a factor, but we should accept gracefully the fact that we are also more amenable to reason and, perhaps, more capable of wise decision than we are normally willing to admit. The burden of our European inheritance and our fascination with our American neighbors tend often to distract us and cause us to be unaware of that reasonableness and that wisdom.

"We forget to our disadvantage, for these are traits that have made Canada a land of freedom. Canadians should pause on occasions such as this to reflect that their country is regarded by others with envy. It is a high place of liberty in the world. It is held in esteem because in Canada respect is paid to the individual; privacy and freedom of thought are honoured."

When the Governor-General was finished, Trudeau tabled a list of 68 bills which, having been referred to in the Speech from the Throne, represented the Government's concerns of the moment: legislation to control air and shipping pollution, cigarette advertising and phony bankruptcies, to guarantee easier bail and protection from wiretapping. The debate which followed, the next day, featured an eloquent address from the Prime Minister on the "Just Society", interrupted by the usual jibes from the Opposition benches. "I've never heard anything like it, it's a lot of bull," cried one MP at 2:45 p.m. that Friday afternoon.

Canada was very normal indeed. And at about that time, Jacques and Paul Rose and Francis Simard turned their car on to a highway in New York State, paused at a gun shop to buy some attachments for an M-1 rifle and headed back to Canada. The Cross affair, they felt, was not being taken seriously enough in Canada. That same Friday, the police decided that if they could find one man who had slipped out on bail earlier in the year, they would find Jasper Cross; they knew now they were looking for Jacques Lanctôt.

On the Thursday of the Speech from the Throne, Premier Bourassa flew off in a Government DH125 executive jet to meet investment dealers and government officials in New York. "We welcome foreign investment," he told them in Rockefeller Center. "The problems at home are not reason enough for me to cancel this trip. I have a plane waiting and ready and Montreal is just one hour away." Americans, he found, were not unduly concerned by the events at home which were occupying Canadian headlines. "In New York, they are used to these things."

Bourassa's airplane was not, however, scheduled to return directly to Montreal. His staff had been assigned to arrange a landing at Boston airport and a trip into the city for a picture-taking meeting with Senator Edward Kennedy. The Senator's staff had been at first reluctant; the U.S. elections were in full swing and Kennedy was running a "low-profile" campaign—the best way to dampen memories of the scandal which arose after the death of Mary Jo Kopekne, trapped underwater in a car the Senator was driving.

Senator Kennedy's staff finally relented and agreed to the picture. On Saturday, Bourassa prepared to go to Boston, but Boston airport was fogged in that day and for four hours Bourassa waited at LaGuardia for clearance to take off. He had changed by this time to a larger F27 jet owned by IBM. After the long, impatient wait, the plane took off, but by the time it reached Boston, fog had once again descended. The plane turned about and headed for Montreal.

When Bourassa and his party stepped out in front of the hanger of Atlantic Aviation, they found the Premier's limousine had failed to show up. They called for taxicabs and the Premier got into one, his bodyguard into the one behind and they drove off to the Holiday Inn for sandwiches. The choice of an ordinary taxicab contained its own irony; only the day before the police had begun to concentrate on finding Lanctôt who with Marc Carbonneau, had been a radical activist in the Taxi Liberation Movement.

On the way up to Montreal in the plane, Bourassa had expressed to one of his companions his surprise that Quebec seemed undisturbed at the kidnapping of Jasper Cross. "Isn't it alarming," he said, "that people aren't concerned."

When Bourassa's jet touched down at the airport at Dorval, the status of Pierre Laporte automatically changed—he reverted to his usual titles of Minister of Labour and Government House Leader. That afternoon, a 1968 Chevrolet was circling around the Montreal south-shore suburb of St. Lambert, and when Laporte came outside, just after 6 p.m., to toss around a football, two men in ski masks appeared and hustled him at the point of a submachine gun, into the car. But for the fog over Boston airport which turned Bourassa around in mid-air and sent him home prematurely, the FLQ would have had in their hands the Acting Premier of Quebec.

2 'Mon cher Robert, my life is in your hands'

In the single moment of Pierre Laporte's kidnapping, the crisis escalated a thousand fold. In the week after the Cross kidnapping, the negotiations with the kidnappers had been carried out as a cool, dispassionate diplomatic exercise. There were days when it was mentioned only passingly in the House of Commons: Stanfield asked one day if there was any news on Cross, and Trudeau said there wasn't. That was the end of it. The kidnapping of Cross at first seemed a single criminal incident but a second kidnapping carried the implicit threat of a third. The crisis was now greater than the sum of its parts. The knowledge of stolen dynamite, caches of guns and training camps in the Laurentians had been interesting recent history at the time of the Cross kidnapping, now they became real and relevant dangers. The greatest and most genuine fear was the fear of the unknown. On the authority of the Prime Minister himself, messages were sent to important French-Canadian men of business and politics who seemed the next most likely victims of vengeance kidnapping. Yves Pratte, president of Air Canada, and Paul Desmarais, chairman of the conglomerate Power Corporation whose personal portfolio includes *La Presse*, were both told from Ottawa: "We cannot be responsible for your personal safety."

In the days following the Laporte kidnapping, the offices were empty at Power Corp., symbol for some of "lackey" French-Canadian capitalism high in the tower of Place Ville Marie. No one was there but the armed guards. Mothers in suburban Pointe Claire drove their children the few blocks to school. On Thursday, Minister of Justice John Turner phoned from Ottawa to suggest to his sister in Montreal that she take the children out of town, to St. Andrews-by-the-sea, perhaps.

Throughout the week, communiqués had flowed from the kidnappers of Cross, setting deadlines and then extending them, appearing to threaten his life, then assuring his safety. At 5:30 p.m that Saturday, half-an-hour before yet another final deadline, Jérôme Choquette went on the air to reject totally any thought of negotiating over the fate of the 23 prisoners either in jail or awaiting trial. There would be no blackmail of the Government or the courts: "This signifies the end of social order . . . . We cannot accept the suggestions about those crimes which have been committed by the so-called political prisoners . . . . But we will consider the cases with clemency."

Pierre Laporte listened to Choquette on the radio at his pleasant suburban home across from the park on Robitaille Street, and he approved. Negotiate once, he had said earlier in the week, and you will have no end of kidnapping. He walked outside, threw the football to his nephew, and the hooded men arrived in the blue Chevrolet. It was a difficult place to find, but the kidnappers had been there before, looking around. The police, when it was their turn, got lost on the way.

The divisions in the Quebec cabinet were deepened by the knowledge they were dealing now with one of their own colleagues, a former rival to Bourassa for the leadership. In the leadership race, Laporte by and large had had the support of the Assembly politicians, Bourassa the money and the party hierarchy. Having just arrived Saturday afternoon at the Simard home in Sorel, Bourassa turned around and returned to Montreal, locking himself behind armed guards on the twentieth floor of the Queen Elizabeth Hotel. In a war of symbolism, it was an injudicious choice. He gathered opposition party leaders around him and got on the phone to seek advice from everyone he could think of. At three minutes to 10 on Sunday night, still behind guards in the hotel, he went on the air; he was as choked on the radio as he had been in his distraught and seemingly aimless telephone calls.

Before he went on the air, Bourassa had seen the pathetic, hand-written plea for his life sent to him by Pierre Laporte. "Mon cher Robert," Laporte had written, . . . "you have the power to dispose of my life." The kidnappings, three, four, twenty of them, Laporte wrote, would only end with the release of the "political prisoners." Laporte also repeated the demand that police activity be called off because if the police did find him "this would result in a murderous shoot-out from which I shall certainly not come out alive." The Laporte note reduced the demands, as previous FLQ notes had already done, from the original seven to only two. "One might as well act now," Laporte wrote, "and avoid a bloodbath . . . " Laporte had also written to his wife: "The main thing is that the authorities move."

The notes seemed at the time the anguished pleas of a man who, being French-Canadian, a liberal reformer and a staunch opponent of Quebec separatism, realized that he, far more than a foreign diplomat, faced the real threat of vengeance from his scraggly, demented tormentors who, he said, were letting him die little by little. Or was it all a clever code? The letter to Bourassa had said Laporte was the sole support of his mother, his own children and his late brother's children—"a dozen people are involved." This was a mis-statement of the number and Laporte added immediately afterwards "I think you will understand!" In his letter to his wife, Laporte put the date as October 12, although it was found on October 11. He was being held in a house on Armstrong St. within hailing distance of a large hanger frequently used by government aircraft at the St. Hubert air base—Hanger Number 12. It was painted in huge figures on the roof.

None of this was in Bourassa's mind, of course, when he made the painful decisions in the Queen Elizabeth hotel on Sunday night and, facing into the microphone, appeared to offer for the first time a way of releasing the 23 prisoners. He did not call them the "so-called political prisoners," as Choquette had done, he called them the "political prisoners" which was perhaps the most obvious concession of all.

"It is because we particularly want Mr. Laporte and Mr. Cross to live," he said, "that we desire—before discussing the demands that have been made—to set up mechanisms that would guarantee, as Mr. Laporte says it will, that the release of the political prisoners will surely result in the safe release of the hostages. That is a prerequisite that common sense forces us to require and it is for this reason that we ask the kidnappers to contact us."

The day before, and before Laporte's kidnapping, Choquette had said that no society could permit the decisions of its courts to be questioned or erased by blackmail. Now the premier was saying "We want to save the lives of Mr. Laporte and Mr. Cross and it is because we want it with all our strength that we are making this gesture." Was it a gesture, an offer of real negotiations involving the men in jail or awaiting trial, or was it a stall for time, a gamble to throw out the appearance of negotiations while the police continued their raids, their searches?

Claude Ryan, editor-in-chief of the intellectual, nationalist Montreal morning newspaper *Le Devoir*, had spoken to Bourassa on the telephone after midnight on the night of the Laporte kidnapping. "Immediately after the kidnapping of Mr. Laporte," he was to recall later, "I could sense that there were two trends among the people in authority. Some were in favor of seeking a negotiated solution and among these I would rank Mr. Bourassa himself, and some other members of his cabinet. Some were in favor of taking a hard line, and one example of this school of thought was Lucien Saulnier, chairman of the Montreal executive committee, who was in favor of resorting to drastic measures immediately after Mr. Laporte's kidnapping.

"From our position at the newspaper we followed the development of opinions in the government from hour to hour. We sensed that Mr. Bourassa was meeting with strong resistance on the part of some of his ministers, at the head of which was Mr. Choquette, the justice minister who was consistent all the way in his own approach.

"There was internal squabbling among themselves for about three days from the Sunday until the Wednesday. Four commentators speaking on the French television network of the CBC immediately after Bourassa's statement of Sunday night interpreted it as opening the way to negotiations, and so did I. But one of my colleagues phoned me immediately after the statement and said 'Don't rush to conclusions; you may be tempted to interpret it as positive. It may just as well be negative.' This fellow was right, because it was deliberately ambiguous."

"On the Wednesday, I learned from Mr. Bourassa himself that he was moving in the other direction. He phoned at one o'clock and he said in his typical Jesuit style—you must not appear to delude anyone—he said there is going to be a little move in the direction of firmness—a *petit virage*, I remember the words well. On the lips of Bourassa I knew it meant more than that. Under whose influence, under the impact of what new facts, I do not know . . . but I realized something was coming."

In Ottawa, Stanfield remembered the tight security in Quebec when he had attended conferences there. As premier of Nova Scotia he had been assigned a body-guard at a premiers' conference in the early 60s and he was astounded to learn no policeman had been in sight of the Laporte home.

On Sunday, Stanfield felt quite in the dark. He went downtown to do an interview for the CBC. "Ron Collister wanted to ask me whether I approved of the way the government was handling the thing and I asked him not to, and he didn't. Our interview was so dull the CBC didn't use it." About suppertime, one of Stanfield's speech writers, Tom Sloan, came out to the house with Bruce Phillips of the CTV network. "Phillips was a bit more hard-boiled and he persisted in the question. He asked me what I thought they should do that they weren't doing, so I said that two men's lives were at stake and I don't propose to discuss this on television. If I have any suggestions to make, any criticisms, I'll go directly to the government." Starved for news, and still having heard nothing from the government, Stanfield stayed home Sunday night to watch the French network and the W5 public affairs program on CTV.

20   On Monday, the Thanksgiving Day holiday across Canada, Stanfield finally took it upon himself to phone Mitchell Sharp. He was a bit hurt that Sharp had not called him already. Stanfield wanted to find out if the government was maintaining its position of no negotiation over the "political prisoners." Sharp assured him that was still the government's position. Stanfield's staff, meanwhile, was pressing him to go after Trudeau, to issue a statement demanding that the Prime Minister stop hiding behind Mitchell Sharp. But Stanfield couldn't see much sense in this proposal. There was nothing to say.

On Monday evening, the sky over Ottawa was filled with the unaccustomed, pulsating roar of helicopters, as 500 battle-dressed, fully armed soldiers arrived from Camp Petawawa and took up positions at public buildings and at the homes of diplomats and cabinet ministers. "It's not a move in keeping with the federal government's restrained performance since the crisis began nine days ago," wrote Douglas Fisher, introducing with some prescience the new phase of heightened tension and mood of crisis.

Stanfield had been told that afternoon that a guard would be placed at his official residence. At about midnight, he came sleepily downstairs in his dressing gown in answer to a knock, expecting that a trooper would be spending the night sitting in the front hall. He was astounded to find a lieutenant with 10 soldiers, a truck and radio equipment. A command post had been established in the Rockcliffe public school. The officer asked Stanfield how many people lived in the house and in which rooms they slept and from then on, they kept the outside lights burning all night. Stanfield never left the house whether for official business or for a brief walk in the morning without a soldier at his side. Tom Sloan from Stanfield's staff came by the house one night, but the sergeant in charge wouldn't let him in, and wouldn't go to the door to check if Sloan was acceptable. Sloan went home, phoned his leader, and came back again. But throughout the crisis, Mrs. Stanfield continued to go shopping by herself, and 17-year-old Mimi Stanfield walked unaccompanied along the Rockcliffe streets to the Elmwood private school for girls.

On Tuesday morning, Finance Minister Edgar Benson arrived at work on Parliament Hill in an armoured car with two military policemen. Marcel Lambert, a Tory MP, went innocently into his back garden in the morning to pick some flowers and found himself looking down the barrel of an M-1 automatic rifle. His next door neighbor was the Minister in charge of the Post Office, Jean Pierre Côté. The soldier who drove to work with Stanfield, clomped into the Parliament Buildings and into Stanfield's outer office.

Horrified MPs reacted immediately. There might be a crisis, but there were also the traditions of the House of Commons, the place not even the King may enter, nor the King's men (which is why the MPs leave their own chamber and go to the Senate to hear the Speech from the Throne read by the Governor-General.) There had probably not been an armed, on-duty soldier inside any House of Commons since the soldiers of Charles II stormed into Parliament at Westminster and demanded the arrest of six members, causing Mr. Speaker Lenthall to issue the famous words which through the centuries have defined the independence of the House of Commons from the executive (the Crown). "I have not eyes to see," he said, "but that which this House gives me," and the soldiers went away. The sentiments on October 13 were the same when Tory MP Gordon Aitken gave vent to his feelings: "The presence of armed troops here revolts me," and the soldiers were quickly withdrawn from the corridors of Parliament.

Although troops were stationed at the Ottawa home of every cabinet minister and at the homes of former Prime Ministers John Diefenbaker and Lester Pearson, one member of the cabinet came and went as informally as ever, free of armed escort. Yet Eric Kierans, of all the cabinet ministers, would have been the most symbolically attractive kidnap victim for Quebec terrorists: a bilingual "English" Quebecker, he had been president some years before of the Montreal Stock Exchange, scene of a tremendous blast of FLQ dynamite on February 13, 1968 which injured 27 persons and wrecked the trading floor. As Minister of Communications, Kierans had been in charge when the Montreal postal delivery contract was transferred from Lapalme to a group of other firms, without, in the first instance, making any provision for the 450 men thrown out of work. A group of Lapalme drivers still met every day at the Paul Sauvé arena in Montreal, still demanding that the jobs which had been subsequently offered them in the Post Office include the re-instatement of their old union; their rehiring had been among the seven demands made by the kidnappers of Jasper Cross.

Eric Kierans lived on a large and lonely, tree-shaded riverside estate, easy prey for kidnappers. But the riverside estate was across the Champlain Bridge from Ottawa, his property was the first house inside the Province of Quebec, which had not yet called upon the federal troops to assist the civil authority. There might be a crisis, but it was not permitted to upset the Constitutional niceties in order to guard the most obvious kidnap victim among federal officialdom.

During the week, troops were moved into camps around Montreal and on Thursday appeared on the streets for the first time, taking up guard duty at public buildings. Members of Parliament from Quebec were offered guards at home if they wanted them; Marcel Prud'homme of the Liberals turned the offer down. His Montreal constituency had voted separatist in the provincial election and he was not about to exacerbate the situation by making it appear he was unsafe among his own people. In Ottawa, it became a common joke that one's status could be judged by the number of soldiers encamped in the garden.

But whatever number of soldiers were deployed, and however conspicuously displayed, they could not solve the essential dilemma, which was: Should *any* bargaining take place involving the 23 "political prisoners"? Unlike the prisoners who had been successfully exchanged several times in Latin America, none of the Canadian prisoners had been convicted of political crimes such as sedition or treason. All had been convicted for physical crimes such as manslaughter, armed robbery and bombing; those awaiting trial had been charged with conspiracy to kidnap the U.S. consul-general. Neither could it be said that the sentences imposed were inconsistent with general Canadian practice unlike, for example, the Roman Catholic priest who poured blood on draft records in Baltimore, Maryland, a minor trespass which did not disrupt government functions, a symbolic crime which was punished with the harsh and patently "political" sentence of six years imprisonment.

Among the "political prisoners" whose release was sought was Edmond Guenette, who was 20 years old when he pulled the trigger inside the International Firearms store in 1964, killing the company vice-president. Convicted of non-capital murder, Guenette was sentenced to life. Serge Demers, an FLQ bombmaker whose products killed two people (but who gave Crown evidence in other trials) was serving eight years and 10 months. Pierre-Paul Geoffroy was serving a life term on 124 charges involving bombs, including the explosion at the Stock Exchange. Robert Levesque was a thief before the FLQ was founded; he had already served time for 18 thefts in Ontario before being sentenced in 1968 to seven years on charges of armed robbery, placing explosives and stealing rifles. It would be difficult indeed to conceive of any of these criminals as the victims of political trials or politically-motivated sentencing. The most obvious "political" prosecution had been the attempt by Quebec to convict Pierre Vallières and Charles Gagnon of murder after the bombing of a shoe factory, but Gagnon had been acquitted and Vallières, free on bail awaiting his second appeal, was not on the list of "political prisoners" for whom the FLQ demanded freedom.

Exchanges in Latin America had quite recently been successful. Five prisoners were released in Brazil in 1969 in exchange for a Japanese consul-general and 15 prisoners later in the same year in exchange for the U.S. ambassador. Forty were exchanged for the West German ambassador. Palestinian guerillas who had hijacked airplanes were released without charge by Britain, West Germany and Switzerland and the guerillas responded by releasing airline passengers held as hostages. In Guatemala, on the other hand, the West German ambassador was murdered when the government refused to release 25 prisoners; and in Uruguay, an American was killed when the government refused to release 150 prisoners.

In 1968, Pierre Trudeau came to the leadership of the Liberal Party as a man of stunning intellect, entirely free of political cant and humbug. He was certainly the first leader in Canada to be propelled into office by a campaign which began in the academic community, a rare enough event in any country. He was impossible to catalogue ideologically: during his leadership campaign he had been denounced by a tiny right-wing rump as a dangerous crypto-Communist (he had travelled to China without going through the ritual of denouncing Mao and all his works) while at the same time he had rejected one of the fundamental planks of the Liberal Party, the universality of social welfare programs. "We've had enough of this free stuff," he told the Liberal Party delegates in 1968, the same delegates who were hearing in an underground whispering campaign that he was a dangerous radical. His style was often of the university common room, more an intellectual exercise than debate, and he drew to his election campaign the same admirers from the campus, both faculty and students, as in the U.S. had flocked to Eugene McCarthy and Robert Kennedy. He had come to power at a time when political separatism was becoming a strong and respectable force in Quebec ("Equality or independence," the leader of the ruling Union Nationale party had said) and now the lunatic fringe of the separatist movement presented their terrifying dilemma. Two men's lives could be saved, at the price, it was said, of establishing the parallel power of banditry.

There was no lack of advice. Réal Caouette, the 25 car-dealer-leader of the Créditistes, demanded that 10 FLQ hostages be taken before a firing squad for every one of their victims. James Eayrs, professor of international relations at the University of Toronto, wrote in the *Toronto Star* that if a leader will sacrifice the life of an individual to any political abstraction, his followers one day "will find themselves not in the Happy Valley of the Just Society, rather in the canyon of totalitarian rule.

"If James Cross is crucified," Eayrs wrote on October 13, "we cannot fairly charge the government of Canada with his killing; the FLQ will have done that. But our government's decision may remind us of another, centuries ago. 'I am innocent of this man's blood; see to it yourselves.' Pilate's ghost stalked Ottawa's East Block Operations Room last week."

It was the greatest intellectual dilemma of Trudeau's life. Here was no exercise in logical alternatives being contemplated in the biting prose of *Cité Libre.* In the short run, two men's lives were at stake. Whichever choice was made—to bluff it out or to begin real bargaining—the country would be changed forever. Real bargaining, the critics said, would lead to ever-escalating rounds of kidnapping, as every bandit gang sought to get its colleagues out of jail but, like all such propositions, it was not subject to proof. On the other hand, if penitentiary prisoners, all of whom would in any event be eventually released, were sent instead into exile, which country would be the beneficiary? If exiled on parole, they could return to Canada only on penalty of serving out their terms. A refusal to negotiate would lead eventually to the release of all 23, none of whom could be deported, since 22 were native-born Canadian citizens and the 23rd was a citizen of Hungary, a country to which Canada will not ordinarily deport and, in any event, it was unlikely Hungary would accept him.

A policy of bluff, of public statements rejecting negotiations while at the same time making small concessions, could not go on forever. There might be any number of possible results, one of which was death. And if death ensued, what would the judgment of the country be? Would the country inflict the harsh analogy proposed by James Eayrs?

These decisions could not be made in the abstract. The facts which had to be weighed were clouded by the great unknown: What would the FLQ do? Would they kill?

Into the midst of this delicate conundrum strode the romantic, extravagant and vociferous figure of Robert Lemieux, a 29-year-old lawyer who in many ways represented within himself the dilemma of identity which afflicts many educated, middle-class French Canadians. Speaking English at home (as had Trudeau) but educated in French to college level (as was Trudeau) his family had followed the practice of "maintaining the culture", but Lemieux (as had many others) assumed an early contempt for French Canadian values. Early in life, his attitude had been "You can beat the system, learn English, get a good job." But he took his law degree at McGill, and there, as others had before, he encountered such half-witted bias against French Canada, he was turned completely around. "Had he taken his law at the Université de Montréal," said a friend, "Robert would have remained an English Canadian. It was McGill which made him a French Canadian."

Fired from a conservative, corporate law firm, he moved into cheap lodgings at the Hotel Nelson and had defended many FLQ suspects, including Pierre Vallières and a good number of the 23 "political prisoners." After the communiqué from the Cross kidnappers, he had busied himself rushing to see his old clients in jail, to ask if they would accept exile to Cuba or Algeria. Some wouldn't, but most would. Lemieux, available to any microphone or camera, announced from the beginning that the deal should go through. Without it, he warned, the FLQ would kill.

René Lévesque thought so too. He remembered the night of the April 29 election and the roaring, furious crowd at the Paul Sauvé arena as the results came in: The Parti Québecois received 23 per cent of the popular vote and won seven seats in the 108-seat assembly; Lévesque, the party leader was defeated. "A lot of our young supporters were in the hall," Lévesque remembered, "and we tried to make them swallow it, but a lot of them went out saying, 'never again, we've seen the way things can be manipulated.'

"We were working our goddamned hearts out trying to keep these guys channelled in the democratic way. It was funny, during all the time of the build-up to the election, there wasn't one single explosion, not a bomb. But when that election was over, and they saw what had been done, a lot of them ... well ... how many of those, I thought afterwards, became FLQ? I don't know."

On the day after the Laporte kidnapping, Lévesque spoke to Bourassa on the phone, urging him to negotiate and Bourassa had, indeed, gone on the air later that Sunday night with a speech apparently opening the way to bargaining, particularly by his reference to the "political prisoners" without any modification. Choquette had already offered safe conduct for the kidnappers themselves to Cuba, but after the Bourassa Sunday night speech, nothing happened. True, the police had charged Robert Lemieux with obstructing justice *before* the Bourassa speech, then the Quebec government had got him out of jail *after* the Bourassa speech and assigned him to do exactly the same thing, speaking for the FLQ, which had, just previously, landed him in jail. By Tuesday, the Quebec government's negotiator, lawyer Robert Demers, had asked for counter-hostages from the FLQ. If there had ever been any intention of negotiating, that signalled the end of it.

On Wednesday, Bourassa paused at the Montreal airport on his way to Thursday's special session of the National Assembly which would end the doctors' strike over medicare. Bourassa put in a call to Lévesque—he had already phoned Ryan to tell him of the *petit virage*, the turn toward toughness. "What the hell's going on," Lévesque shouted into the phone, "are you negotiating or aren't you?" Bourassa replied that they were, that Trudeau was keeping him fully informed and that Trudeau was still willing to confirm safe conduct out of the country for the kidnappers. "Jesus Christ!" Lévesque exploded, "that's what Choquette said *last week*."

Recalling the conversation later, Lévesque said, not without sympathy: "Honestly, he sounded like a man everybody was harassing. He said he had problems in his cabinet and he added 'I have the police on my back.'

"That's one very important fact," said Lévesque, "we had a rather inefficient police set-up. The police high command were trying literally to indoctrinate them with their demands for extraordinary powers, the same thing they did with Drapeau and Saulnier after the police strike.

"About the kidnappers, Bourassa said: 'Those kids, after all, those kids are from our own neck of the woods and basically they aren't bad, they won't kill.'

"That was his assessment. Whether or not he sold himself on that to support the gamble, I think that was the view they finally decided on: The kids won't kill.

"Our assessment was different, because of the quality of the communiqués, they looked like dedicated fanatics. And this Quebec frustration—once they start copying this sort of thing from the outside, they want to be taken seriously. If they aren't taken seriously, they will go the limit."

Lévesque picked up the phone and called Claude Ryan at *Le Devoir*. He hadn't spoken to him in more than six months and Lévesque was, to put it mildly, fed up with Ryan. He felt Ryan had rejected the Parti Québecois platform in the last election, then had supported the same points in the Liberal platform. The members of the Quebec leadership elite all know each other, and know each others' needs and responses. Lévesque, for example, was at university with Michel Chartrand; Chartrand went to private school with Trudeau; Trudeau chose Pierre Vallières as editor of *Cité Libre*, the links were endless. These associations are less corrupt than the Cliveden Set, less insidious than the "old boy net" of the English public service, but they serve the purpose of making possible the ever-shifting alliances of Quebec politics. Lévesque shared some jokes on the phone with Ryan about their recent animosities and then said: "What's your assessment?"

They came to the same conclusion: the "soft line" of negotiation was being abandoned, if indeed it had ever been adopted. Both knew that in Toronto that day, Ontario Premier John Robarts had gone out of his way to tell the press the Quebec situation was "total war" and the time had come to "stand and fight." Robarts with his declaration of "total war" was preparing the country for the War Measures Act, whose use at that moment was being prepared in Ottawa. Lévesque and Ryan may have had their differences, but they agreed on two points: Ottawa was forcing the Bourassa government into a tough stand, and the statement from Robarts was a mischievous intrusion into Quebec affairs. "Maybe it would be useful," Lévesque said, "and anyway it can't hurt, the way things are going, to put some pressure on Bourassa."

Lévesque suggested some names and Ryan suggested others and within a few hours they had organized a remarkable coalition: Louis Laberge, leader of the international unions in Quebec; Marcel Pépin, leader of

29

the national unions, others from the credit unions and teachers' federation, 15 in all. By that evening, they were meeting the press at the Holiday Inn to issue a statement urging negotiations and deploring the "atmosphere of almost military rigidity which one can blame on Ottawa, which risks reducing Quebec and its government to tragic impotence."

They could hardly have imagined what impact their statement was to have, not in the direction they hoped, but in steeling Trudeau's nerve to counteract what he was to call "confusion" in Quebec, what other Liberals were to call the erosion of the will to resist.

"We were scared," Lévesque said later, "Our assessment was that if the kidnappers were not taken seriously, they would kill."

A calm assessment of the situation depended not only on the current circumstances—what could be gleaned from the communiqués—but also on what could be learned from the FLQ's past and what could be expected from it in the future. In six years there had been some 200 bombings in Quebec. Six deaths resulted from terrorist bombings and holdups and while all were legally murders, none had been a planned assassination. These experiences, while serious, could hardly compare with the recent history of violence in the United States where, in the 15 months ending in April of 1970, there had been 4,300 bomb explosions, 1,475 attempted bombings and, as a result, 43 deaths, 384 injuries and $21 million in damage. In the same period, New York City had a bomb incident on an average of once every other day.

Government decisions, in the absence of any clear knowledge of what the FLQ was, had to be based in part on the history of previous terrorism in Quebec and in part on informed guesses at what the kidnappers would do. One prediction, put forward by, among others, Premier Bourassa and his Minister of Finance, Raymond Garneau, was that the next step of violence was to be "selective assassination" which, it was said, had been revealed by Lucien Saulnier in an appearance before members of Parliament. (See Chapter 9, The Four-Point Plan.)

A second fear was of riots in the streets of Montreal, a fear which was heightened when 2,000 students in the arts and social sciences faculties of the University of Montreal (about one-third of the student body) voted on Thursday to close their school in support of freedom for the 23 "political prisoners." The administration building was occupied at the Montreal campus of the University of Quebec.

In addition, the arts and social science students at the University of Montreal, (but without the support of law and science students who are traditionally more conservative) planned a mass rally for Thursday night. A typical news report (from *The Toronto Telegram* of October 15) declared that this rally "raised the possibility of violent street demonstrations in support of the Front de Libération du Québec." Denied a meeting hall at their own university, the students walked to the Paul Sauvé arena, waited around until the anti-administration municipal party, FRAP, had concluded a fund-raising auction and then, with the consent of the FRAP leaders, took over the arena for their own meeting. Robert Lemieux rushed up from one of his endless series of press conferences at the Hotel Nelson, together with labour leader Michel Chartrand and Pierre Vallières.

There were a few raised fists, and some chants of "FLQ, FLQ" in response to one of Chartrand's typically hectoring, insulting and rambling speeches. Bourassa, he said, has the courage of Cross' convictions. He made the usual puns on Trudeau's name (waterhole) and said the presence of federal troops was analogous to Vietnam where "in order to stop communism, you bomb the people." But, said Chartrand, "I don't think the FLQ wanted to replace the government in this instance."

Instead, he said, the revolutionary goals represented by the FLQ were gaining new popularity among the people of Quebec. "There is no doubt," he said, "that there are infinitely more people now in accord with them, who understand and sympathize with the objectives of the FLQ than there were in 1963 and 1966.

"Journalists agree that 50 per cent of the people of Quebec sympathize with the aims of the FLQ. Even the trade unions of which I am a part, bourgeois capitalists that we all are, went so far as to actually demand the release of the prisoners, which for trade unionists around here borders on the extraordinary. That's the most fundamental change, it's an extraordinary mental change." The worst time to strike, Chartrand added, drawing on his trade union experience, is when the boss wants you to strike. And with a few more chants and shouts the meeting broke up and the students went home. It was after midnight, early in the morning of October 16; there had been no riot.

In Ottawa, the wheels of government were already turning. The full cabinet had met twice during the day and had authorized its security and intelligence committee (essentially, Trudeau, Sharp, Turner and Mc-Ilraith) to meet at 10:30 p.m. to make the final decision. In the middle of the night, an assistant secretary to the cabinet drove to Government House to get Governor-General Roland Michener out of bed.

Raymond Garneau at this point was able to take a level-headed and sophisticated view of the strikes, rallies and sit-ins at the campuses in Montreal. He had been holding meetings with student leaders and Garneau reported: "We all know that in normal circumstances during the month of October—I've been a student myself—the month of October is conducive to student activities. It is obvious that there was a possibility that mass action could be taken. In large part, this would have been to take a few days holiday and demonstrate, which is perfectly understandable in the student milieu. It is obvious to me after the conversations I have had with student leaders that are not involved in the terrorist movement—and that is the large majority—that they are very hesitant because they are aware of the seriousness of the situation and they do not want to risk their academic year. Neither do they want to risk the breaking-up of Quebec society." Such sober-sided analysis was rare in the middle of October and (so far as the authors can determine) was never published in the English-language press.

An attempt to predict what the FLQ would do on the basis of past terrorism was as fruitful as consulting the astrology tables. There had been some 200 bombing incidents in Quebec between 1963 and 1970. Groups calling themselves the Liberation Front or the Liberation Army had gone through five separate phases, each distinct from the other, and the chief lesson of this experience was that an incredible amount of damage can be caused by a handful of people, or indeed, by one person. A flurry of bombings in 1966 suddenly ended in 1967, not because of any ideological regrouping but because young Serge Demers stopped making bombs. Another year-long series of bombings which included army offices in Montreal, the Liberal Reform Club, the Montreal Stock Exchange and the federal government bookstore, ended early in March of 1969 with the arrest of Pierre-Paul Geoffroy, who was responsible for at least 31 explosions and who eventually was sentenced to 124 terms of life imprisonment.

Later in 1969, bombs began to explode again, although many seemed less for the cause of "liberation" than for the cause of the CNTU construction workers in Montreal who, contrary to the advice of their top officials, were resisting a wage settlement. The central office of the CNTU was bombed, so was the office of the Minister of Labor. Other explosions were ludicrously amateurish, such as the green-house at McGill University. Others were narrowly-avoided disasters, including the 4 a.m. bomb which wrecked the modest home of Mayor Jean Drapeau on September 28.

Within two weeks of the explosion at Drapeau's house, the Montreal police staged a one-day strike, leading to a two-million-dollar downtown riot. Although explosions at such disparate targets as a trade union office, a university greenhouse and the mayor's home seemed hardly to display a common purpose, there was a pattern emerging in official thinking. Lucien Saulnier gave voice to it in 1969 when he told MPs in Ottawa that a revolution was beginning on the streets of Montreal. At about the same time, Mayor Drapeau came, not surprisingly, to the same conclusion and he also decided what had to be done.

After his home was bombed, Drapeau said to one of his liberal friends: "See, this is the result of the kind of liberties people like you are advocating."

"Do you have any idea who did it?" his friend asked.

"No," Drapeau replied, "and we won't have unless and until we are given more extensive investigative powers than we have now. In some European countries, they can pick up 500 people in erratio (at random) and keep them in jail for two, or three, or four weeks, as long as they refuse to talk. This is the way we must deal with the situation, but nobody wants to accept it in this country."

At 9 p.m., on Thursday, October 15, Bourassa repeated the offer of safe passage out of Canada for the kidnappers of Cross and Laporte, adding that Quebec would recommend to the federal authorities parole for five of the "political prisoners" who were already eligible for parole. He demanded an answer by 3 a.m., a time which coincided with the arrival in Ottawa of the letters from Quebec and Montreal requesting special powers to cope with an insurrection. The decision of the security committee of the cabinet had already been made, and so D. F. Wall, an assistant secretary to the cabinet, drove from Parliament Hill to Government House to get Roland Michener's formal signature on the document which would, as of 4 a.m., invoke the War Measures Act and give force of law to a set of regulations the like of which had never been seen in Canada's peacetime history: Support of the FLQ was a crime subject to five years' imprisonment but anyone, supporter or not, could be jailed for three weeks without any charge. Those charged could be held at least three months without bail, and for longer periods upon the word of one official, the attorney-general of Quebec.

Television and radio sets stayed on throughout Canada on that Friday, October 16 as teams of policemen brought into jail everyone from Pierre Vallières and Robert Lemieux to a hapless member of the Liberal Party in Hull (together with his vacation slides) and a photographer, Ronald Labelle, who had sold pictures to *Perspectives* and *Weekend* of two Quebeckers taking rifle training with the Palestinian Liberation Front.

The audience around the radio at 5630 Armstrong St. that Friday afternoon was particularly attentive. In the next room, within earshot of the news, Pierre Laporte lay on a bed, one set of handcuffs binding his wrists, another set securing him to the bed, his eyes smarting from the pain of his ever-present blindfold. He had arrived at that house with his eyes bound by Kleenex and tape and, except for brief moments of exercise, eating and letter-writing, he had been blindfolded for a week. A few days before, in one of the hundreds of raids which had been conducted even before the War Measures Act, the police visited a house not far from 5630 Armstrong St., which had frightened Pierre Laporte no less than his captors.

The first morning in this little house in St. Hubert he had eaten a ham sandwich and some tea. Occasionally, he had some tea after that but for most of the time he ate nothing, because there was nothing to give him. The $60 in his pocket he had offered to his captors and much of it went to pay for Paul Rose's taxi rides around Montreal to plant communiqués from—as they now described themselves—the "Chenier financing cell."

The Chenier financing cell of the Front de Libération du Québec was founded in an old yellow Valiant on a highway in the state of Texas on October 5, the day Jasper Cross was kidnapped in faraway Montreal. The news came over the radio. "That's crazy" exploded one of the passengers, "the government will never give in for a guy like that." The car turned around and headed non-stop for Canada, retracing in less than four days the leisurely trip that had taken almost two weeks.

Mrs. Rosa Rose, whose yellow car it was, had been pleased to leave Montreal with her two sons Paul and Jacques. A loving, working-class French-Canadian mother, she had been proud of her sons, one of whom had become a teacher, but displeased at their activities in the past two years in organizing flamboyant displays against the private American-owned fishing lodges in the Gaspé. When Jacques appeared in September with a $600 cheque from the Canadian National Railways, she had joined Paul and Jacques in what she thought was a permanent move to the U.S. The finance companies were after them, and now, with an amount of cash that seemed a small fortune, she was ready to start a new life. The dream ended as the car swung around and sped back home, with Paul and Jacques taking turns at the non-stop driving with their friend Francis Simard. They had tried to buy revolvers in the U.S., but without success. In New York State, as they began the last leg of the trip home, they bought some attachments for an M-1 rifle and, home at last on October 8, they had breakfast at a Woolco store with their mother, and then drove her home. From a pawnshop on Rue Notre Dame, they bought two M-1 rifles and a 12-gauge shotgun.

The house on Armstrong St. was waiting; Paul Rose had rented it the previous April under the name of Alain Blais as a pad to share with an old friend, Lise Balcer. They picked up a friend, 19-year-old Bernard Lortie, and made their preparations: they cut a hole from the garage through a wall into the house, so their victim could be brought in without being seen. Francis Simard put on a false moustache, Paul Rose a blond wig, Jacques Rose a gray wig, Bernard Lortie pulled down the flaps of an army cap, covering his face with a piece of cloth into which he had cut eyeholes. They had already decided on Laporte and had driven past to see that he was still home. They waited for Jérôme Choquette's Saturday afternoon speech and when they heard his strong denunciation of compromise (" . . . for this is the end of social order . . . ") they set out for Laporte's house. On the way back to St. Hubert with

Laporte covered in trench coats on the back seat, a police car passed them. They stopped, let out Simard, who went off to deliver the communiqué they had already prepared.

A week later, Laporte still lay on the mattress from which he was allowed up for only brief minutes of exercise. Listening on that Friday afternoon to the radio reports of the massive arrests under the War Measures Act, Laporte came to a desperate decision. Slipping out of his handcuff, he lunged for the window, breaking the glass with his pillow. His body was half way through, with shards of glass cutting into his wrists and chest, when Jacques Rose ran into the room and pulled Laporte back in. Lortie bound the wounds with bits of torn-up sheets, then headed in to downtown Montreal to find Paul Rose and tell him the news.

The debate in Parliament, beginning on the Friday morning, continued all day Saturday and into the early hours of Sunday, the debate which could have but one conclusion, Parliament's approval of the proclamation which had already sent hundreds into jail. Around midnight, the Speaker called for order as the buzz of conversations from the floor and from the galleries made it difficult to hear. At 12:45 a.m. Robert Borrie, a Liberal backbencher from B.C. rose to speak. Some, he said, had expressed concern because the War Measures Act gave too much power to the Prime Minister. "I say the power could not be in better hands." And then Borrie became the first to say what everyone in the chamber by that time knew. "A body has been found . . . it is Mr. Laporte." Borrie wound up his speech at once: "We are not dealing with political dissenters; we are dealing with organized murderers."

3 The debate in Parliament: non-facts and non-decisions

Parliament was like a small window, permitting the public to see some of what was taking place during the Cross-Laporte kidnap crisis. Through the daily question period and in rare instances during the debates on the proclamation of the War Measures Act and the subsequent legislation to replace the regulations, little glimpses were seen and pieced together. That, after all, is one of the functions of Parliament. It is a place where public information is exchanged. If the glimpses were irritatingly tiny, however, it should not be assumed that they left a great deal more to be revealed. The nature of the Cross-Laporte kidnapping crisis meant that there was precious little information at all. The news media chased rumours, spent a great deal of their time interviewing each other, and speculated.

One notable characteristic of Parliament is that it reflects, to a great extent, the mood of the Canadian people. It is more sensitive than most people think and it is especially good in reflecting emotions. As the country responded with horrified concern, so did Parliament; as the country was careful and restrained, lest the kidnappers carry out their threat to kill, so was Parliament.

The country's antagonism toward the kidnappers knew no bounds and no matter how slight the criticism of the government, each questioner and doubter among the Members of Parliament went through a careful ritual of disapproval of the actions of the FLQ lest he be confused with their supporters.

On October 16, the day the War Measures regulations were announced, Eldon Woolliams, a Calgary lawyer and Conservative Justice critic, was harpooning the government as much as he dared while still retaining the right to vote in its support in the test which was to come. But, he assured the House: "We want to be just as tough with the FLQ as the government. In fact, two years ago we wanted to get even tougher."

In its desire for information, the country began to look to Parliament. Questions were restrained, but asked as often as the circumstances allowed and the Members dared. The day after Cross was kidnapped Opposition Leader Stanfield asked Mr. Trudeau for comment. Trudeau had none except to say there was close consultation between the governments. Then Stanfield wanted to know about a reported halt in police activity. Trudeau said he had heard about it too.

Then the tentative, apologizing question, by Stanfield: "I do not wish to pry into something that I ought not to pry into, but I would ask the Prime Minister whether he is indicating that he himself does not know the reason for this report? Is the Prime Minister indicating that he does not know why there has been a halt in or a suspension of police activities."

If Stanfield had been asking to be reproached, he would not be disappointed. The answer came: "Mr. Speaker, I am rather disappointed that the Leader of the Opposition would press me on this point. Perhaps he can conjecture a little bit, that if the police do not want the life of Mr. Cross to be endangered they are calling off their activities—or perhaps they are only pretending to. I do not know."

The game had been played. A few debating points had been made and no one was further ahead in information. But the game had its cost, for if the credibility of a halt of the investigation was important so as not to endanger the life of the kidnapped British Trade Commissioner, Trudeau's crack, "or perhaps they are only pretending to," was not among his more intelligent utterances.

The proponents of capital punishment in the House did not lose one day in reflecting their particular segment of public opinion. Its reintroduction was suggested in two questions, one by Martial Asselin, a former Conservative cabinet minister from Charlevoix, Quebec, and another from Réal Caouette, Ralliement Créditiste leader who introduced his own bill to impose the death penalty for kidnapping on October 20.

The searches and the communiqués and responses stretched to the end of the first week when Pierre Laporte was kidnapped in an escalation of the crisis. The atmosphere grew tense. On Monday evening, October 12, following the Saturday kidnapping of the Quebec Labour Minister, military guards appeared around public buildings, watching over the homes and families of senior officials and diplomats, including the Cabinet. It was in this military atmosphere that the government dropped out of step with the events.

After the House met at 11:00 a.m. on the 13th, there was tense expectation in the air. Mr. Stanfield asked a restrained question, in keeping with the mood. "Mr. Speaker, I should like to ask the Prime Minister whether there is any further information he can give at this time with regard to the kidnapping cases?" And then, as if to make his solicitude very clear, he added: "I ask this question in full knowledge of the possible delicacies of the position and responsibilities of the Prime Minister."

The Prime Minister needed the question to make his statement, but paused to acknowledge that there had been the required deference to the situation. He answered: " . . . I appreciate the way in which the question was asked and I shall attempt to answer it as best I can." He went on to say that his government agreed with the Quebec approach to establish, through negotiation, the mechanism for the release of Laporte and Cross.

Then came a theme he also repeated outside the House along with his attack on those who wanted to give the kidnappers all or some of what they asked: "I do sometimes wish," he added, "that the media—radio, television and press—would exercise a bit more restraint in talking about these problems. It is a mistake, I think, to give them publicity, which is the thing they hope for most. I also think it is a mistake to encourage the use of the term "political prisoners' for men who are bandits."

By that Tuesday, after the Thanksgiving weekend, the pressures mounting on the Bourassa government were being felt with almost as much force in Ottawa. Later evidence indicates that by that date a plan had begun to evolve for a drastic shift in tactics, for a show of strength which would leave no doubt about who was in control. The plan would involve the reputation and prestige of the Trudeau administration and would be a transfusion of strength to Bourassa's, ending internal dissension and public feeling that the government was powerless to act.

The plan must have weighed heavily on the consciences of the senior members of the cabinet and Trudeau himself. The dangers were many, but the cause was worthwhile and the alternatives, as seen from Parliament Hill, were worse.

To buy the time necessary to put the plan in motion, Bourassa and Trudeau decided to stall. Robert Lemieux was released from his jail cell at about noon and "negotiations" were set up. The statements flew back and forth as press conferences took the form of separatist rallies. It was important that the kidnappers keep the feeling that there was still hope to make a deal.

Facing the television cameras in the late afternoon, Trudeau talked tough when asked about the soldiers. "Well, there are a lot of bleeding hearts around who just don't like to see people with helmets and guns. All I can say is, go on and bleed, but it is more important to keep law and order in the society than to be worried about weak-kneed people who don't like the looks of . . . "

He was interrupted by a reporter: "At what cost?" he was asked. "How far would you go with that? How far would you extend that?" Trudeau's mind was full of the plans being proposed to him. Plans of which Parliament had not yet heard. "Well, just watch me," he retorted. The next day his "bleeding hearts" and "just watch me" remarks were recalled to him in the House by Mr. Stanfield. He asked if consideration was being given to "the declaring of emergency police powers of the sort, for example, to permit the police to search without warrant and arrest and hold individuals for questioning without having to lay a specific charge or justify any such action?"

He received the answer that the government had been considering all possible types of action, including the one asked about, but that there was no decision made along those or any other lines "which is not obvious to the country and to Parliament." Stanfield pressed him for an assurance that no action of that nature would be taken without the approval of the House of Commons. The answer did not satisfy a worried Opposition. The following exchange indicates that by Wednesday October 14 the course was set. "I believe, Mr. Speaker, that this is a matter of law. Quite frankly, I do not think this type of suspension of civil liberties, if I understand the Leader of the Opposition, would be possible without some amendment to our statute or some action by the government which would have to be brought before the House at some point."

Stanfield: "Will the Prime Minister give the assurance that even if the government has this authority in law, no such action will be taken without seeking the approval of the House of Commons?"

Trudeau: "This is completely hypothetical. I repeat that if such action were ever contemplated it would certainly be discussed in the House of Commons. Whether it would be immediately before or immediately after would depend, of course, on . . . " There was an interjection of disapproval at this point. He then continued: "I am sorry to observe the lightness with which the opposition treats this question. It is obvious that if urgent action is needed at some time in the middle of the night we cannot ask Parliament to approve it first."

Thomas Bell, a New Brunswick Conservative, tried to get the last word by remarking: "All these things happen in the middle of the night." But the last word was John Diefenbaker's who must have been aware of what Trudeau had in mind: "You have no power to do it," he warned, "except through Parliament."

As Parliament moved on to the day's business, Bourassa's representative, lawyer Robert Demers, met with Lemieux. And at the Holiday Inn, later that day, a different sort of meeting took place—one which, unlike the lawyers', was not planned or approved by Trudeau. It would be to his distinct dislike.

Parti Québecois leader René Lévesque, Claude Ryan, editor of *Le Devoir*, Marcel Pépin and Louis Laberge, the leaders of the two major trade union groups in the Province, and eleven others of like mind had their press conference at the Holiday Inn in Montreal. Their statement was still being written as the reporters arrived. They pressed the government to release the prisoners in exchange for the two kidnapped men. They urged flexibility and negotiations and clearly placed the lives of the two kidnap victims in the highest priority of all.

The next morning, Thursday, October 15, Parliament met at 11:00 a.m. to continue the Throne Speech debate which had taken much of the day before as well. It must have seemed irrelevant and disconcerting to Cabinet members weighing and pondering what they were about to do. But there was a chance on Wednesday to discuss their specific plans, and they came close to doing it. The press had been full of speculation that day that the government planned to proclaim a state of insurrection under the War Measures Act. It was not widely believed.

John Diefenbaker, who had called for repeal of the War Measures Act in 1947, whose Bill of Rights contained measures which, he had hoped, would prevent its abuse and whose promise to study it by the use of a committee was never fulfilled, was waiting for the Prime

Minister on Thursday. "I now ask the Prime Minister whether the government has given consideration under the War Measures Act to bringing in emergency powers. In particular," he went on, "has the government secured from the law officers of the Crown, inasmuch as the Prime Minister described what is happening as a result of the kidnappings as 'this emergency', any opinion on whether or not the present situation falls generally within the wording of the Act to which I have referred which empowers the Governor-in-Council to do and to authorize various things because of the existence of 'real or apprehended insurrection'? Would the Prime Minister take Parliament into his confidence with reference to this matter?"

Trudeau: " . . . Therefore I would not be truthful if I said that we had not considered such measures. However, the fact that we have not taken them indicates that we have not considered them in a way that would cause us to act upon them, at least at this time." That was said as the War Measures regulations were being drafted. They were proclaimed seventeen hours later. He continued his answer. "As to the more precise question whether I have sought advice on this matter, the answer is that we have discussed the matter because in considering the various possibilities we have to know what are the conditions. I would suggest to the hon. gentleman that he would agree he has raised not only a legal question but, perhaps even more importantly, a question of fact which can best be understood and discussed by people who are aware of politics in this country as well as those who are aware of the law."

The Prime Minister then asked the former Prime Minister for his views either in the House or privately. Diefenbaker pressed on, trying to pin the government down on the War Measures Act, which Trudeau countered by again asking for the opinion of the leaders of the opposition parties, and his questioner as an ex-Prime Minister "who has a distinguished record in the matter of civil liberties." Trudeau finally provoked an outburst from Diefenbaker by suggesting that it was the latter who had suggested that the War Measures Act might be called for.

Except as a focus for speculation, the House was of little use to the country as a place to satisfy the thirst for information. The government's answer to the suggestion that it was helpless would come in the night. Under conditions of top security, squads of police were being briefed, letters to establish the record for the sake of formal correctness were drafted, signed and sent. The proclamation and the regulations were drafted and ready. The necessary personnel, key assistants to the Prime Minister, the couriers, were all there, counting on the excitement to help them fend off sleep, and waiting.

At 10:30 Thursday evening, Trudeau took the leaders of the opposition parties into his confidence as to what he intended to do. He neither asked for nor received agreement as to his proposed course of action and they departed to wait until the next day, when Parliament would enter into a debate of events already past and decided. But the facts would still elude it.

If the members and the country learned no more in the two days that followed the Prime Minister's announcement of the proclamation "that apprehended insurrection exists and has existed as and from the fifteenth day of October, 1970" it was because there was no more to know. Parliament had acted, the regulations passed and the police sweep had begun. Now there was a new focus of attention.

Parliament was the news. The government had acted and while the doubts were murmured in the background, a groundswell of public support began, as the people of Canada rallied around the only concrete event since the kidnappings. In the security of seeing something happening, Canadians would offer their support and the Members of Parliament soon saw this.

Robert Stanfield arrived earlier than usual on Parliament Hill that Friday morning. He had been told at the meeting in Trudeau's office the night before what was going to happen; now it was all over the radio. The only missing ingredient, Trudeau had told the party leaders, was the arrival of the formal requests from Quebec, the three letters all employing the word "insurrection." Bourassa's last offer to the kidnappers had expired at 3 a.m. and, as if by magic, the letters arrived in Ottawa at 3 a.m. and the Cabinet invoked the War Measures Act at four. A typist filled in the figures 3 and 4 in a press release that was already prepared, and the police in Montreal were on their way to homes all over the island well before five.

Stanfield, with 10 soldiers encamped in the grounds of his official residence in Rockcliffe, had already changed his daily routine. In the mornings, he no longer asked his driver to let him off at the Macdonald-Cartier Bridge so he could walk the last 20 minutes down below the Mint and along Sussex Drive to Parliament Hill. He felt he was a logical target for kidnapping, but that was not why he stopped the morning walks; rather, he felt embarrassed and conspicuous striding alongside a battle-dressed soldier, rifle at the slope. "I changed my habits," he said, "it was a little public to walk along Sussex Drive with a soldier with a gun." Instead, he took quick little walks in the morning along the shaded, more private streets of Rockcliffe, soldier in tow of course, many of whom to Stanfield's delight turned out to be from the Maritimes.

On Parliament Hill that morning, Stanfield moved to consult with the two sources of power in his party, and in the appropriate order. First he went in to see John Diefenbaker, author of the Bill of Rights and the party leader he had replaced, then he met with his caucus. In Diefenbaker's office, Stanfield related his understanding of the proclamation from the night before: The FLQ was to be outlawed, its advocates were being arrested. By this time, dozens of people in Montreal and other parts of Quebec were already in jail, the score for the day was 242, but the two men who would be most responsible for moulding Canadian public opinion, next to the Prime Minister himself, still did not know precisely what the law said. Neither did those in jail.

Diefenbaker was most concerned about the attempt to outlaw membership in an organization. It is not always easy to define what membership means. Not all members subscribe to every aim of an organization, they may not even know some of the aims. People join up or go to meetings for all sorts of reasons—out of curiosity, to make friends, to seem fashionable, or because their brother-in-law is going. Diefenbaker's concern about making membership a crime was of long standing. He, one of Canada's most ardent anti-communists (of the 'free the captive nations' school of thought) had stood against this method of dealing with the domestic Communist Party even in the early days of the Cold War. Diefenbaker's concern was a noticeable feature of Stanfield's speeches later in the day.

Stanfield had expected that by nine or so that morning he would have a copy of the regulations which were already sending people to jail. His staff phoned several times to try to hurry the government along. The Prime Minister's staff replied there had been a typographical error, and a copy of the regulations did not arrive until after Stanfield began to meet with his caucus at 10. At 11 that morning he would be called upon as leader of Her Majesty's Loyal Opposition to give the House of Commons, his party and the country his considered opinion on the most extraordinary grant of power any Canadian government had ever taken in peacetime. When the regulations arrived, the staff ran off a few copies on the office Xerox, mindful of the warning that the material was still secret. The caucus tried to reach a consensus, but Stanfield had to excuse himself early, explaining he had to go and make a few notes for his speech, and "I really haven't had a chance to read the regulations yet."

As he prepared his notes, Stanfield could not guess at the waves of popular support, the mail, the telegrams, the full pages of letters in the newspapers, which would soon break around him as the country rallied to the War Measures Act, and to Trudeau its sponsor. "We may be in the presence of a political giant," wrote Charles

Lynch for the 850,000 readers of the 11 Southam newspapers in a not untypical judgment. Stanfield's judgment on that Friday had to be based on what he had been told by the government, in briefings the first week from Mitchell Sharp and in the second week from Trudeau.

There were no great secrets. The party leaders had been told almost exactly what the House of Commons would be told, not on that first day, but in the days ahead as Trudeau slowly played out the facts and the reasons which had influenced the government. But men do not act on facts alone, like so many punch cards in a computer, they respond to their impressions of the facts, and Stanfield had his own impressions of the government's impressions. 49

On Wednesday, Ryan, Lévesque and the others had issued their statement urging negotiation, some kind of exchange involving Cross and Laporte for the "political prisoners."

"This obviously increased the pressure on Bourassa," Stanfield recalled later. "Laporte's letter (*Mon cher Robert*) put great pressure on, it had quite an effect on members of the Quebec government. That, and the fact that Mme. Laporte wrote personally to members of the government.

"When Bourassa first spoke about parole (an offer for five of the "political prisoners" made the night before) I thought that Bourassa was really breaking down, was really on the verge. The concessions were mounting. I think the government in Ottawa became really concerned about how long the Bourassa government could stand up."

There was at this time an obvious solidifying among the elite of Quebec's opinion-makers who were urging negotiation. "I suspect," said Stanfield "that this was a source of great concern to Mr. Trudeau. Relations between the government of Quebec and the Government at Ottawa had become extremely difficult. The federal government wouldn't release prisoners, it wouldn't do what the government in Quebec was asking with regard to releases, it wouldn't sanction that kind of negotiation. Relations had become very difficult; in fact, the government in Ottawa had got into a virtually impossible position to continue to resist. I could see it would be a source of tremendous concern, but whether it is a justification for the War Measures Act is another question."

The party leaders had been told in their briefings about the stolen guns and the dynamite and the ruthlessness of the FLQ. But, as Stanfield was to say later to an interviewer: "I doubt more and more whether the FLQ is an organization. It sounded to me more like an idea, I think it is an umbrella, but not an umbrella exactly, I don't know what word to use. Those kids, the Rose boys and their mother, hearing on the radio about Cross and coming back from the States—I think they just constituted themselves a 'cell' on the spur of the moment, they gave themselves a name and identified themselves with the FLQ. I am sure there is not much more to it than that, although when I say that, I don't minimize the effect of terrorism."

Always, in every public utterance, there would have to be that disclaimer; always, when any scepticism or doubt crossed the lips of a public man, he felt required to add that he was not voting for the FLQ. Stanfield was soon to lead his party members in a unanimous vote of approval for the invocation of the War Measures Act, and later, a unanimous vote (save for one member) to replace it with the slightly-patched-up Public Order (Temporary Measures) Act. As a sophisticated party leader, he could see that a large part of the crisis was the political strain between Ottawa and Quebec—the "extremely difficult" relations as he put it—with Quebec verging on negotiations but Ottawa, which held almost all the cards (in its jails) refusing to negotiate. That was the political segment, and as for the terrorist content, Stanfield could see that, without for a moment discounting the seriousness of two crimes, the FLQ was more an idea than an organization.

His unease showed clearly in the two major speeches he made that day, the first when he rose in the House of Commons after Trudeau about 11:15, the second on television to the nation that evening. He thought afterwards that he had given a poor performance in the House: "I'm not ashamed of what I said, but I didn't deliver it well. I wasn't feeling for a position, but I was sort of putting things together as I went along." Which was understandable from a party leader who had had the wording of these extraordinary regulations in his hand for only an hour, who had to glean on the run, from his staff, from the radio, from the reporters, what was happening in Montreal.

Stanfield's position in that first speech in the House was that he did not deny the government's legal right to invoke the War Measures Act, but it was the government which would have to take the responsibility. He could not say whether there was an "apprehended insurrection" in Quebec; Trudeau, apparently, had not convinced him. "A special danger exists," he admitted, but the government should have brought a bill to the House of Commons; properly done it could have been quickly passed. He would have co-operated, but he most certainly would not have voted for a bill presented to the House which contained the same provisions they faced today in the government's War Measures regulations. Certainly, he was in favor of prosecuting criminals and violent revolutionaries but—and this was the key to it, taken from Diefenbaker's office—"I am not prepared to see it made a crime to be a member of an association," particularly since the regulations made it a crime for someone to have gone to a meeting a long time ago at a time when the meeting and the association were perfectly legal.

Stanfield was to describe that speech later as an attempt to keep his options open; it had all happened so rapidly and so little information was available. They had to learn from the news reports how the powers were being used in Quebec at the very moment they spoke.

The arrests had reached over 200 by the time they recessed for lunch, but no one told them that in the House.

Diefenbaker's role was curious. Having told Stanfield in his office of the danger of making membership a crime, describing to Stanfield how he had once stood almost alone against it, Diefenbaker then never mentioned the subject in his speech. Instead, he railed against the government for not having acted sooner. He demanded to know why Michel Chartrand had not been arrested weeks ago, "when he has been issuing statements that were seditious and against the law." He attacked Jerry Rubin and foreign agitators the government had permitted into the country. "The government of Canada let these people run wild."

If Stanfield's speech in the House that morning was designed to keep his options open, his speech on television that night was more definite. He recognized there was a need for special legislation but "*under no circumstances* can we accept the idea that anyone should be deprived of his freedom in this country simply because of his opinions or because of his expression of them, unless this is seditious or otherwise unlawful. That is repugnant to every ideal that we have ever held about free speech . . ." The Conservative Party—he made it a "pledge"—would "do its utmost" to preserve "the delicate balance between security and freedom."

If the Conservatives were going to preserve the delicate balance between security and freedom, that was not, Stanfield was soon to discover, what the people of Canada wanted at that hour in their history. He went to a Conservative meeting in London, Ontario that Saturday, where a few Tories expressed concern over the upcoming vote, but Stanfield did not yet feel any great pressure. And then, later on Saturday night, the police pried open the car trunk at the St. Hubert air base, revealing Pierre Laporte's body, strangled with the chain of his own religious medal. Stanfield was at home on Sunday, insulated by his unlisted telephone number, but his Members were exposed to the full weight of an outraged nation.

On Sunday morning, the crowds gathered early on Parliament Hill, a rare event in Canada, a country which very much believes in allowing its leaders to lead. The crowd was quiet, there to gather the memories of being within sight of momentous events, to watch Ron Collister of the CBC and to see the Cabinet Ministers come and go. With the exception of one pro-separatist sign carried by an English-speaking Ottawa housewife (soon taken from her grasp and ripped) there was no doubt of the emotions which moved the crowd, standing there in the warm autumn sunshine to give surrogate expression to the bitter revulsion of all Canadians. 53

It was the second political murder in the history of Canada, the only one since a Fenian shot down Thomas D'Arcy McGee on the streets of Ottawa in the first year of Canadian nationhood, 102 years before. To his assassin, McGee was, in the French slang of a century later, a *vendu*—a sellout to the English. The Fenians boasted of having "executed" McGee, the same word the FLQ was to use in its threatening communiqués. "McGee," wrote W. G. Hardy, "was a martyr to his Canadianism," a phrase that was to be heard often in the days following the death of Pierre Laporte. Rare as political murder was, Canadians felt on that Sunday a sense of shame, born in part perhaps from watching with detached fascination all the political murders which had happened someplace else, from Medgar Evers through Robert Kennedy, and now it seemed that all that horror had descended on Canada in a single day. The vote on the War Measures proclamation, after debate from Friday into early Sunday, was to be taken on Monday morning. There was no doubt now what had to be done.

At nine that Sunday morning, Hugh John Flemming, a gentlemanly MP from New Brunswick and a former provincial premier, was sitting in his office on Parliament Hill listening to a church service on the radio and sipping a sherry with a friend. Within 20 minutes, the phone rang three times; each call brought Flemming another complaint about Stanfield's speech on Friday night, the speech in which he had pledged his party to maintain the balance between security and freedom, to refuse under any circumstances to agree to make political expression a crime. A typical caller to Flemming that morning said: "What's your leader humming and hawing over this one for?" Flemming made up his mind, no matter what his leader did, he would support the government.

The Cabinet met that morning, and as each Minister came down to the rotunda he picked up his soldier. Donald Jamieson couldn't find his soldier, Gerard Pelletier's soldier couldn't find him. He was walking in circles around the rotunda crying "I've lost my Minister, I've lost my Minister." The departures were sometimes less than ceremonious, Jean Chrètien sped down the Hill in his little white Volkswagen, a soldier in full battle-dress filling the front seat. But as each Minister left he got a cheer from the crowd.

On Monday, there was nothing left but the formalities. They had already made an arrangement for Conservative M.P. Robert Coates to withdraw his amendment which would have limited the War Measures regulations to the next 15 days, less than the 21 days of confinement-without-charge the regulations made possible. It had put the Tories in an impossible position: They were saying that "under no circumstances" would they agree to imprisonment for the public voicing of political ideas unless, of course, the circumstances were 15 days of imprisonment instead of 21. But for the three days, at least, the Tories were almost virgins. The Liberals agreed to introduce within a month new legislation which Parliament could debate and the two parties—one profiting and one smarting from the rage of public emotion—made their deal.

Stanfield paid his tribute to Laporte: "We must ensure that his death will be a milestone in the struggle for Canadian unity." And then he slid quickly back from his previous pledge. "The questions I raised on Friday last," he said, "remain as important to me now as then, but this is a day for unity and I hope that we can show it." Less than an hour after the sitting began, the members rose in their places on division to approve 190 to 16 "the action of the Government in invoking the powers of the War Measures Act to meet the state of apprehended insurrection in the Province of Quebec as communicated to the Prime Minister by the Government of Quebec and the civic authorities of Montreal . . . . " All the Tories, all the Creditistes and four of the New Democrats voted with the government.

When it was over, with the memories fresh but the sting removed, Robert Stanfield gave every indication of being a man who felt he had done his duty, and in so doing had allowed the chance for greatness to pass him by. He could hardly help but wonder what the outcome might have been, and particularly what the judgments of the distant future might have been, had he maintained his bold stance of Friday night: "It has been proven time and time again that ideas cannot be smashed for long by official force . . . . (these regulations) could be turned into an instrument of oppression."

"If you discuss it in terms of principle," Stanfield said, much later, "I suppose I changed in the sense of a compromise. I think I would have to concede that. The circumstances changed somewhat following the Laporte murder . . If I had followed what I had said, strictly speaking, on the Friday, for example, I wouldn't have accepted the outlawing of the FLQ. However, I felt it was sufficiently narrowed that I could accept it, and Mr. Diefenbaker does too, despite the strong opinions he expressed about the outlawing of associations."

Stanfield was in the old trap. The FLQ had killed Laporte and at the time of the Parliamentary vote still held Cross. How could a party leader vote against outlawing such bandits? It was fruitless, as both Stanfield and Diefenbaker knew, to attempt the argument that outlawing the FLQ would in itself catch no brigands and would chiefly succeed in bringing to jail a few friends,

55

relatives, casual hangers-on, fools, half-wits, curiosity-seekers and—as the events were to show—a very large number of the innocent.

"It seemed to me more important following the murder of Laporte," Stanfield related, "to achieve some reasonable display of unity in the House of Commons if we could. That was the first factor. The second factor was that if we had voted the way the NDP did against the bill, we might very well, in that atmosphere, have destroyed the Conservative party. It probably would have been such an emotional reaction that things would have gone flying in all directions."

The outraged reaction to Stanfield's speech, exacerbated by Laporte's death, did not descend directly on Stanfield himself. "I get at least an intuitive feeling about the state of opinion," he said, "I'm not that oblivious to it. There was no doubt in my mind that there was a furore of righteous indignation in the country, and particularly among Conservatives." At the same time, the Government was anxious to have Tory support for the War Measures regulations, and so the trade was made. "There was no difficulty getting those assurances that the bill would be forthcoming in a month," Stanfield remembered, "and so we weren't actually confronted by the decision about what we would have done if the government had refused to make such a commitment."

The end result was that the Tories failed to get a single comma changed in regulations their leader had said were "dangerous" and "a very blunt instrument indeed to be wielding under the present circumstances." More important, they failed in what is usually the Opposition's function: to create the issues the country cares about.

"The government has the support of a very, very substantial majority of the Canadian people," Stanfield conceded in November, "and the people don't even ask themselves—*they're not interested*—in whether or not the government was justified in any way at all in invoking the War Measures Act, other than that *some-*

thing had to be done and they were delighted, for a variety of reasons, that the government had reacted vigorously.

"They say such things, as 'it wasn't the most appropriate tool but it was the only tool that was around.' They are not asking themselves what the implications of invoking the War Measures Act might be, not yet anyway." Ever cautious, Stanfield added: "I have been quite careful not to say that the government was not justified, because," and this was weeks after the decision, "I still do not know what all the facts were."

While he was certainly inclined to agree that some form of special police power was needed, Stanfield was obviously appalled at the mass detentions, incommunicado, of people whose names were not revealed. He and his wife went one night during the crisis to the home of old friends in Ottawa. "What would you say," Stanfield said, challenging his host, "if you'd been picked up?"

"I hope I'd be able to recognize," his host replied, "that even though it was a mistake, it was necessary." In telling the story, Stanfield paused, rolled his eyes heavenward, said "well . . ." and emitted that soft, patient sigh which means "What can you do?"

In Toronto, an ebullient Tory lawyer, E. A. "Eddie" Goodman, chairman of the convention which had chosen Stanfield, was impressed by what he regarded as his leader's firm opposition to another example of Liberal excess, and he was anxious to send his support. Stanfield, on the other hand, was more conscious of his retreat from the "under no circumstances" position of Friday to the "unity" position of Monday. "Bob!" cried Goodman into the telephone, "congratulations on your stand."

Stanfield, an amazingly introspective and self-effacing man, smiled wanly at the other end of the line as he replied: "Which one?"

Public pressure came quickly and definitely to Parliament Hill. Also, a security blackout on news and some real fears in the media that they could be in violation of the regulations resulted in the familiar round robin of rumours.

The kidnappings were a fact. The FLQ notes were a fact. The obvious inability of the police to find the kidnappers or their victims was a fact. There was a fear, based more on the impression of the authorities as to the tactics of the FLQ than on hard evidence, that there would be more kidnappings and possibly destruction of property.

Then there were the unstated facts. Some were hinted at, some came out later and some were held in reserve, to support the argument that someday they might be known to justify the unprecedented use of severe emergency powers in peacetime. "This step," Trudeau assured the House, "was taken after consideration of all the facts, and particularly of letters received from the Prime Minister of Quebec and the authorities of the city of Montreal reporting a state of apprehended insurrection."

The letters were tabled. The alarm they expressed was in keeping with the mood of the country and the House, and was acceptable and credible. But in a different mood, they do not reveal hard facts, any more than Mr. Trudeau's speech did. The letters were obviously carefully planned for content. From Montreal, on October 15, QPP Director Maurice St. Pierre wrote to Mayor Jean Drapeau and the Executive Committee chairman, Lucien Saulnier using all the right words. He warned of an "extremely dangerous subversive organization" which has the intention of overthrowing the legitimate government "by seditious means and eventually armed *insurrection.*"

The kidnappings, he wrote, were the first stage of its seditious plan 'and of activities "leading directly to *insurrection.*" Therefore the investigation must include all activities of the various cells and not just be confined to a mere search for the kidnappers. The resources of the police department had been, he said, taxed to the utmost by the necessity of checking and searching in the face of the internal structure, divided into many autonomous cells.

He pointed to the extreme urgency "of obtaining concrete results" and stated that it was essential that higher levels of government come to the assistance of the police if they were to carry out their enormous task, "without resorting to unhealthy and undesirable repression."

He stated that the slow pace of procedures and the restrictions resulting from "legal machinery" did not allow his forces to meet the situation, and requested "the means which in their (higher levels of government) estimation are suitable and useful to enable us to gather and submit the evidence necessary to protect society against the seditions and insurrectionary activities triggered by the kidnappings."

Every police officer is impatient with what he regards as the slow pace of procedures and "legal machinery." His function is to carry out an important role within, and as part of, that "legal machinery" and he works because of it, not in spite of it. The policeman is not society's only, nor indeed even the main, instrument of law enforcement. This is a function which society has given to the courts. The letter was an appeal for the Valhalla of which all policemen dream; the police were to be let loose like kids in a candy store, to enforce laws they had asked for as they saw fit. They would not be hampered by "legal machinery"—meaning lawyers, judges, bail, courts, presumptions of innocence or public scrutiny of their actions or their prisoners. The letters' vivid descriptions provided the factless 'evidence' which Ottawa needed to set up the grant of extraordinary power. It simply planted the word "insurrection" often enough.

What it also said almost as clearly, was that if the cumbersome necessity of dealing with suspects according to the law could be dispensed with, they could pick up a great many people without overtaxing their already strained resources. Even without the War Measures regulations the police could have searched as many premises as they wished using ordinary search warrants, which are easily and secretly issued by a simple procedure. In reality, the only substantial new power they acquired was the power of internment.

The Saulnier–Drapeau letter merely confirmed that the police had indeed sent the letter and joined in the request for "every measure of assistance the federal government may deem useful and desirable in order to carry out the task of protecting society and the lives of citizens in this difficult period." But still it gave no facts.

Bourassa was more specific in what he sought. "I request that emergency powers be provided as soon as possible so that more effective steps may be taken. I request particularly that such powers encompass the authority to apprehend and keep in custody individuals who, the Attorney General of Quebec has valid reasons to believe, are determined to overthrow the government through violence and illegal means.

"According to the information we have and which is available to you, we are facing a concerted effort to intimidate and overthrow the government and the democratic institutions of this province through planned and systematic illegal action, including *insurrection*." (The one word which was common to all three letters was "insurrection".)

Bourassa was not asking for the creation of a new offence of being a member of an illegal organization, the FLQ. He was asking for power to detain those who his Attorney General had "valid reasons to believe" were seditious in their intentions and already guilty of the crime of seditious conspiracy.

If the Attorney-General had "valid reasons" to believe that certain persons were determined to overthrow the government through violence and illegal means, the Attorney-General had, in the words of the Criminal Code, "reasonable and probable grounds" to make arrests under the existing law. Bourassa's request was really for the *internment* of Canadian citizens.

The pre-trial procedures could be altered a bit, to satisfy Quebec's need for internment and Trudeau would not appear to go too far. So a new offence was created to give a patina of respectability to the detentions. In effect it was detention in the guise of pre-trial procedures.

The new offence was used as justification for the holding of the accused persons in police custody for up to 21 days before the charge was laid and the resulting appearance in court was necessary. It permitted the Attorney-General to control bail right up to the time of trial. In normal circumstances, arrest of an accused is not intended for the purpose of removing him from society. It is to secure his attendance at his trial. Bail achieves the same purpose. Both are based upon the presumption of innocence and both recognize that imprisonment even before trial is punishment.

Clear facts of actual insurrection would have been needed to justify detention or internment. There were many liberals who would not have supported such a move. But arrest and charge implies that at the end of the process there will be a fair trial and that the guilt or innocence of the accused will be established. It is easier to support. But with the safeguards based upon the presumption of innocence taken away, it becomes detention. It was detention powers which Bourassa requested and it was detention, under another guise, which he got.

In Parliament and elsewhere the question was repeatedly asked, what was the information "we have and which is available to you?" Was it the St. Pierre letter or were there some hard facts on which the Prime Minister and his cabinet based their action?

In subsequent days Trudeau was to answer numerous questions in the House of Commons as to the information on which he and the government acted. In the first week oblique reference had been made outside of the House to "confidential reports" and intelligence information which had been acted on. It was galling to the opposition parties, who had been forced to debate the government's resolution confirming its action without any such information. A typical exchange took place on Friday, October 23. NDP leader Douglas asked the

Prime Minister whether he would make a statement in the next few days as to the course the government intended, that is, whether or not he would give the House, publicly or privately, the "basis of the information upon which they took the step they did in determining there was a state of apprehended insurrection."

Trudeau: "By now I would have thought this information was in the hands of everybody. We have at various times explained why the War Measures Act was brought in at the time it was. The first fact was that there had been kidnappings of two very important people in Canada and that they were being held for ransom under threat of death. The second was that the government of the province of Quebec and the authorities of the City of Montreal asked the federal government to permit the use of exceptional measures because, in their own words, a state of apprehended insurrection existed. The third reason was our assessment of all the surrounding facts, which are known to the country by now—the state of confusion that existed in the province of Quebec in regard to these matters."

Later, he added, "There are other facts which have been made known to the public—that a great quantity of dynamite has been stolen in Quebec during the last year and not recovered, that there is a great quantity . . of rifles and small arms that have disappeared."

In reply to a further question from Mr. Stanfield, he explained his early reply that the facts upon which the government acted were known to the public. Then he left the impression that there had indeed been further facts.

"Mr. Speaker, what I said was that the facts that I have recited and which are known to the House were sufficient for us to take the steps we did. I am not saying that beyond that there are not other facts which may or may not be known to the public. It is a matter that will be left to the police as far as I am concerned. I say that the facts that are known to the House are the facts on which we acted, and it is on that that we stand."

The following Tuesday, the furore arose again with Trudeau being pressed on news reports that the government had been aware of a plot to replace the Bourassa government with a provisional government. (The details of this plot are in Chapter 10.) Stanfield asked: "Mr. Speaker, may I ask the Prime Minister whether the government invoked the War Measures Act because, among other reasons, it believed that a group of influential Quebeckers had set out to see whether they might supplant the legitimately elected government of the province of Quebec?"

Trudeau: "Mr. Speaker, I gave in the House yesterday the reasons why the government invoked the War Measures Act and I also gave them last Friday. They are the same reasons, and among them is not included the reason alluded to by the hon. member."

The distinction between a "reason" and an unstated influence was not lost on the more perceptive Members of the House. Much earlier, the two-day debate on the regulations commencing on Friday, October 16 had revealed some interesting glimpses of what was in the Government's mind the day the War Measures Act was invoked. There may have been other facts. There may have been reasons other than security. On that day Justice Minister John Turner told the House: "It is my hope that some day the full details of the intelligence upon which the government acted can be made public, because until that day comes the people of Canada will not be able fully to appraise the course of action which has been taken by the government." This intelligence, the existence of which was later denied in successive statements by the Prime Minister, was not referred to by Turner in his major address of Wednesday, November 4, opening the debate on the new legislation. " . . . the country already knows the facts upon which we based our decision. We received written requests from the government of Quebec and from the civic administration of Montreal for immediate assistance in the face of what they called apprehended insurrection. A Quebec minister and a British diplomat had been kidnapped and governments had been held to ransom. Large amounts of dynamite had been stolen, were ready for use and had been used before. Arms and ammunition were in the possession of terrorists."

In his earlier speech of October 16, in reciting the "list of events that have contributed to the rapid acceleration of this dangerous situation in Quebec," Turner had referred to the bombings and the increase in thefts of dynamite and, continuing the list: *"More disturbing,* we have a type of erosion of the public will in the feeling among some sincere people that an exchange of prisoners for the victims of the kidnappings would somehow ease the situation."

And again on November 4: "All this, was against the background of an erosion of public will and confidence in the ability of the institutions of government and law enforcement agencies in Quebec to respond to this crisis. We do not have to explore plots or allegations of provisional governments to appreciate the acute sense of apprehension and fear in Quebec in those days preceding the proclamation of the War Measures Act."

The circumstances and the government strategy could not have worked out better. If, as was increasingly suspected, there were no hard facts on which to base a finding of an "apprehended insurrection", the alternative political motive comes to the forefront. Perhaps a combination of the desire to reinforce the Bourassa government, to combat the "erosion of public will" and to solve the kidnappings, while at the same time reacting firmly against the FLQ, combined to contribute to the "value judgment" which Turner said the decision involved.

The War Measures Act had been proclaimed and the regulations were in force and had been acted upon when the Commons met on Friday morning to hear Trudeau's dramatic announcement in a Liberal-dominated Parliament.

The sudden release of tension as the country watched

something happen at last accrued to the government's benefit. Assured of strong support from the Ralliement des Créditistes, the move also received the support of the Conservatives, whose leader feared the split that any other position would bring within his party. Only the New Democratic Party was prepared to buck the tide. Even their numbers were lessened in opposition as four voted for the resolution.

Early Sunday morning October 18, Stanley Knowles of the New Democrats was speaking in the House of Commons. The death of Pierre Laporte had already been announced in the House and around one a.m. an emotional outburst forced a stop to the debate. Marcel Prud'homme of the Liberals rose on a "question of privilege" and said: "Under the circumstances the best thing the hon. member (Knowles) could do would be to offer his silence for a better united Canada." Mr. Knowles, who had been cut off during a plea for greater understanding between French and English Canada had no intention of dignifying meaningless interruptions by allowing an irrelevant debate on his right to speak. He backed down gracefully. "I do not quarrel with the hon. member, I was in the midst of my last sentence. I shall say no more. We are all very sad tonight."

The government soon introduced its promised new legislation which would be passed after debate in the House of Commons and which would be little improvement over the old regulations. All it did was give an aura of legitimacy to the emergency powers so arbitrarily taken.

It placed the opposition in a position of getting what it wanted and therefore being less able to criticize. The Conservatives and the New Democratic Party had based their criticism on the fact that the measures the government sought should have been brought before Parliament and not passed in secret cabinet session. Eldon Woolliams even suggested an *in camera* session of Parliament would have been appropriate, as was done in wartime.

No one wanted to quarrel with the need for the

legislation, although considerable criticism was levelled at the government for failing to disclose a factual basis for its decision. That criticism centred on the need for the War Measures Act. By bringing a new measure before Parliament, the government was blunting the opposition attack.

But things could never be quite the same. Events had gone too far to restore Parliament's authority over the problems raised by Bill C181, "An Act to Provide Temporary Emergency Powers for the Preservation of Public Order in Canada."

When the act became law almost all of the arrests and abuses of civil liberties had taken place. The abridged time limits and changed procedures could not and did not accomplish any real good except to salvage a little bit of the government's civil liberties image. The debate began on the 4th of November and continued until the bill went to the Senate. It was passed and received Royal Assent on December 3, 1970, the same day that James Cross was recovered alive and well in Montreal North and his kidnappers given safe conduct to Cuba.

In spite of their assurances that they would welcome opposition suggestions, the government repeatedly rejected proposed amendments to its Act. Only one amendment, by New Democrat John Burton, to ensure that military personnel would be under civilian control, actually carried, and that was in a session of the House in committee when the government benches were depleted during Monday evening, November 1.

A Liberal backbencher moved a number of amendments in an attempt to improve the Act. A lawyer and former private secretary to Pierre Trudeau when he was Minister of Justice, Pierre de Bané of Quebec City risked his political career as his various suggestions were turned back, one after the other, by the government majority.

One of the amendments proposed in committee and rejected by the government was to cause some embarrassment on the following weekend. Conservative Eldon Woolliams had moved for a federally appointed administrator to be authorized under the statute to "inquire into and report to Parliament from time to time upon the administration of this Act and of the Public Order Regulations, 1970." The administrator would have had the power to interfere on bail matters and to fix a time for trial of detained persons.

Woolliams' amendment followed a lengthy debate on David Lewis' proposal to establish a supervisory commission of three with authority to interview persons arrested to ensure they were treated according to law, that they had access to counsel, that they were not further detained without adequate grounds and that they had been given the opportunity to contact their families. It too had been rejected.

Meeting in Ottawa on Saturday, November 21, the National Liberal Policy Conference voted 492 to 424—and thereby made it Liberal Party policy—that a review board be established to serve as a check against abuse of powers under the new legislation. The government still refused to amend the bill.

In opening the debate, NDP Leader Douglas summed it up in advance: "After all, we are not faced with the choice of this legislation or no legislation; we are faced with the choice of this legislation or continuing under the War Measures Act and the regulations enacted thereunder."

Government intransigence was made possible by the overwhelming mood of support in the country. The Prime Minister had gone directly to the people by television: "I am speaking to you at a moment of grave crisis . . . " The country responded; no other issue had ever raised such a flood of favorable mail and telegrams to the Prime Minister's office. The House of Commons lost its leverage; in this crisis, Parliament was largely irrelevant.

4 'Get your clothes on, you're coming with us'

Pauline Julien's living room is on the second floor of an 69
old house on the first rise above Sherbrooke Street
toward the mountain. It is filled with faded, rumpled
furniture, with a rattan bird cage in the open upper
window facing the morning sun. A very French room on
the "English" side of Montreal.

When she enters, gay, expressive, cat-quick, with
those beautiful high cheekbones and a few wisps of
curly hair falling free, we test each other for a moment
to see if English must be the language of our
conversation. It must, and I realize then that I can never
really join the laughter nor understand the passions of
this entrancing woman and I am lessened by it, because
to understand her must be one of the shared delights of
those who know her.

Instead I trip on the TV cord and stumble halfway
across the room, almost into her arms; she apologizes
quickly on behalf of the room, but my mind for an
instant is filled with all sorts of humiliated racial
symbolism: the bumbling, stupid, awkward English, so
gauche in the company of grace. I am being only partly
silly because I know that she knows, or thinks she
knows, that I represent that class of people, the
uptight-English-and-their-lackeys-with-the-French-names
who have so recently exerted their power.

A few days later her teenage children are to express
almost precisely those sentiments I find so inhospitable
within myself.

As I hunch down in the crinkly old chair and sip a morning beer and she darts back and forth to answer the phone, a great malaise of unreality grips me, for I am not here because she is an intense and sensuous woman, I am not here because she sings so hauntingly of the mysterious seekings of the sexes, I am not here because those quick phone calls are finishing the details of her next concert in one of the great theatres of Canada. I am not even here for the simple pleasures of a morning beer, nor to enjoy a woman's company; I am here, for God's sake, because this woman has been in jail. This room is the scene of one of the great bungles of the War Measures Act, it is here they all gathered in their nightshirts at five o'clock in the morning while the police rummaged around, being, oh yes, polite enough to let her find a housecoat. And that television set over there is the one they turned on and all of them watched while they learned of the secret new law which allowed the police to stomp into lovers' bedrooms in the covering darkness before the dawn.

—R.H.

70

"These are strong powers," the Prime Minister of Canada said late on the night of the day they took Pauline Julien to jail, "and I find them as distasteful as I am sure you do. They are necessary, however, to permit the police to deal with persons who advocate or promote the violent overthrow of the democratic system."

After the invocation of the War Measures Act by the federal cabinet at four o'clock in the morning on Friday, October 16, 1970 (though it was not published until 11 a.m.) 497 Quebec citizens were rounded up by the police, and many dozens more were detained for short periods and did not enter the official statistics. Among those who were officially catalogued, the average period of detention was about a week. All but a handful were released without any charges being laid and, in most cases, with only perfunctory interrogations. But the most noticeable characteristic of the 497 detainees was their diversity, ranging from Pierre Vallières, the philosopher—patron of violent revolution, to university student Les Lasko who was unlucky enough to be working on a public opinion poll for the McGill sociology department.

While the extraordinary powers of arrest without charge and detention without trial were needed, the Prime Minister said, to permit the police to deal with persons advocating violent overthrow of the government, the police, for their part, were subject to the *if only* disease. Like the American generals in Viet Nam who could win the war *if only*, the police of Quebec could solve the kidnappings of Jasper Cross and Pierre Laporte *if only* they had more power. "I have the police on my back," Premier Bourassa told Réné Lévesque on the Wednesday night before the Friday morning invocation of the War Measures Act.

It is as misleading to put all the people who were arrested into the same paragraph (or into the same jail, for that matter) as it would be to list together the Mafia and the Chamber of Commerce because they both are in business. One of the results, intentional or otherwise, of the events after October 16 was to blur the distinction between all the varieties of dissent in French Canada. Newspapers fell into the habit of referring in their headlines to the "FLQ sympathizers" who were in jail, and they wrote about the round-up of "suspected terrorists."

Some were. But as Pauline Julien said, 99 per cent of those who ended up in jail were opposed to terrorism, although a more accurate statistic would probably be about 90 per cent. Leaving aside obvious errors and confusions over similar names, those who went to jail covered the political spectrum to the left of Jean Drapeau. In between Pierre Vallières at one end, and the polling student at the other, a fair sampling of those who went to jail would include:

— Nick Auf der Maur, a story editor on a CBC public affairs television program who had consorted with leftwing groups in Montreal, both as a journalist and as a friendly camp-follower;

— Michel Chartrand, the loudmouth Montreal labor leader about whom no one can be neutral: Auf der Maur sees him as a beautiful person, René Lévesque sees him as an adolescent, who breaks everything he touches;

— The two candidates in the Montreal civic elections a week away who had the best chance of beating the Drapeau supporters, including Dr. Henri Bellemare, a leading specialist in internal medicine who was taken, also in the pre-dawn darkness, from his broadloomed, split-level suburban bungalow;

— And of course Pauline Julien, whose songs of Quebec pride and independence are as sensuous as her love ballads, and her partner Gérald Godin, a professional writer and editor who, while loathing violence himself, had published Vallières' first book.

In their third-floor bedroom in the old house in Montreal, Pauline Julien and Gérald Godin woke at five in the morning to the sound of voices nearby. "Are there any anywhere else?" one voice said, and another: "Did you go around the house?" In bed, the two mumbled to each other something about there must be a fire, and Godin slipped on his trousers to look. On the threshhold of his bedroom he found three policemen.

"Why didn't you ring?" Pauline asked from bed and one of them replied, "We did but you didn't hear us."

"You must be crazy," she cried, more incredulous than angry, "Do you go places and not ring the bell?"

Godin asked if they had a warrant, and one of them replied with what Godin described as a smiling, triumphant tone: "We don't need a warrant any more, sir. A special law's been voted and we can search where we want without a warrant. Listen to the radio, you'll see."

One policeman asked how many people were in the house and Pauline Julien replied with a gay laugh she didn't really know; her daughter often brought friends home, they'd have to look and find out. There were six people in the house that night as it turned out, and now they were all gathered in the second floor living room with four policemen, two from the Quebec Police Forces and two from the city police. Then they began a two-hour search into books and papers, mainly of the publishing co-operative *Parti Pris* of which Godin is secretary-treasurer.

"They asked nothing," Miss Julien recalled, "they said, 'You stay here.' But I refused and I said, 'I'm going to accompany you everywhere because this is my place.' They were not so bad, they were not so savage here as I hear they were at some other places."

By 7 o'clock the search was over and the police had carried out two typewriters, a personal list of phone numbers and a pile of papers from the publishing business. They did not, however, seize the Bell Telephone Montreal directory, as they did at some houses (since people have a habit of marking their friends' names in the book). And then they said: "Come on, get your clothes on, you're coming with us." Pauline Julien exploded with surprise, *What!* for it was only then she realized that she was to be detained.

When she asked, she received an intriguing explanation from the policemen in her living room. Pauline Julien says she believes the explanation. Others may wonder if it was an explanation offered out of politeness by men anxious to transfer to others the responsibility for what they had been ordered to do.

"We have nothing against you," she quoted one of the policemen as saying. "We didn't know you were here, we didn't know you were at this address. We didn't have any request for you but we just called the *prefecteur* and he said, 'All people you get, bring them in.'"

As an explanation, it leaves much to be desired although, as she says, if her name was on a list, why her and not any of half-a-dozen other French-Canadian singers? In any event, the Montreal telephone directory lists P. Julien at 1627 Selkirk, and it lists Gérald Godin at the same address and the same phone number. If the explanation was true, that it was all an accident of the bed-chamber, it does not serve to explain the arrest of Miss Julien's two teenage children, not on October 16 when she was arrested, but eight days later when the police came back to the house on Selkirk St. and took away her children only a few hours before Miss Julien herself was released, a source of anguish that hardly needs to be described.

It was all done, as almost everyone who was detained has said, completely without rancor. As they drove down St. Catherine Street in an old blue, unmarked Chevrolet, Gérald Godin discussed current movies with the policeman beside him. When they entered the underground garage of the Quebec police headquarters and detention centre on Parthenais Street—where there was a traffic jam of police cars waiting to discharge their passengers—a passing Montreal policeman made some remark to Godin; it was the only rudeness he heard in eight days of jail. But however circumspect the guards and however hygienic the walls, it was still a jail.

By 7:30 a.m. Godin was in a common bullpen in the new building, a room with a red cement floor and yellowish walls, except for one wall which is all bars.

There are about 10 men in the small room when Godin enters, but soon there are 35. No one has eaten, and it is not until 1 p.m. that three guards bring in a basket full of ham sandwiches, biscuits and coffee. There is nothing to do and they have already felt the strangeness of being cut off from news or contact with the outside world; after lunch they try to lie down but there is not enough room around the walls for all of them to lie down, so they take turns, and they sustain each other with the inevitable jailhouse humor. "There," says one as he stands up to give his place to another on the cement floor, "I've softened the mattress for you." And another: "I've warmed the bed."

They form up teams to play football with the blown up sandwich bags, trying to make jokes of the rules. Anyone who gets a penalty will have to leave the cell. They begin to refer to themselves as prisoners of war and they ask the guards, "Is the war over yet?" But the guards do not answer. They are being held incommunicado, and they are beginning to understand what it means.

Speaking of it afterwards, Godin says his feelings on that first day are of rootlessness, of floating in absolute uncertainty. "Why am I here," he asks himself, "if only they would ask me questions I would at least know what it was about. Are there some things I may have said, some things I may have written or published? But for the moment everything is absolutely empty under me, I have no place."

Godin began his career as a newspaperman in Three Rivers, the city where Pauline Julien was born; he also worked on dailies in Montreal and was the chief story editor of a *Radio-Canada* daily television public affairs program *Aujourd'hui*, leaving there to work on a National Film Board feature on the Quebec textile industry. In October, 1969, he joined the editorial board of *Québec Presse,* a union-sponsored popular tabloid full of lively coverage of movies, sports, television and, of course, politics. It is not hard to guess, however, why Gérald Godin was in jail: the co-operative publishing house he directs published in 1968 Pierre Vallières' haunting account of his slum childhood *Nègres blancs d'Amérique,* a book which, after a slight hiatus around October 16, is still sold at the McGill University bookstore, not only for the insights it offers into Vallières desperation but also as the work, whatever his politics, of a great natural writer.

There is, at the same time, no doubt where Gérald Godin stands on violence: He regards it as suicidal to the interests of the Left. "From a Leftist point of view," he said not long after his release from jail, "terrorism is not the way to save Quebec, but the way to kill Quebec, to destroy it. Quebec terrorism is brinkmanship of the extreme Left. The realistic Left cannot agree with that, it has been proved wrong every two or three years. Quebec's neck is put on the guillotine by a group of guys who make a very wrong analysis of the situation. Now, there is a new and broader consensus among the moderate Left, and one of the tasks of the Left will be to make a critical analysis of terrorism as a suicidal way."

Godin's criticisms are not, of course, confined to others of the Left. "The political equivalent of terrorism," he says, "is demagoguery, and I am sure we will still have politicians stupid enough to use demagoguery." (He is obviously referring to politicians such as Montreal's Mayor Jean Drapeau and the federal cabinet minister who had visions of the FLQ having infiltrated into the highest places in Quebec, Jean Marchand.) "In the face of such demagoguery, you push people to despair and to a sense of impotence, and then anything can happen. That's why I hope a sense of responsibility will at last come to our statesmen and they will not resort to those methods any more. In the short term, they give a sort of electrical shock to the public, but in the long run it can kill society itself."

While Gérald Godin was in a bullpen at Parthenais Street playing football with the sandwich bags, Pauline Julien shared another floor with 36 women, a slightly better place, since there were eight small cells off the common room where they could take turns lying down. Not everyone wanted to, however. Pauline Julien herself felt too anxious to lie down and, as often happens to people in such circumstances, everyone began to talk and a sense of community quickly developed.

"We tried to learn their stories," she recalled afterwards, "and for some of them it was because their husbands or their boy friends belonged to the PQ or FRAP (Parti Québecois or Front d'Action Politique). Some helped, but some had nothing to do with that, they just kept the children. There was one American girl who answered a little advertisement at the university to get a room. She rented the room from a girl at the university, and that girl's boy friend was in FRAP or the PQ or something, and that caused the room to be raided."

On Friday evening, Godin and five others from the

bullpen were led out, happily assuming, quite wrongly, that they were to be liberated. The paperwork of the prison was in obvious disarray and the six men were held for an hour in a tiny four-by-four foot transfer cell. The guard was lounging outside in the corridor thumbing through the *Reader's Digest*, but the cell itself was so small the men could not even kneel down.

Pauline Julien, at almost the same time, was being transferred to the Tanguay women's prison, also a new building, "like a convent for young girls," she called it. Montreal has more new jail cells than new units of public housing.

At Tanguay, the three dozen women detained under the War Measures Act could gather in a games room, watch television and read the current newspapers. They did gymnastics, danced, worked with fabrics and played dominoes. They also organized discussion groups, with heavy emphasis, of course, on politics and Women's Lib. There were two young women there, Pauline Julien remembers, whose student-husbands often handed out pamphlets in Sherbrooke, "but the two women, they were absolutely not interested in politics."

Back at Parthenais Street, Gérald Godin and the five others in the tiny transfer cell, which is really part of the hallway, are finally taken out, released, taken upstairs to the real jail on the top floors, where they are stripped, searched, and then given back their own clothes including, unlike most jail prisoners, their ties, belts and shoelaces. Godin's cell is nine by five feet and, except for his interrogation on Saturday, and a shower, he is in it all Friday night and Saturday.

An FM radio station is broadcast into the cells, but as soon as the announcer begins to read the news, it is turned off. On Sunday, the prisoners can see the flags outside at half-staff; someone important is dead but they do not know who it is. The next day, a prisoner coming back from the infirmary reports that he was able to sneak a look at a newspaper: Pierre Laporte is dead. But he gets it wrong: he says Laporte has been shot twice through the head. That night, either by mistake, or because the news was out anyway, the prison allows one news broadcast to come over the loudspeakers.

Back at Tanguay meanwhile, the women were holding their meetings, and making their little prison jokes that they should be talking about women's *liberation* at a time like this; they were watching television and reading *La Presse* and *Montréal-Matin* but they were still incommunicado. One woman was worried about her cats, she had six of them and the police had locked them in the toilet as they left. Another woman had left four children at home, her husband was away on business, and she had a chance only to give a quick word to a neighbor she hardly knew as she left for jail. Without news, not being sure what had happened to her children, she hardly ate or slept for three nights.

Over the weekend, a matron came to the women with an offer to phone out messages. Pauline Julien remembers her saying: "I can ring for you, not saying who I am and not saying where you are, but saying to the person whose name you give me, please take care of the cats or the children."

"She took all the names and by Monday she came back and said OK your cats are being taken care of by your friends, and your children are with the neighbors."

Henri Bellemare also discovered the differences in treatment between the men at Parthenais Street and the women at Tanguay. While the matron at Tanguay was telling the women they could have a message sent out, a guard at Parthenais St. told the men that those who had been picked up on the street, or away from home, could have a message sent to their families saying they were safe and alive. Although Henri Bellemare was arrested in full view of his family, he thought he might as well try to get a message to them. "No," the guard said, "you were arrested at home. No message." But the women at Tanguay did not, at this point, know that they were, at least to this extent, already more liberated than the men at Parthenais Street.

Henri Bellemare is a handsome, 38-year-old specialist in internal medicine and a founder and director of a community-run medical clinic in east end Montreal where for $2 a month the families of St. Jacques get access to the services of five doctors, three psychiatrists, three or four dentists, as well as prescription medicines. He is of a rare breed in Canada: a socialist doctor who lives his creed.

The civic politicians of Montreal have plenty of reason to have Dr. Bellemare on their hate list: among other recent campaigns, he attempted to convince City Hall to vaccinate children against measles, as is done in such suburbs as Outremount, Montreal North and Ville LaSalle. He exposed the fact that the City health department made a practice of telling parents in more affluent parts of Montreal that their children's shots did not include measles, and that vaccination could be obtained from a private physician for $12 while neglecting to tell anything to poorer parents, who couldn't afford it anyway, and would only worry if they knew.

In his campaign as a candidate for the Front d'Action Politique, Bellemare told the voters of St. Jacques that the City of Montreal spends more on its police horses than on the health of its people. One of his slogans was: $3 million for health, $33 million for the police. And he must have been on more than one list on October 16, because four Quebec police arrived at his door at 5:10 a.m., and just as they had finished searching the kitchen, four city police arrived on the doorstep, also under the command of an Inspector. The city police searched the kitchen all over again, including a careful examination of the refrigerator freezing compartment.

The trademark of the police everywhere that morning was the green plastic garbage bag; they came well supplied, and from Dr. Bellemare's comfortable bungalow they removed two full bags of material, including the complete list of voters in the electoral ward of St. Jacques, perhaps the most public document then around, since bits of it were posted on utility poles throughout the ward. They also removed the Bell Telephone directory, although Dr. Bellemare does not make a habit of marking the names of friends in the book. They did not take his personal list of phone numbers. "They took a lot of books," Dr. Bellemare recalls, "they took any books that looked a bit socialist, but they were not very good at it." Into the green garbage bags, went Samuelson's *Economics: An Introductory Analysis*, the most widely-used textbook in its field in the United States and Canada, but not Karl Marx's *Das Kapital*. By 5:45 they were at Dr. Bellemare's office, all eight policemen in tow by now, and five searched his office while three sat in the waiting room with him.

The search at home had been thorough. The police had felt along the undersides of all the drawers in the dining room sideboard, had picked through his wife's lingerie, and had looked under the mattresses of his children, except for the mattress of the seven-year-old who was still asleep. But by the time they got to his office, Dr. Bellemare could sense that the search was becoming perfunctory. The police seized his appointment book for last year, but not the one for the current year. When he told them a filing cabinet contained his patients' records, they did not open it. But they searched along the backs of the pictures on the wall.

For Dr. Bellemare's children, five girls between seven and thirteen, the stress began not when the police were in the house—they found that rather interesting—but after their father was gone. He sat with them in the dining room while the police rummaged through the house and told them he would probably have to go downtown for an identification parade for a little while and of course the police didn't say for how long he would be away; they didn't know.

"As the days passed and they had no news," Dr. Bellemare says, "the girls thought I was on bread and water like they see in the movies and they thought I was questioned under a big spotlight and things like that. When the police were in the house it was more a curiosity, but the stress came for them afterwards."

His 11-year-old cried in the mornings and refused to go to school, the nine-year-old raced home from school out of breath, crying, "He's here, he's here," but he wasn't.

Until he was deposited at the Parthenais St. headquarters, Dr. Bellemare was in the company of eight policemen for two hours, the equivalent of two mandays not spent on other police tasks. The two officers who eventually questioned him went through a three-page printed form, asking him the color of his wife's eyes, what political groups he belonged to. He told them FRAP. They asked him if he had kidnapped James Cross or Pierre Laporte and if he had any dynamite, but they did not bother to complete the third page of the form, which Bellemare already knew from other detainees contained questions about the occupations of brothers-in-law. It was all very polite, very friendly, and the police were laughing as they went through the routine.

Six days later when he was released he was given back his two green garbage bags full of assorted junk, and he also obtained, probably by mistake, the police list which went with it. Two hunting knives were described on the list as daggers (poignard) with a careful notation of which drawer they had come from. Another notation said: "Nothing incriminating, a lot of socialist literature."

In the Montreal civic election three days after his release, Dr. Bellemare was the most popular of the FRAP candidates, but still unsuccessful in an election in which Mayor Jean Drapeau received 92 per cent of the vote and saw supporters of his Civic Party elected to every council seat. "I may have offended Mr. Drapeau or Mr. (Lucien) Saulnier," Dr. Bellemare says, but he is reluctant to believe, since he was one of only two FRAP candidates arrested, that the explanation is quite that simple.

"I am an independentiste, you call a separatist, I am a member of FRAP which is a socialist party. And maybe my name is on a list from the old RIN. When they pass a law that they don't need any warrant, and someone says go out and arrest 400 people this night—and don't touch any crook, any bandit, any protection racketeer—that's not easy to do. Maybe they have IBM cards, maybe they get out every card that has three notations on it."

Curiously, the press commented almost universally on how nice the police had been to Dr. Bellemare, how polite the guards, quickly accepting as a norm the jailing of a candidate who, far from advocating violent revolution, had joined in the electoral process that very week. And while the police were polite in the broadloomed expanse of Dr. Bellemare's suburban bungalow, they were not quite so polite at the home of the other FRAP candidate they arrested, the bearded, informally-dressed director of a leftwing printing co-operative on the other side of St. Lawrence Boulevard.

"The first thing I remember," says Jean Roy, a FRAP candidate in St. Louis district, "was being pulled out of bed. I was held up by two men and there was one man yelling, 'Police.' They had a gun pointed at me from the end of the bed. Later that night, I realized I had marks on my arms where they had grabbed me."

There were no polite knocks on the door at Jean Roy's rundown print shop and home. The police came into the basement at 5:15 a.m., where they found Michel Lavoie working on the press, turning out pamphlets. He was manacled by the ankles and left with a policeman while the press spewed ruined pamphlets on to the floor and the rest of the party ran upstairs to awaken Jean Roy, his wife and children and others who were asleep in the house.

"Oh yes," says Henri Bellemare, "elsewhere they broke down doors and woke people with machine guns in their ribs and all that, but at my house they never showed their guns. There still exist class distinctions, you know."

The green garbage bags were also much in evidence at the home of Michel Chartrand, where the police also arrived in the first 5 a.m. wave and found, quite by accident, a young friend of one of Chartrand's sons who had spent the night there, as well as an organizer in the construction branch of the Confederation of National Trade Unions, who had come home with Chartrand after a late meeting the night before in the Paul Sauvé arena. The young man worked at a magazine edited by Pierre Bourgault to which Pierre Vallières had from time to time sent articles; in his personal list of phone numbers in his pocket, he had the numbers of Vallières and Bourgault. Off he went to jail, and so did the union organizer.

Of all the men and women rounded up on the dark morning of *les mesures de guerre,* none roused such contradictory feelings as black and snappish little Michel Chartrand, president of the Montreal central council of the CNTU who had made a habit of hanging around the action in the first ten days of the Cross-Laporte crisis. He had said, in his particularly direct and, to many, insulting way that everyone was worried about the drugs James Cross needed for his high blood pressure, but few worried about the medications which society denied every day to the poor. His worst scene occurred outside the home of Pierre Laporte, the night of the labor minister's kidnapping. Chartrand drove by out of a desire to be where the excitement was, and when a radio reporter recognized him and put a microphone before him, Chartrand said Mr. Laporte had been sent to do penance (it was frequently translated in the English press as penalty box) and now would have time to think things over.

Chartrand had reason to be annoyed with Laporte's Labour Department, since the construction unions of the CNTU, to whom he acted as an advisor, had been involved for many months in a protracted argument on many sides concerning wages to be paid outside Montreal, a city where the generally higher-paid inter-national unions predominate. But not even Chartrand's best friends could lightly forgive him that gaucherie into the microphone, which appeared even worse a week later when Laporte was dead.

The 13th in a family of 14 children, Chartrand grew

up in the middle-class surroundings and aspirations of a family headed by a minor Government official. His father was an accountant in the court system. As a boy at St. Jean de Brébeuf, the proud and arrogant Michel hissed at a student a few years his junior, 'Speak French,' which Pierre Elliott Trudeau already did well. Chartrand entered the Trappist order for almost two years, although few today would believe he once was in an order with vows of silence. He spoke at that time an elegant and polished French and it was not until he was a mature man that he vulgarized his language and discovered the rough humour which made him the folk-hero of many a labor battle to come.

There were curious dissimilarities in the police tactics in the raids of October 16: Pauline Julien was permitted to phone a friend to say the police had arrived and she would be unable to keep an appointment to go to Sherbrooke that day; Simone Chartrand was not allowed to use the phone while the police were in her house. She had wanted to phone her brother who is a judge, as was her father. It was also odd that one of Chartrand's more conciliatory speeches of the period had been made the night before his arrest, at the student meeting at the Paul Sauvé arena, which was to become a feature of the Drapeau campaign for re-election, because Vallières was also there. Chartrand had told the students there were a lot of foreigners in town (the troops) and they should be kind to these people who were standing all over the place, they should offer them chairs. This was one of Chartrand's typical inside jokes, based on the fact that regulations of the City of Montreal require that shop employees who must stand at work should have a chair and the chance to sit down every three hours. And, Chartrand said, drawing further on his union background, the time to strike is not when the boss wants you to strike. The students took his advice and went home.

For Pauline Julien, the experience was not over when she arrived home from jail at 10 a.m. on Saturday, October 24. In the dining room she encountered that scene of so many frightening plots: the table set for dinner but never used. Her two children, 15-year-old Nicholas and 18-year-old Pasquale were nowhere to be seen.

The police had been back to Pauline Julien's house three times during the week when she was in jail, searching for more material from *Les Editions Parti Pris*, apparently, but without success. Then, at 7 p.m. on Friday, October 23, not long after Miss Julien had phoned her children to say she was being released, the police arrived again and said, "Come with us." But for chance, the children would have been alone. Their aunt, Miss Julien's sister, had arrived about five minutes before to give the children some money. She then decided to stay with them for supper, but she too ended up in jail.

"It was completely crazy," Pasquale was to say later. "We're children you know, my brother is 15, and I'm 18 and my brother isn't even interested in politics or things like that . . . "

The police, of course, did not have to explain why the safety of the state required the jailing of a 15-year-old boy, his sister and his aunt but they did, on this one occasion, confirm that Nicholas was in jail when Miss Julien arrived home the next morning and found the house empty. Nicholas got home from jail at 8 p.m. that night and Pasquale at 10.

Pasquale blamed the neighbors, the English neighbors: "Everybody these days is making trouble for people they don't like." And Nicholas, who may not have cared much for politics before, became suddenly much more interested. "The War Measures Act is a good act for Canadians," he said, "but not for us."

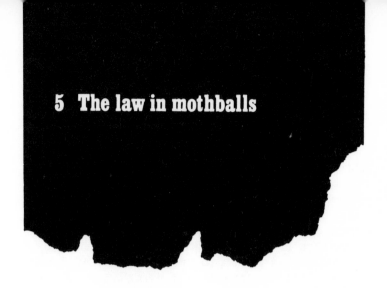

5 The law in mothballs

When Archduke Franz Ferdinand was assassinated at
Sarajevo, Sir Robert Borden was packing his bags for a
patronage-dispensing trip to Halifax. He was Prime
Minister of Canada, but still a minor figure. He faced a
hostile Senate, a disenchanted Quebec and, in Sir Wilfrid
Laurier on the Opposition benches, a leader who clearly
outclassed him. Undeterred by some foreign gunshot,
Borden went off to Halifax. Then, filled with innocence
and indecision, he returned for a vacation in the
Muskoka Lake district of Ontario. Tired and ill, he
could not make up his mind whether to retire or
continue in office.

An urgent cable brought his indecision to an end and
he was back in Ottawa on August 1, 1914. He began
immediately to plan for the war which was now inevitable, which Britain declared on August 4. Eventually, he
was to emerge with new stature for himself and for the
country he led.

A special session of Parliament was called to deal with
the emergency, but in the meantime orders-in-council
were invoked by the cabinet to deal with those
difficulties which could be anticipated, such as detaining
enemy ships and prohibiting trade with the enemy.
Borden's law officers set to work to draft a Canadian
version of Britain's Defence of the Realm Act.

The regulations under the British act were specific in
the emergency powers they granted. Working late into

the humid August nights in Ottawa, Borden's legal advisors tried to draft regulations which were similarly specific, but their work was rejected by Borden, who could not decide what he wanted to leave out and what he wanted to include. Rather than incorporate the details into a bill for the consideration of Parliament as he originally intended, Borden gave instructions to bring in a bill that would allow him to decide later, as the need arose, what powers he needed. His last act of indecision in affairs of state gave him and his cabinet unprecedented powers to run the country as absolute rulers. They had far greater powers than His Majesty's government in Great Britain, which faced an actual physical threat from the war and, of more lasting importance, the powers Borden took unto himself and his cabinet were to live past him, unlike the emergency legislation in the United Kingdom, which died on the day of victory.

Almost three weeks after Borden's return to Ottawa, the extraordinary new legislation was ready for Parliament, which was prepared, indeed eager, to pass it.

Parliament truly reflected the flush of enthusiasm in Canada to go to war for the honor of Empire. Apart from the minor South African experience (and the opposition to it in French Canada) the country had no great familiarity with bloodshed. Laurier's patriotic speeches from the Opposition side made the process painless. Borden was given, and accepted, a blank cheque to make the laws Parliament usually makes and there was no protest. The war had to be won; leaders were there to be trusted. The House of Commons readily accepted an explanation from Charles J. Doherty, Borden's Minister of Justice, as to why the Commons was to be by-passed in the future and, indeed, why Parliament could not be told then the areas in which emergency orders might be made in the future.

"It is true," Doherty said, "that with regard to certain matters, it might perhaps have been possible to realize just what present conditions require and to enact direct legislation with regard to them, or to provide in a specific manner for authority to the Governor-in-Council to deal with them in a particular way. But, after giving the matter the fullest consideration" (read procrastination) "and listening to and carefully thinking over the numerous suggestions that came to the Government from many quarters," (read indecision) "it appeared to us that the wiser course was to ask this House to give to the Government of the day the power to exercise its own judgment as regards the requirements that the various conditions which we have to apprehend may call upon us to meet."

The debate lasted just over half an hour on that Wednesday, August 19, 1914. The lone Opposition speaker supported the bill but asked the government to reconsider the absolute right to deal with arrested and detained aliens without permitting bail, a regulation which effectively denied habeas corpus.

When the bill came back on Friday after consideration by a Committee, it took only five minutes of debate for Borden to assure an Opposition member that the Germans would not be able to collect royalties on their patents from Canadian businessmen, and then the bill passed. The Senate took even less time and the Duke of Connaught, Governor-General of Canada, returned from a Banff holiday in time to give Royal Assent the next day.

It is fitting that blanket legislation leaves nothing uncovered and Borden's law officers had Parliament ratify for the government "all acts and things done or omitted to be done prior to the passing of this act and on or after the first day of August . . . " All things done or undone, whether known at the time or not were all deemed to have been done or omitted to be done under the authority of the act which was given the name "The War Measures Act."

Nothing of importance has been changed to this day. In 1960 a review procedure on the motion of ten members of Parliament was added as one of the features of the Canadian Bill of Rights. Otherwise, the Bill of

Rights does not apply to acts taken under the authority of the War Measures Act.

The War Measures Act permits the cabinet to make such orders and regulations as it deems necessary or advisable by reason of the existence of real or apprehended war, invasion or insurrection. It comes into force on the proclamation of the Governor-in-Council (the cabinet) that war, invasion or insurrection, real or apprehended, exists. No independent check, except for the 1960 *ex post facto* review, exists on the power of the Cabinet to declare the emergency and then act upon its own declaration.

As though to underline the absolute power that is given to appropriate absolute power, and to ensure no outside interference, the act declares that: "The issue of a proclamation by Her Majesty, or under the authority of the Governor-in-Council shall be conclusive evidence" that the state of events described in the proclamation exists until, by a further proclamation, it ceases.

While the power is general and cuts across all of the basic rights of the provinces, there are some that are listed. They are those that Borden and his cabinet could think of but to which they didn't want to be limited. They include, censorship, arrest, detention, exclusion and deportation, control of harbours, ports and territorial waters, movement of vessels, all transportation, trading, exports, imports, production and manufacture, and complete power to deal with property, including appropriation, forfeiture and disposition. Since it was first enacted, proclamations have brought the act into force on two occasions, September 1, 1939 and October 16, 1970.

On September 1, 1939, the Mackenzie King government proclaimed that a state of apprehended war existed as and from the previous August 25. If the War Measures Act did not exist, one would have had to be invented. But it was there. As author Ralph Allen later described the event: " . . . in one of his most dazzling constitutional exercises he proclaimed a state of 'apprehended war' and announced his intention of making use of the War Measures Act, a sweeping mandate for absolute rule of the Cabinet which no one had remembered to cancel after the 1914 war."

In 1945 the war was clearly over. There was none of the haziness of dates brought on by lengthy negotiations which followed Armistice Day of 1918. Victory was decisive and the dates were definite. The powers under the War Measures Act were terminated, but the act itself was not repealed. To provide for a gradual phase-out of the powers taken and an orderly reconstruction of the economy, the Government extended its powers on an annual basis by special legislation bearing the cumbersome title, "The National Emergency Transitional Powers Act."

The use of a special act to continue wartime powers after 1945 was flimsily based on a near-precedent from the first world war. Then, the Borden government sought to introduce special legislation to extend wartime powers in 1919 because it was feared that the formal declaration of the end of the war, tied to the peace negotiations at Versailles, might occur when Parliament was not sitting and catch the government as it was phasing out its programs. The delay overseas made the move academic and Meighen either as Minister of Justice or Prime Minister never actually put his bill through the House of Commons. Mackenzie King, then aspiring to the Liberal leadership, was a keen observer of what went on in the House, and the precedent was there for him to use as Prime Minister a quarter-century later.

The War Measures Act was never intended to be permanent legislation. Britain's Defence of the Realm Act, which inspired the Canadian Act, clearly limited the extraordinary power it granted the government to a period "during the continuance of the present war." It was passed four days after England declared war on Germany and there was no mistake possible. It expired with the war.

Then tied in foreign but not in domestic affairs to the authority of the United Kingdom, Canada's government recognized that its authority to make and enforce regulations under the War Measures Act might end by the act of the British government declaring war at an end. In April 1919, the Borden government sought to introduce special legislation to extend the wartime orders-in-council because, in the words of Arthur Meighen, then acting Minister of Justice, "we have no knowledge as to when the proclamation terminating the war may issue." The bill was withdrawn when it became clear that a formal proclamation of peace was long enough away to permit orderly decontrol.

However, the Canadian law didn't extinguish itself, it stayed on the statute books. That was an accident of history, the product of the urgency felt in 1914 of

getting something into law to justify both the actions that had already been taken as well as those to come. No one intended it to last any longer than the English law which inspired it and it is clear from the debate that no one thought it would. In the opening words of its originator, Justice Minister Doherty, it was needed "to meet those conditions that have arisen or may arise by reason of the state of war which now prevails."

But its language allowed it to be resurrected by a simple proclamation of Mackenzie King's government in 1939 and that wily leader took credit for a constitutional coup which made it possible to take major steps to mobilize for war while members of Parliament were still catching their trains to Ottawa for the special war session.

At the end of World War II Louis St. Laurent, then King's Minister of Justice, replaced the government's powers under the War Measures Act with the National Emergency Transitional Powers Act, which like the British wartime legislation had to be extended year by year. In giving his reasons for this move on November 23, 1945 he told the Canadian House of Commons:

"I believe it was intended to delegate these powers for the purpose of enabling the Governor-in-Council to take such expeditious measures that might be required to secure the safety of the state against the immediate dangers resulting from a state of war; and though it might be technically correct, it would not be within the general intent of that statute that the Governor-in-Council exercise under that statute extraordinary powers to protect the safety of the state against dangers arising out of the economic disturbance consequent upon war.''

St. Laurent, the crusty corporation lawyer from Quebec City, was saying quite explicitly that even the national emergency of transition to peace should be accomplished by new laws specifically passed by Parliament; technically, the Government could still use its wartime powers, but it preferred to follow the obvious intention of Parliament: to use wartime powers in wartime and to pass new legislation for the powers needed in peacetime. It was then that the distinction between the British and the Canadian practice became most distinct: in Canada, the War Measures Act did not die, it went on the shelf awaiting another constitutional expert who might find it useful not to have to consult Parliament.

While King's interdepartmental committee was hurrying to draft wartime regulations during the summer of 1939 so was a committee especially appointed by the British government. The difference was that there was no accident of history to give the British Cabinet the right to enact new laws without further reference to Parliament.

The English had been much more careful of civil liberties. The rights given in time of war by the Defence of the Realm Act were largely military in nature and the Crown was generally considered to have already the prerogative to do what was necessary to defend itself. During the first world war the House of Lords ruled that this power did *not* extend to interfering with the rights of the subject. Requisitioning ships was one thing, personal liberty was another.

It was not until 1920 that Parliament enacted a peacetime power to proclaim an emergency. Under the Emergency Powers Act the U.K. government was given the right to make the proclamation on the basis of action taken or threatened by some person or body of persons of such a nature and on so extensive a scale as to be calculated, by interfering with the supply and distribution of food, water, fuel, or light, or with the means of locomotion, to deprive the community, or any substantial portion of the community, of the essentials of life. As a peacetime measure, and intended for purposes other than national security, its proclamations were limited to one month at a time.

The war clouds of 1939 caused the British government to examine its powers and to conclude that something suitable for time of war was necessary. It enacted the Emergency Powers (Defence) Act on August 24, 1939. This act empowered the Cabinet to make defence regulations by order-in-council for the purpose of securing the public safety, the defence of the realm, the maintenance of public order, the efficient prosecution of any war in which the Crown might be engaged and the maintenance of essential supplies and services.

The Home Secretary, Sir Samuel Hoare, went before the House of Commons at Westminster on August 24, 1939 and asked the representatives of a people who were certain to feel the war more sharply than the Canadians across the sea for emergency powers to last no longer than one year. The powers, he said, "must be wide, drastic and comprehensive." He headed off criticism that the powers might last for too long a period by providing that they could not extend past twelve months and that they could only be continued past that time by a resolution of both Houses, in effect, new passage.

As a further guarantee, Sir Samuel told the House, "that we have no intention whatever of using these emergency powers for peace-time purposes." The Emergency Powers (Defence) Act passed both the Commons and the Lords and received Royal Assent the same day. At the end of the war, both Britain and Canada recognized that their wartime legislation should not be used, although the economic reconstruction of the country, and the dangers it presented amounted to an emergency. Special legislation was brought in to extend the life of the various orders-in-council.

Under the act, the British government assumed wide powers to control national security, industry, the economy, shipping and commerce in general. However, the British Government took pains to ensure that this statute would not be one which could be forgotten and permitted to lie dormant at the war's end. It was originally limited to remain in force one year. At the year's end, on an address to both Houses of Parliament, the act was extended for a further year. Again, the next year the process was repeated, even in the midst of war, until finally in 1945 it was extended for the last time and it expired on February 24, 1946.

To allow for reconstruction, certain regulations were kept in force by special statute in a procedure similar to that adopted in Canada. In Canada, however, the War Measures Act was left alive, to be used again without reference to Parliament. In England, an address to both Houses of Parliament would have been necessary to resurrect the parallel legislation. In order to guard against even that happening, the Emergency Powers (Defence) Act of 1939 was formally repealed in 1959.

In the United States, each branch of the Federal Government is subject to a system of checks and balances and the executive and the Congress have their power limited by the courts, which in turn derive considerable authority from the Bill of Rights. There is no permanent legislation authorizing the executive to exercise war emergency powers, but a system of Presidential decrees has been used in both world wars to accomplish the same purpose.

The test by the United States Supreme Court of the Espionage Act, enacted by Congress in June of 1917 resulted in the landmark "clear and present danger" doctrine enunciated by Justice Oliver Wendell Holmes. The Espionage Act, which was upheld constitutionally, contained provisions for postal and military censorship. Its companion, created by amendment in May, 1918, but usually referred to as the Sedition Act, was more comprehensive and included a prohibition of criticism of the government. In many ways these acts paralleled the censorship regulations passed in Canada during the first world war which culminated in the consolidated orders respecting censorship of May, 1918.

In the United States, more than 1,500 people were convicted under the Espionage and Sedition Acts during the war. Among them was Schenck, the secretary of the Socialist Party, whose case tested the validity of the law, unsuccessfully, but gave Holmes the opportunity to enunciate the "clear and present danger" doctrine. Free speech could be curtailed by law only where the speech created a "clear and present danger". The Socialist leader Eugene V. Debs was also convicted. In spite of the extremes of feeling which gave rise to these laws, there was no interference with procedural guarantees nor the right to habeas corpus.

The notorious Palmer raids and the accompanying anti-Red campaigns, the wholesale deportations to Russia and the general hysteria, caused a backlash which resulted in the election in 1920 of Harding and a "return to normalcy". One of the results of the "return to normalcy" was the repeal of the laws which had been used in the Palmer campaigns.

During the second world war the country gave, and Roosevelt took, almost absolute power to operate under Presidential decree. The courts had the right to review, and did exercise some control over his actions. The Supreme Court upheld the constitutional validity of the mass internment of the Japanese-Americans. Its decision declaring the military government imposed on Hawaii illegal came after the war had ended.

For both sheer volume and importance, the various regulations made under the War Measures Act since it first came into being are unsurpassed in Canadian legal history. Only in times of war would Canadian politicians feel free to legislate into every nook and cranny of the life of the country.

In the first world war, the Borden government found

it necessary to protect security-sensitive locations, guard against espionage, protect means of transportation, prevent trading with the enemy, register aliens, prohibit publications containing comment on the war "contrary to the actual facts" and influencing persons against the cause of the United Kingdom or in favour of the enemy, appoint a censor of publications, and control the supply and trade in various commodities. It also used its power after the war had ended to establish the Canadian Wheat Board and to pump public money into the Grand Trunk Railway which was later taken over completely by the government, along with others similarly assisted to become the Canadian National Railways.

The preparation for mobilizing and controlling the nation to fight the second war began before it was declared. In the summer of 1939, King had a departmental committee hard at work deciding what was needed and drawing up a multitude of orders-in-council creating regulations. The Defence of Canada regulations were ready and were brought into force on September 3, 1939, the day Britain declared war. These regulations provided for all the protections in the name of national security which were present in the earlier war together with powers to intern and detain at will and powers to outlaw organizations. The regulations were considerably more thorough and detailed than their predecessors and they were more vigorously employed. However, the vast majority of the volume of regulations concerned the economic control of the country. The cabinet created controllers and boards of controllers in every important area of commerce. Rents and prices were controlled. All essential supplies were controlled. The resulting mobilization was the envy of the Allied world, so complete was the effort. Using its enormous powers, the Government set aside provincial discriminatory legislation, so that Orientals could for the first time work in British Columbia lumber camps on Crown land; it also interned 20,000 persons of Japanese ancestry, even those who were native-born Canadian citizens, in what remains one of the grossest single acts of racial discrimination in

Canadian history.

As early as the first war, the entry of the federal government into the control of the commercial life of the country and into the right of the provinces to legislate brought support from the courts. The courts held that the power to enact such laws in a time of emergency could not be doubted and was part of the right and duty of the federal government to pass laws for the "peace, order and good government" of the nation. This was so, even though provincial rights were clearly infringed.

The extension of wartime powers to reconstruction was accomplished by special legislation in 1945. But in 98 1918, the special powers drifted with the peace negotiations and companies affected by some of the regulations tested them in the courts. Although the courts upheld the right of the Governor-in-Council to decide for itself when the emergency would pass, there was at least one case in which the Supreme Court of Canada applied its common sense instead of taking the Government's power at face value. On the grounds that the war emergency was over, it struck down a Cabinet order-in-council giving a paper controller extreme powers.

"The common knowledge," the Court said, "possessed by every man on the street, of which courts of justice cannot divest themselves, makes it impossible to believe that the Governor-in-Council on the 29th day of January, 1920 deemed it (the power) 'necessary or advisable for the security, defence, peace, order or welfare of Canada . . . by reason of the existence of real or apprehended war, invasion or insurrection' ".

"Advisability or necessity, however great, arising out of post-war conditions is not the same thing as and should not be confounded with advisability or necessity 'by reason of the existence of real or apprehended war' ".

The court set aside an order made under the authority of that regulation.

The courts have hinted that there might be grounds for reviewing what the cabinet does under the authority of the War Measures Act, but only on "very clear evidence." The consistent view of both the Supreme

Court of Canada and the Judicial Committee of the Privy Council is that the decision as to whether or not the Act ought to be invoked is a matter of statesmanship. The courts are loathe, they say, to interfere in matters which the Executive is best able to handle. The courts point out that Parliament has granted the authority and that it is capable of reviewing the exercise of it.

In considering the many regulations which have come forth under the authority of the act, liberal interpretation is also the rule. The prevailing attitude was well represented by Mr. Justice Plaxton who upheld the forfeiture of certain securities brought into Canada by a man named Wheeler contrary to the Foreign Exchange Control Order. Wheeler was taking advantage of a higher price being quoted for the shares on the Toronto Stock Exchange than on the New York Exchange and was bringing them across the border to sell. Wheeler argued that stock certificates were not "goods, wares or merchandise" and therefore not subject to forfeiture under the order. It seemed like a good technical argument. Not so, said Mr. Justice Plaxton of the Exchequer Court of Canada. " . . . the powers of the Governor-in-Council under Section 3 (War Measures Act), coming into play as they do during a time of great emergency, are of the most sweeping character, and are certainly to be most liberally construed."

Entering into the spirit of the regulations is part of the court's function, even if some very basic rights are affected. For example, lack of knowledge that you are committing an offense is no excuse.

Thus, a Quebec City druggist, Charles Duquette, was convicted of selling codeine without a doctor's prescription contrary to an order made under the authority of the War Measures Act, notwithstanding the fact that the sale was made by an employee, in Duquette's absence and that he was able to prove that he had issued explicit instructions to the contrary. The court even found that the sale had been made by mistake, but convicted anyway on the theory that the administration of these regulations required strict liability.

Equally startling is the case of Douglas Stewart, advertising and circulation manager of The Clarion, a Toronto left-wing newspaper. In one of the earliest applications of the new Defence of Canada Regulations, Stewart and three other staff members of the paper were prosecuted for publishing an issue in November, 1939, containing the Manifesto of the Executive Committee of the Communist International, issued on the 22nd Anniversary of the October Revolution, November 7, 1939.

He and the others were convicted by a judge and jury in Toronto on January 17, 1940 of publishing reports or statements intended or likely to cause disaffection to His Majesty, tending to prejudice recruiting and prejudicial to the efficient prosecution of the war. All of this occurred despite evidence that he had no idea what was in the paper and that the first time he had seen the offending article was when the paper arrived at his home after publication. They each received two years in penitentiary.

In judging the 1970 Canadian crisis and the response of the federal and Quebec governments, there is one prerequisite: no government can employ the War Measures Act in ignorance of its casual political history and its very rigid legal one. Somewhere in the Cabinet file reserved for this act should be placed the words of Ontario's Chief Justice Meredith, uttered when the act was barely one year old:

"It is also, as a matter of law, quite immaterial what the opinion of any Judge or other person may be respecting the wisdom or unwisdom of conferring such powers, or of the wisdom or unwisdom of the way in which the power is exercised, provided it is exercised in good faith; but it should be plain to everyone that in the stress and danger to the life of any nation in war, the Courts should be exceedingly careful not to hamper the action of those especially charged with the safety of the nation . . . It is not a time when the prisoner is to have the benefit of the doubt; it is a time when, in all things great and small, the country must have every possible advantage, a time when it must be the general safety first in all things always; until the final victory is won; even though individuals may suffer meanwhile."

On Sunday, October 11, 1970, the day before Thanksgiving and the day after Pierre Laporte was kidnapped, Prime Minister Pierre Elliott Trudeau and some of his key advisors began to consider the responses which would be possible. As the holiday weekend passed into the following week, the options were explored and assessed, the advantages and disadvantages weighed and weighed again.

Finally, the decision for surprise raids was taken. For the police to be able to move without fear of transgressing the law and also to preserve their deteriorating image, new powers were needed. Those powers were in the hands of the federal government and would have to come from the War Measures Act if secrecy and effectiveness were to be preserved. The motive clearly was secrecy and it was on this basis that the government acted.

Nothing in its history, in the discussions of it in Parliament or in the courts, nor even a casual perusal of its language would support the suggestion that the apprehended insurrection mentioned in it could be anything short of an all-out civil war. It was designed and intended to support a military action, not a police action. It was never intended as a tool to root out criminals, whether they be self-styled terrorists or just thugs.

With the move no longer secret and no element of surprise left, the government found it expedient to "give in" to the opposition's request and replace the regulations with other measures which were not based on questionable historical, let alone legal, foundations.

They chose legislation which was deceptively similar to the regulations but which contained some "improvements" which were meaningless to those already detained or charged, and some other "improvements" which substantially improved the position of the prosecution in the trials which were yet to come.

6 Big fish, little fish

As usually happens with social democrats, the New
Democratic Party got it from both sides. Pierre Vallières
had denounced the NDP; when the party gets close to
electoral victory, he wrote, that only proves it is getting
closer to the bosses. On one occasion a group of FLQ
thugs broke into the NDP office in Montreal and stole
the mimeograph machine. From then on, a great deal of
FLQ literature was turned out on this machine stolen
not from the capitalist exploiters, but from those who
opposed them democratically. Then, three days after
the invocation of the War Measures Act, the Montreal
police came to the NDP offices with a raiding party of
half-a-dozen.

At the time of the raid, the New Democratic Party
was the official opposition in the legislatures of British
Columbia and Saskatchewan (where it once held office)
and it was the governing party of Manitoba. Its members
were a minority but significant force in the Ontario
Legislature and in the federal Parliament. The NDP National leader, T. C. Douglas, was one of the three opposition party leaders Prime Minister Trudeau brought to his
office on the night of October 15 to be informed that
the invocation of the War Measures Act was virtually
inevitable. A police raid on NDP offices in Toronto,
Winnipeg or Vancouver would create a major scandal; in
Montreal, the raid went virtually unnoticed.

At 1:30 p.m. on October 19, a Monday, Joan

Banfield heard half-a-dozen men come into the NDP offices and move through to the back. She left her own office and went into the office of the NDP secretary. "May I help you?" she asked.

"As soon as I said it I realized how silly it was," she recalled later, "because they were in the back already. They just came right in. They said 'no' in answer to my question, and then they didn't say anything else. They just ignored us. They started opening files and looking into everything. They didn't take anything, they did it all as if we weren't there."

The police went through NDP party files but did not appear to be searching for anything in particular. "One

of the files wouldn't open," Miss Banfield recalled, "and they got very suspicious. It was just stuck, and they finally got it open, but there was nothing much in it, just a few papers.

"They went into the back and looked around, and they found a safe belonging to the NDP, which was locked. They asked for the combination, and were told it, but they still couldn't get it open. This seemed to disturb them very much. But they seemed to be finished then, so they asked all of us for our identification."

Miss Banfield and five others in the office were in Montreal working on behalf of the United Farm Workers, the California agricultural union led by Cesar Chavez. The famous grape boycott had ended a few months before with the signing of labor contracts at Delano, California. Now the union was organizing workers in the lettuce fields; its major adversary was Bud Antle Inc., a huge agricultural business much indebted to Dow Chemical.

The police came to the NDP offices equipped with little cards which they said it was necessary for them to fill out at each raid. They took everyone's name, address, phone number, driver's license and, since the workers in the lettuce boycott who were in the office had all come to Montreal from the U.S., the police also asked for immigration details.

The process had taken about half an hour and the

police seemed ready to leave when they asked one of the men in the office, Juvencio Garza, to return with them to the back room for questioning.

In the investigation of FLQ kidnappings and (by that time) murder, Juvencio Garza was about as ludicrous a suspect as could be imagined. A Mexican national, he speaks not a word of French and only halting English. He had been in Canada precisely 10 days, arriving from the California lettuce fields on October 7, and he knew practically nothing about Canada. (After Juvencio and his wife returned to the United States, Mrs. Garza was asked if she would ever return to Quebec. "Where is Quebec?" she asked, "I only know Montreal.")

Joan Banfield, knowing that Garza spoke no French and little English, moved toward the back room to help him, but she was kept out by one of the officers. The police had Garza in the classic stance up against the wall for searching, the only one of those in the office to be searched. Finally, when Joan Banfield and the others could hear that Garza and the police were having great difficulty in communicating in their imperfect English, they got into the back room and tried to explain who Garza was and why he was in Canada. The police then began to take Garza away and when they were asked why, one of the policemen said: "He resembles one of the suspects."

Since Garza has plainly Mexican features, is small of stature, and the officers did not decide to question him until they were preparing to leave, those in the room got the impression that it was a last-minute decision made by a group of not-very-experienced policemen who needed a justification for the raid should there be future complaints. "It was," said Miss Banfield, "as if, when they couldn't find anything, they decided they should go away with something, so they looked pretty hard for something to be suspicious of. And they chose Juvencio. They'd been there half an hour before they decided to even question him."

The police left with their utterly confused, 32-year-old "suspect", leaving behind his 18-year-old wife, whose English at least was sufficiently proficient that she was terrified. Half-an-hour later, the police were back to have another try at the NDP office safe. Still later, three more policemen returned to pick up Mrs. Garza and this time they had another justification for detaining Juvencio: there was a falsification or a discrepancy on his landed immigrant papers. When Garza crossed the border, an immigration officer copied the date of his arrival in Canada (October 7, 1970) into the space for "Date of birth". Juvencio Garza's papers showed that he was 10 days old. Mrs. Garza, ordered out by the police, left the NDP office in tears.

At the station, the police called in an official from the Mexican consulate. When Mr. and Mrs. Garza returned to the NDP offices after about three hours of detention, they told their colleagues the police had advised them to leave Canada. "Both the Garzas told me," Miss Banfield reported, "that the police had told them it would be better if they left the country, because if they were stopped again they wouldn't be bothered with all this questioning, they'd be put in jail for six or seven months."

Mrs. Garza herself said: "The man who did the papers at the border put the day we got into Canada instead of the day Juvencio was born. So it said he was born on October 7, 1970. The police were very upset about that. The (Mexican) consul told us it was better for us to go back to the United States because the police were going to be picking up many people and if they saw him again they were going to put him in jail."

Juvencio Garza and his wife were reassigned by their union to the Boston area. Whatever else might be said about the War Measures Act, it was a complete success in this instance: it removed from Montreal the two genuine farm workers engaged in trying to convince Canadians not to buy non-union lettuce.

The War Measures Act had other incidental successes. The combined anti-terrorist squad moved into a house in Pointe-aux-Trembles where they found, not terrorists, but terrible whisky. The occupant, who was operating a still with a two-gallon a day capacity, was arrested. Much the same occurred in Ville LaSalle, where another illicit still and 100 gallons of liquor were seized after being discovered accidentally by a police raiding party.

In Ottawa and elsewhere, much was made of the fact that the Government proclamation did not invoke all the powers possible under the War Measures Act. There was, for example, no official censorship, but this did not deter the Royal Canadian Mounted Police from visiting a number of university newspapers across the country to check their contents. At the University of Quebec in Montreal, a student group met to discuss, quietly, the War Measures Act. On November 11, by which time any misunderstandings about the act were supposed to have been ironed out, the police arrested Bernard Mateigne, the student who had presided at the discussion. The rector of the university, who personally supported the invocation of the War Measures Act, issued a statement criticizing the arrest. "The main danger I am trying to point out," said Leo Dorais, "is that of no longer being able to express any point of view for fear of denunciation or arbitrary imprisonment."

The period immediately after the invocation of the War Measures Act offered everyone an opportunity to get at his favorite target; a time of hippie-bashing, the *Globe and Mail* called it. Montreal's Mayor Drapeau had long been at odds with the Quebec movie censor, known as the Cinema Supervisory Board, and he soon drew to their attention his distaste at the movie *Quiet Days in Clichy*, which had been passed by the censors and had been showing for several weeks at two movie houses on principal streets, one on Sherbrooke, the other on St. Catherine. Approximately one week after the passage of the War Measures Act, Mayor Drapeau began the first of a series of phone calls to the Cinema Board, which refused to alter its decision. By that time, the Board, a creation of the previous Union Nationale government, had been in operation three years as an autonomous arm of the Quebec Government and, in line with the current thinking in the rest of Canada, had been more concerned with classifying films for the type of audience that could see them than with censoring out objectionable passages. Finally, Mayor Drapeau warned the Cinema Board that if *Quiet Days* was not withdrawn, the Montreal police would raid the 7:30 p.m. performance on November 5, would cast into jail everyone in the audience at the Festival Theatre and Cinema V, as well as all members of the Cinema Supervisory Board, and would charge them all under Section 152 of the Criminal Code, which prohibits an indecent performance. The movie, an adaptation from Henry Miller, contains several explicit sexual scenes and had been approved by the Cinema Board after its customary consultations with theologians and others able to define "public order" and "good morals". The mayor, and Montreal City Attorney Michel Côté believed that several prosecutions against magazines had failed because the Cinema Board was permitting nudity in movies. Said the mayor in one of his phone calls to the Cinema Board: "You are through humiliating the police."

When Mayor Drapeau demanded the withdrawal of the film, it had been showing in Montreal some six weeks, and the War Measures Act had been in force one week. After a discussion in the Quebec cabinet, the film was taken out of the two theatres. As the letters came down from the marquee of Cinema V, the cop on the beat walked over to the manager and said it was the best film he'd seen in years, "Why in hell are you stopping that movie for?"

The statement from the Cinema Board on November 9th was a classic example of the way all will to resist official pressure, in whatever area, evaporates in times of repression. The Quebec government, said the statement, had received protests over the movie. (Only when the crisis had passed was it revealed that the protests were from Mayor Drapeau. From the public, the censorship board had received precisely one letter of criticism of *Quiet Days*.)

"Realizing that a bitter dispute might ensue," said the

statement, "and above all taking into account the troubled times through which the people of Quebec are now passing, the president of the board (André Guérin) decided to recall the film for further examination . . .

"The board will obviously not be in a position to undertake a further review of this film until the present tense climate has subsided and calm is restored." Those Canadians who wrote letters-to-the-editor by the hundreds during the period of the War Measures Act saying: "My civil liberties have not been curtailed," did not, apparently, take account of a citizen's right to choose his own entertainment free of secret and arbitrary censorship. Among the last people in Montreal to see *Quiet Days* on the screen was the mayor's private secretary, Paul Leduc, who took his wife to the movie entirely unaware of his employer's campaign. Some of Leduc's friends had said it was well worth seeing.

Many a timorous bureaucrat decided the safest course was to avoid any controversy at all. The Canadian Broadcasting Corp. postponed a documentary called *The Legacy of Lenin* scheduled for October 27, directly as a result of a question posed by a Tory Member of Parliament, Lloyd R. Crouse, who asked: "Since we as Canadians are experiencing the agony of a wave of revolution against our democratic government, will the Secretary of State consider the cancelling of the program *The Legacy of Lenin* to be projected by the CBC tomorrow night?" Only a few hours later, the film was screened for Eugene Hallman, the CBC's Toronto-based head of English-network TV. Hallman had once removed a song by Pauline Julien from the CBC's public affairs program *Weekend*, apparently because of her separatist politics. Even earlier, he had cancelled the broadcast of an exclusive radio interview with Fidel Castro shortly before his capture of Havana. Batista's ambassador in Ottawa had complained.

The Legacy of Lenin, a straightforward documentary on Lenin's influence on the arts, was removed from the next night's schedule with a statement from Hallman which attributed the decision to the "concern and anxiety" in the country. The unmistakable slur on those who had created the film, the idea that they had produced and the CBC was about to broadcast something subversive, was firmly established, at least until the film was actually broadcast the next month.

Perhaps even more significantly, the publicly-owned network also postponed a clever and imaginative documentary on the Hollywood Ten, the story of American film writers and directors who were blacklisted from work in the motion picture industry during the anti-Communist hysteria of the 1950s. For most of them, their crime had been to follow government suggestions to insert favourable references to Russia in wartime films made after 1941. A film about the victims of indiscriminate smear was not, the CBC decided, something the Canadian public should see in the month of October, 1970.

CBC news reporters in Ottawa received a directive that they were to broadcast only those stories which could be attributed to an identifiable source. While on the surface this could be defended as an attempt to keep rumours off the air, its effect was to confine CBC news to official reports from the Government, or to the restrained comments the opposition parties were willing to make on camera. The doubts and the concerns of many members of all parties could be broadcast only if the MPs were willing to attach their names. CBC "personalities" were reminded in another directive that they were not to allow their names to be identified with political statements.

In the context of the times, these events were simply more subtle versions of an incident which occurred at Jarvis Collegiate, a high school in Toronto. A group of students was given the use of the school mimeograph machine to turn out a petition to be sent to Prime Minister Trudeau supporting the invocation of the War Measures Act. When another, smaller, group asked for the use of the machine to produce a petition in opposition, they were refused, and when they objected they were told: "Your freedom of speech is being preserved by your right *not* to sign the petition." The concept that the right to remain silent was the only acceptable expression of dissent was common throughout Canada, although not always expressed as clearly as in that high school in Toronto.

Many people got in a shot at their favorite targets. The Alberta movie censors refused a Quebec-made film *Red*, the story of a Métis who leaves the reserve and goes to Montreal. In Vancouver, the City Council took under consideration a motion, inspired by the War Measures Act, to ban all "subversive gatherings". John Turner, the federal Minister of Justice, had already felt it necessary to warn the Attorney-General of B.C. that the War Measures Act was intended only for the specific situation in Quebec, and any extension of its use "beyond that purpose might very well be harmful."

The attacks on the CBC in Parliament were endless and any broadcast that hinted at a less than unanimous spirit of support for the War Measures Act was immediately challenged, particularly by the Creditistes and the Western Tories. A TV panel discussion in which Mr. Justice Samuel Freedman defended the need for such measures and the novelist Morley Callaghan offered wry and witty dissent was attacked in Parliament the next day by E. B. Osler, a Winnipeg Tory (and former CBC director) as being "of doubtful taste". Another Tory wanted the CBC to stop broadcasting the words of any person who could not be admitted to Canada—he had Timothy Leary in mind particularly—which would have had the interesting result of putting the Immigration Department in charge of broadcasting.

There were innumerable outcroppings of firm anti-FLQ action in British Columbia, the province furthest removed from the trouble. The province passed an order-in-council banning any teachers from tax-supported schools "if they advocate the policies of Le Front de Libération du Québec."

The order-in-council was designed more for domestic political purposes in B.C. than for the maintenance of law and order. Many members of the B.C. cabinet had over the years criticized the "socialist ideas" they feared were spread in the classroom. The Minister of Municipal Affairs, Dan Campbell, had said teachers who expressed concern over pollution in the province were "preachers of doom and gloom". An official pronouncement calling for the dismissal of British Columbia teachers who advocated the policies of the FLQ could not help but convince the people of B.C. that a real and present danger from such a source actually existed.

There were, indeed, two isolated incidents in British Columbia upon which the government could rely. In the high school of Dawson Creek, students were invited to line up in the hallway and sign a telegram to Prime Minister Trudeau supporting his use of the War Measures Act. They were also invited to contribute five cents each to the cost of the wire. One of the teachers went down the line-up asking several of the students what the FLQ was. Not a single one of them had the faintest idea. He initiated a discussion in his classroom during which he offered the view that there was not much difference between the Russian invasion of Czechoslovakia and the situation in Quebec. Whatever the wisdom or otherwise of his views (T. C. Douglas chose instead the analogy of the Reichstag fire) the Dawson Creek school board was not prepared to allow its students the educational experience of debating challenging ideas. The telegram went off to Ottawa, signed by students who didn't know what it meant, and the teacher was promptly fired.

At the University of Victoria, assistant professor Ronald Kirkby issued a statement declaring that Trudeau's actions were responsible for the death of Pierre Laporte, a brutal assessment perhaps, but one also shared by René Lévesque, whose political party was supported by almost one-quarter of the voters of Quebec. The police came around to the offices of The Martlett, the University of Victoria student newspaper, and warned them not to publish a letter from Kirkby. They didn't.

Premier W. A. C. Bennett of British Columbia was

certainly the most ingenious public official in exploiting the FLQ crisis. The provincial Treasury Board, which in effect is Bennett himself, announced in early November that officials of the health department would not be permitted to attend an Ottawa meeting to discuss research grants, because of the crisis in eastern Canada. No one was really fooled; there had been a restriction on travel east of Winnipeg, in order to save money, since early summer.

Just as Premier Bennett used the crisis of political crime in Quebec for his own local purposes, others found material for advancing all sorts of assorted causes. It might be, said the Minister of National Defence, Donald MacDonald, that Canada's policy of cutting back its armed forces would have to be reconsidered (although the 7,500 troops used in Ottawa and in the province of Quebec were less than half the ground troops in a total force of 90,000).

The validity of defence expenditures had been suffering some criticism because of the 125 million dollar expenditure on an airplane whose role, at best, was questionable for Canada's defence purposes, the CF-5. It is an excellent airplane for short-distance attacks on an advancing enemy army, but unless there was another classic European ground-war, the airplane's only functions were for reconnaissance or as an expensive trainer. Many of the planes, as they came off the Montreal assembly line, were put into storage. In the first week after invocation of the War Measures Act, the Department of National Defence announced that "an undisclosed number" of the CF-5s were engaged in photo-reconnaissance missions as part of the hunt for the Cross-Laporte kidnappers. The planes were strip-filming the southern part of Quebec in attempts to spot unusual activity, but the number of sorties and the exact locations were, of course, "classified information". In the mood of October, 1970, this particular bit of nonsense was received without comment (as if kidnappers' cars produce a different kind of exhaust or different tire tracks than anyone else's car). Canadians could rest assured that the CF-5 had proved its worth.

The Government of Quebec steadfastly refused to divulge the names of those detained, although nothing in the War Measures proclamation required such secrecy. And Quebec continued to keep the names secret in the face of several proddings from the Federal Minister of Justice, John Turner, who could see no reason for the secrecy. Jérôme Choquette offered no reason. The names of arrested persons ordinarily become known because of the necessity of bringing them "before the first court of competent jurisdiction." There was no need to bring anyone to court, nor even to accuse him of anything, for 21 days, and so the names remained secret.

The notable names soon became known, of course, because their friends and admirers were accustomed to dealing with the press: Pauline Julien, Michel Chartrand, Henri Bellemare, Serge Mongeau, and a host of others. If any "terrorists" were arrested (although none was charged as such among the first several hundred detainees) those arrests could hardly be secret from their colleagues. The only names which were secret were the Government's mistakes.

Jim Leitch had studied at McGill University and a year before moved to Vancouver. He was back in Montreal on holidays in October when he and his friend Pierre Fournier, who is getting his M.A. at McGill, went over to the University of Quebec on the Friday of the War Measures Act to watch the action. They spent an hour or so in a restaurant and then walked back to the administration building, the Louis-Joliette Pavilion, which was being cleared that day of its student sit-downers. Leitch picked up a pamphlet along the way, no more than a souvenir, since he is unconcerned with politics and speaks and understands almost no French. A helmeted motorcycle policeman zoomed in front of the two as they walked along, and within seconds had them stretched up against the wall for searching, first making sure they removed their shoes. "Move, you bastard, and you'll get shot," the policeman said, in French. Leitch didn't understand what was said; Fournier told him about it afterwards.

The pamphlet was soon discovered in Leitch's pocket—he hadn't had a chance to look at it himself yet—and the two young men were taken to the nearest police station. The police made a point of reading parts of the FLQ manifesto to Leitch and explaining to him it was anti-English. After four hours at the station, Leitch and Fournier were driven to Fournier's apartment where the police made a thorough search, finding nothing. There seemed no reason for picking them up other than their long hair, although it was no longer than the current fashion among Quebec students.

Fournier, being French-speaking, was questioned more extensively than Leitch. "The guy who was interviewing me was really quite human," Fournier recalled, "he felt uneasy about what he was doing and he felt the need to justify what he was doing. He recited the Drapeau political creed which goes something like 'there will always be the poor and there will always be the rich, it's just the way it goes and it's much worse in other countries.' He gave me the feeling he was uneasy about what he was doing and felt to some extent that he was being used."

Fournier and Leitch did not, of course, appear among the official number of 497 detainees; they were but two of many who were questioned and released, at what cost in man-hours no one will ever know, as the police experimented with their new powers to pick people up as the mood seized them.

Les Lasko had spent most of the summer on a survey of Quebec voting habits for which the Canada Council had given a grant to Professors Guy Lord and André Bernard of the University of Quebec. After the invocation of the War Measures Act, several students were picked up by the police as they went from door-to-door asking people: "Did you vote in the last election?" "Why didn't you vote?" Lasko was in a high-rise apartment-building on Saturday, October 17, when two policemen got off the elevator and demanded he come with them.

At Number 17 police station, Lasko was held for some five hours and questioned for about three. "Well," the detective said to him for openers, "what do you think about democracy these days?" Then he was asked if he was in favor of the War Measures Act. Lasko said he wasn't, that it reminded him of Duplessis' attempts to run the Jehovah's Witness group out of Quebec; a lot of people were harassed but it didn't get rid of the Jehovah's Witnesses. The police went over his questionnaire (as it happened, he had the English-language version with him that day and some time was spent in 116 translating it) and one policeman suggested that some of the questions would tend to falsify the results. Lasko pointed out other questions which were designed to get as accurate a picture as possible. The questionnaire, being used by Lasko and several other political science students, was designed as part of a university project to delve into that favorite academic exercise, the correlation between socio-economic status and voting habits.

"Tell me," said one of the interrogating detectives, "do you think it is possible to impose an ideal division of society on that society?" No, said Lasko, but you have to have an ideal to work towards. "Have you ever been to Cuba?" he was asked. "No," he answered. "Why," the policeman asked, "are sociology students always the first ones involved in campus political activity?"

The police weren't even bothering to write down the results of this aimless political questioning. They took him back to his apartment, searched it, and then let him go. Lasko was one of three or four engaged in the same survey who were picked up as they made their rounds, obviously on the complaints of suspicious householders. McGill Professor Pauline Vaillancourt received a phone call from a ranking Quebec police officer after some of her students engaged in the survey had been detained. "He asked me," she reported, "if we had permission to do a survey and I said I didn't think you had to have permission under the War Measures

Act. And he said you have to have permission to do anything."

7 Philosopher of the revolution

When Pierre Vallières was seven years old, his father took him across the Jacques Cartier bridge to look at a tarpaper shack which was to be the family's escape from the slums of east end Montreal. It was the first time Pierre had ever left the city. His father worked for the railway, in the repair shops of the CPR hard by the grubby third-floor flat where they lived, but even for him it was his first trip to the South Shore of the river across from Montreal, an area which some 20 years later was to be served by a subway.

By the time the Metro subway came under the river to Longeuil, Pierre Vallières' father was dead of cancer at 53, and Vallières was in jail, continuing to write of the revolution he seems to believe was born within him as he watched his father go down to defeat under the smothering passivity of an uninspiring and duty-laden Catholic wife. The symbolism which Vallières was to attach to his wretched childhood is abundantly clear: his father is Quebec, grimy with toil, exploited and exhausted; his mother is the unknowing instrument of the forces which must inevitably grind Quebec into the dirt—the English capitalists and the French bourgeoisie.

"My mother never went out," Vallières wrote in his book *Nègres blancs d'Amérique*. "She could have made real friends among her neighbors, but refused to do so. Nothing roused her interest. Nothing appealed to her . . . . except her Sacred Duty which in her mind was the obligation to be continually on guard against any 'accident'. That is why she did not want my father to get involved in politics, why my brothers and I were not allowed beyond the immediate vicinity of the house. Anything that disturbed her habits was a terrible anxiety to her. She never ran a risk or took a chance.

"Within a few years she changed into the boss of the little family of which she was the principal servant. She became a slave to fear and tried to subjugate my father, my brothers and me to her need for security. Security took precedence over freedom, economy over love, resignation over hope."

Vallières' portrait of his father (Pierre was the oldest of three boys) is of a politically aware labourer, popular and gregarious at work in the Angus Shops but silent at home. He had gone to work at 14 to help support 13 brothers and sisters when their own father was paralyzed. He then got his job in the CPR shops in 1938, where there were still many workingmen around who had learned their communism in the depths of the Depression, and Pierre Vallières' father learned it from them.

No one, the eldest son seemed to be saying in the words he wrote from jail in the 1960s, was going to defeat *him* as his mother had defeated his father. "Sometimes it seemed to me that my father was ashamed of himself, and that my mother was afraid of her own desperate eagerness to preserve present security and ensure it in the future . . . to accept this state of things was a crime against oneself and against others . . . " The misery of the working-class family, Vallières came to believe, arose from "centuries of exploitation of man by man." Or that at least is the explanation he offered when he was 27 years old, in jail, and writing the revealing autobiography, *Nègres blancs d'Amérique*.

Another view of Vallières is that he was a self-indulgent dropout. Most of the miseries of his youth of which Vallières complains were the miseries of others or miseries to which Vallières was a volunteer. He notes that other fathers in the east-end slums near the railway shops worked out their frustrations by getting drunk on Saturday night and beating up their families. Pierre's father never did. He complains of his father's long overnight hours of work, but these were overtime hours with a unionized railroad. From 1938 to his death in 1965, his father never missed a day of work. Somehow, Pierre sees this as an example of exploitation. His father used his money and his spare time to build a house in the suburbs at the first available opportunity. This was no doubt a crushing experience in the corrupt political atmosphere of postwar Quebec when the money for watermains and sewer-pipes went not into the ground but into the pockets of the local political bosses. Through it all, his two younger brothers came to far different conclusions than Pierre did and in his adolescence stopped speaking to him. And, like many aware working-class families, Pierre's parents insisted on an education for him; when he dropped out of school he was not expected to go to work; he was sent to another school. From these experiences Pierre Vallières became the philosopher of revolution and more than any other person gave an aura of respectability to violence. He saw himself as the product of a racist, exploitative capitalistic society. He was, but he may also have been the product of those terrible tensions the family in any society imposes on its eldest male sibling.

At the age of five, Pierre Vallières ran with a gang in the Hochelaga slums which specialized in turning in false alarms and setting fires in other people's backyards. The fantasies of arson weave in and out through many of his own childhood memories. "In this violent universe," he wrote, "in which children dreamed about gigantic conflagrations, terrible murderers of women and kidnappers of babies, going to school was, to say the least, a boring diversion." Sent to the hallway to meditate on some classroom crime, "I said to myself that one day I too would have my own gang . . . and that this school would be razed to the ground."

It was a violent neighborhood, where families often

fought with iron bars, chains and baseball bats, particularly in Harbour Alley, which was forbidden territory for Pierre and his brothers. One of the violent children who hung around the sheds with Pierre was Ti-Rouge, who one day tore a braid of hair from a little girl's head, sending her home screaming and blood-soaked. Pierre sees himself as being repelled by this violence, although he is obviously fascinated by it. He recounts his own bravery when, for example, a milk truck ran over his foot, and Pierre, although he had to be carried home, refused to admit he was hurt. The year the war ended, the Vallières family moved away from their slum neighborhood. "When my parents decided to emigrate to the other side of the river," Vallières says, "the Cold War had come to the rescue of capitalism by preventing the war factories from grinding to a halt." This is a silly oversimplification. Canadian postwar recovery, beginning in the year in which Vallières was seven, had little if anything to do with defence expenditures and in fact depended on a program which directed investment into heavy capital equipment and into consumer products.

The postwar housing occupied by the Vallières was a terrible example of the corrupt Duplessis era at its worst. They were allowed to buy the house and move in, although it was served by neither water nor sewers. Around each house on Saint Thomas Street in Longeuil-Annexe (now Ville Jacques Cartier) ran ditches filled with black stinking water, host to flies and hordes of buzzing insects. Money appropriated by the provincial government of Maurice Duplessis for local improvements went someplace, but not for services to Saint Thomas Street. New ditches were dug for the water service, and remained open and empty for years waiting for the pipes to arrive. Water was sold by the pailful, almost within sight of Canada's largest city.

At the age of 11, Vallières refused to go to the school his mother had chosen in Longeuil, a school with a good reputation run by a Catholic order. Rejecting the demands which would be made upon him at such a school, he chose the local primary school, where the teachers were incompetent and the discipline and organization non-existent. He quit even there at 13. Entering a classical college he headed his class, but left at 16 and got a job as a clerk with, of all things, a stock broker. He was there for two years, the longest he was ever to stay at one job.

By the age of 18, he had written, and destroyed, three novels. Full of adolescent confusion, talent and energy, he became a novice in the Franciscan order, quit that and left for France. He returned to Quebec in 1963, shortly after the first FLQ bombs and the toppling of the Wolfe monument in Quebec City. Duplessis had died the year before, and Vallières found a new excitement in the province he had previously rejected. Unable to appreciate that he was now a bit older, and more travelled, he says of his return: "I had not changed much, but the situation in Quebec, *that* was really beginning to change. *Cité libre* was in power . . . Now revolt was coming out of the catacombs."

In the summer of 1963, Pierre Trudeau and Gerard Pelletier invited two men to dinner at Chez Son Père, a fine little restaurant just off Rue Nôtre Dame in Old Montreal. Trudeau and Pelletier had more than a decade before founded the monthly review *Cité libre* which through all the days of Duplessis corruption and repression had remained the leader of dynamic, intellectual dissent. Now the two founders were ready to move into active politics; they had been wooed by the New Democratic Party but they had opted for the party which offered them the more pragmatic appeal of access to power, the Liberals. It was time to turn the magazine over to younger men and they chose Pierre Vallières and Jean Pellerin.

Trudeau and Vallières must have had misgivings about each other. Not long before, when *Cité libre* produced a special issue on independence for Quebec, Vallières submitted an article which, unlike the others in the issue, did not reject separatism. Vallières argued that the existence of the issue offered Québecois an opportunity to assert themselves, making their own history rather than suffering it. Trudeau personally rejected it. The same issue contained a long article by Trudeau himself which, according to Vallières, had been roundly criticized by the *Cité libre* editorial board. Trudeau refused to change so much as a comma. Years later, Vallières could not bring himself to shrug off this experience nor to ascribe it with a smile to the natural arrogance of editors. He sees it all as part of the dark, satanic plot of the Liberal party and the French *vendu*. Trudeau was nonetheless a great admirer of Vallières' style and at a student meeting had compared him to his favorite writer, John Stuart Mill.

Despite his rejection of Vallières' article on separatism, Trudeau published several other essays by Vallières, but Vallières later concluded contemptuously that Trudeau and Pelletier did not understand what he was saying. It was after their publication (under such titles as *To awake to the depths of our existence*) that Trudeau announced the names of the two new editors at the end of 1963. Among those in the audience was Vallières' friend, Charles Gagnon, a sociology professor at the University of Montreal who, just three years later, was to face a murder charge with Vallières arising from the bombing of the La Grenade shoe factory.

Trudeau was not the only intelligent and important man to be impressed by Vallières. Gerard Pelletier, who was to become Secretary of State in Trudeau's cabinet, helped make him editor of *Cité libre* and also hired him as a reporter on the mass-circulation Montreal afternoon daily, *La Presse*. Vallières became an officer of the union at the newspaper and one of the leaders in a long strike. In France, he had discovered Marxism as his personal philosophy but had rejected the cynical bureaucracy of the Communist Party. Now he rejected what he believed to be the equally entrenched and self-serving bureaucracy of the Confederation of National Trade Unions.

During the seven-month *La Presse* strike, Vallières was a delegate to the CNTU convention, where he took the opportunity to distribute copies of *Révolution*

Québecoise which contained a paragraph accusing the CNTU president, Jean Marchand, of spending more time cultivating his own political ambitions than caring for the needs of union members. A resolution was prepared, but never presented, demanding the expulsion of Vallières from the CNTU. The resolution which was passed gave only *pro forma* support for the *La Presse* strike, and Vallières was ordered to stop selling his revolutionary tracts at the CNTU convention.

In the period of a year, Vallières had managed to confront and offend three men who were to become the three most important Quebec representatives in Ottawa. His editorship at *Cité libre*, sponsored by Trudeau and Pelletier, lasted barely six months before the editorial board asked him to resign. His job at *La Presse*, which had been offered by Pelletier even before the editorship of *Cité libre*, did not prevent Vallières from taking a great deal of time away from work to organize demonstrations against the Vietnam war and other causes of the day. Then, at the very time the strikers at *La Presse* needed the assistance of their central labor federation, Vallières managed to insult Marchand, calling him, in essence, a union phony. In 1964, the year of these crucial confrontations, Trudeau, Pelletier and Marchand were on the verge of their entry into federal politics. Six years later, Trudeau was Prime Minister and Pelletier and Marchand were regarded everywhere as his two most knowledgeable ministers on the intricacies of Quebec politics. When the provision for detention without trial was invoked by the federal cabinet in October of 1970, Vallières was jailed within the first hours of its operation. No persons had been so savagely attacked in Vallières' book, *Nègres blancs*, as Trudeau, Pelletier and Marchand.

The 1964 strike at *La Presse* appears to have given rise to Vallières' first advocacy of bombing and terrorism as political weapons. "The mistake made by the journalists at *La Presse*," he says, "was to be content to negotiate without bringing pressure to bear on the adversary by demonstrations and reprisals against, for example, the property of the company's administrators. By negotiating with kid gloves and with respect for bourgeois legality, the strikers at *La Presse* lost a great deal." Similarly, his denunciation of Trudeau and his associates as "traitors" was excruciatingly explicit: "Some day they will have to take all the consequences of this betrayal."

The strike at *La Presse* ended in January of 1965 and that same year Vallières and a group of his friends, in Vallières' words, "joined" the FLQ. More accurately, they re-created an organization which had already been through three generations. The first was centered on Georges Schoeters, a naturalized Canadian citizen of Belgian birth whose group planted the first dynamite bombs in mailboxes, army centres and other symbols of "English" Canada. They were soon arrested in late 1963, and early in 1964 a second group took over; at least two of their members were brothers of those arrested in the first group. They were, concerned almost entirely with robbery and within six months had secured more than $100,000 in cash and military equipment. When they, in turn, were arrested, the equipment was intact but most of the money was gone. They had lived well and, being more pirate brigands than revolutionaries, they stole in the name of the FLQ and then bought furniture and booze like the most dissipated bourgeois.

They too were soon arrested, whereupon François Schirm came upon the scene, a former sergeant in the French Foreign Legion who set out to find guns for his "training camp" by holding up a firearms store. Five men entered the International Firearms shop on August 29, 1964. They had fortified themselves with a few beers; it was for all of them their first robbery and it was over in a few minutes: the vice-president of the company was killed, then an employee of the gun-shop ran into the street with a gun in his hand to seek help; he was shot by the police and killed. Schirm and his four accomplices were all arrested, all were sentenced to life.

In the period which ended with the International

Firearms holdup in August of 1964, the FLQ groups had been more military and adventurist than the groups which were to follow. Their activities and the language of their pronouncements bore a striking similarity to wartime resistance groups in Europe, for both Schoeters and Schirm had lived through wartime occupation of their homelands. Some members of these early groups had been in the Canadian armed forces, which gave them skills, discipline and the realization that the French language is subservient in official Canada. There were indeed "training camps" in the woods, a dozen youths huddled around a few pathetic tents. The sophisticated military equipment stolen from the armouries was recovered elsewhere, intact and unused. 127

It was a tactic of propagandists such as Pierre Vallières to lump together all the criminal activities over a seven-year period, as if all had been centrally directed to a common cause. Thus, shortly after he "joined" the FLQ, Vallières wrote: "One of the objectives of the FLQ was and still is to accelerate (the) process of becoming conscious, to make men aware of the necessity of fighting to the death against the despotism of the capitalist system . . . " By the time Vallières came to the FLQ in 1965, most of the earlier "members" were in jail. Few of them had ideological convictions. Few were able to intellectualize their criminal activities, except that almost all had suffered the deep hurt of being put down by English-speaking Canadians.

Vallières was adept at romanticizing the past and creating the illusion of a continuing, underground, political-terrorist movement. He was successful in inspiring his followers and in frightening his enemies.

In April of 1966, a group of seven men met at the home of Serge Demers in St. Philippe de Laprairie, where Vallières was boarding. They met all day Saturday and Sunday and came to two basic decisions: they designated themselves as the central committee of the Front de Libération du Québec and they decided to announce the rebirth of the FLQ by planting a bomb at the H. B. LaGrenade shoe factory, which had continued in operation despite a strike by a CNTU union seeking a first contract. Of the 84 workers (being paid, in 1965, 90 cents an hour for women, $1.05 for men) 20 stayed with the company and 64 walked out. Daily demonstrations continued into 1966, but the situation was in a hopeless stalemate. The meeting of April 1966 was crucial: the events of that meeting became the central issue in deciding whether Pierre Vallières was merely a revolutionary theoretician who spoke and wrote of violence or, in fact, the plotter of a fatal bomb blast which, as Quebec tried to prove, would make him a murderer.

On May 5, 18-year-old Gaetan Desrosiers left his school at lunch hour to keep an appointment with Serge Demers, at whose mother's house the meeting had been held the month before. Demers arrived at the school on his motorbike with what appeared to be a shoebox strapped to his back; in fact, it was a dynamite bomb Demers had made and, as was usual with this particular FLQ group, an adolescent was assigned to undertake the danger.

(Two months later, 16-year-old Jean Corbo approached a Dominion Textile plant with another bomb made by Demers. It exploded prematurely and he was blown to bits. When Pierre Vallières appeared at the University of Quebec during his brief period of freedom in 1970, a woman student shouted at him: "You're the murderer of 16-year-old boys, that's what you are.")

At a small park near the LaGrenade building, Demers connected the wires of the bomb inside the shoe box and young Desrosiers carried it into the shoe factory posing as a messenger. His boss wanted his shoes fixed, he said, and would telephone later with instructions.

From a pay booth a few minutes later, Demers phoned a warning to evacuate the building. It was lunch hour and Henri LaGrenade himself was manning the switchboard; he had received other bomb threats, and this one he ignored. When a 64-year-old spinster-secretary Thérèse Morin returned from lunch, the shoe box exploded in her face. The FLQ had another victim;

like all the other victims, she was not an exploiter of the working masses, and she spoke French.

A notable feature of the FLQ activities in Quebec had been the high "success rate" of the police. In short order, all those who had been at the meeting in Demers' house were in jail. Less than a year after the LaGrenade explosion, five of the seven had been sentenced to terms of three to eight years for that and other offenses.

Police complaints during the 1970 crisis that the ordinary processes of the law were insufficient to cope with FLQ violence did scant credit to their earlier successes in solving virtually every FLQ crime. There were several reasons for this success. The FLQ needed to boast about its crimes, and there was always a high rate of defection, particularly among activists who became disillusioned at the slaughter of innocent victims. One of these was Demers, who quit making bombs even before the heat was on for his arrest. His resignation as FLQ bomb-maker was the chief reason the year 1967 was singularly free of violence, fortunately for the tourist business during Expo. That, indeed, is where Demers got a job, at Expo 67.

The remaining two of the seven members of the "central committee" were Pierre Vallières and Charles Gagnon, who enjoyed two distinct advantages: they had a following in the academic-intellectual community in Quebec, and the prosecuting authorities, anxious no doubt to land the big fish, turned their trials into a mockery of justice, an opinion which was shared, although not in those words, by a unanimous Quebec court of appeal. Nothing so popularized Vallières and Gagnon and nothing gave so much credence to the term "political prisoners" as the over-eagerness of some judges to convict, and the misuse of the trial process by the prosecuting officials. When in 1970, Prime Minister Trudeau said that extreme measures taken by the state can often be "a trap", justifying in some minds the conclusion that revolution is the only route to justice, he might have been speaking as well of the devious procedures at the Vallières-Gagnon trials.

Two months after the LaGrenade bombing, Vallières and Gagnon went to the United States where, in September, they picketed the United Nations and gave out radio and TV interviews, although they knew they were wanted by the police in Quebec. They were arrested for illegal entry to the United States and held for four months at the Manhattan House of Detention. They were returned to Canada by a curious manoeuvre: released from jail on January 13, 1967, they stepped onto the sidewalk, and were immediately picked up by the U.S. immigration service and hustled onto a plane for Montreal.

Their preliminary inquiry was held jointly in Montreal in February of 1967 and trial set for March 18. Then it was put off until May, then September, then November, then to January 1968. The two tried, during this period, to get the transcript of their preliminary hearing, which was denied them. When they did appear for trial on February 26, 1968, the Crown announced it wanted—after a year of proceeding jointly—separate trials. It opened the trial of Vallières, and Gagnon was put off again. Gagnon had to wait another year and-a-half for his murder trial, all of it without chance of bail. He eventually came to trial for murder in August of 1969, almost three years after his arrest in New York.

The nub of the murder charge against Vallières was that he had been at the meeting in Demers house in April of 1966 where the central committee had been formed and the plans made to bomb the LaGrenade factory. Demers and Marcel Faulkner testified that the bombing plans were drawn up while Vallières and Gagnon were away from the house visiting Montreal. After the two returned to the house, Demers testified: " . . . they were informed of our decision to form a central committee. They were asked whether they wished to continue working with us. They were asked to deal with propaganda, to analyze the economic and social situation in Quebec, to advise the Front in matters involving the formulation of policy, to see to the political organization of the members. They then accepted."

The prosecution sought to extricate itself from the embarrassment that, despite a delay of a year and half, it had no evidence that Vallières had any knowledge of the LaGrenade bombing. It piled the tables high with examples of Vallières' inflammatory writings, which were read to the jury at great length. As the Quebec court of appeal was to say later, those writings might well contain evidence for some other charge, but they contained no evidence of a specific murder. This issue was raised immediately at the trial by Vallières, who was defending himself with the assistance of Robert Lemieux.

"Does the Crown prosecutor wish to put a political organization on trial?" Vallières demanded. "Does he wish to put colonialism on trial? Does he wish to put Quebec militants on trial? Does he wish to put the *Revue Parti Pris* on trial, or does he wish simply to try the FLQ?

"I would like him to answer these questions because I am accused simply of murder. I am willing to have a trial on my political ideas, which I have never hidden; I am willing to review all of my political activity in this trial, but let us start over, let us have another trial than this one . . . .

"There is no reason to include the 1917 Russian Revolution in the LaGrenade case, or for that matter the Algerian Revolution, the Cuban Revolution, the Chinese Revolution, the organization of the FLQ, the organization of any political party, the structure of the electoral machine, the structure of traditional political parties, the organization of strikes, the organization of picketing—what the hell do they have to do with this trial? Are we putting everyone engaged in demonstrations on trial; are we preparing tomorrow a trial for those who demonstrated at the Seven-Up plant last night?"

The inordinate delays and the attempts to bolster a weak case by reading from Vallières' revolutionary writings became the central themes around which action groups were formed to free "political prisoners". Insofar as Vallières and Gagnon were denied fair and prompt trials, they were political prisoners. The concept of "political prisoners" gained credibility from the Vallières-Gagnon trials. The term was to be grossly misapplied to various bandits and bombers during the 1970 crisis, and those who were unfamiliar with the Vallières-Gagnon trials (mainly in English Canada) found it difficult to understand why the term seemed so credible to many in Quebec.

The Vallières trial was replete with errors and excesses by both judge and prosecutor. After the Crown had closed its case, the judge on his own volition changed the charge against Vallières from "the intention of exploding a bomb" to "counselling, procuring, or fostering through his attitude, actions, writings or otherwise" the explosion at the shoe factory. This injudicious manoeuvre had the effect of tailoring the charge to meet the Crown's case, instead of the other way around. The Quebec court of appeal pointed it out, but in view of all the other errors did not find it necessary to rule on it.

The Crown attorney made a passionate, inflammatory address to the jury. He concluded by reading long passages from Vallières' work *Qu'est ce que le f.l.q?*" which included the statement: "Every one of us has his small share of responsibility to assume, and to translate into action. The sooner we unite, fellows, the more quickly we will conquer. We have already lost too much time in useless recriminations; we must now move on to action."

The Crown attorney paused, faced the jury, and declared: "Gentlemen, free Vallières and you know what will happen." Lacking evidence, the Crown was using histrionics. The Quebec court of appeal agreed that "This is simply an appeal to passion or prejudice or fear tending to divert the jury from their principal problem, which is whether the Crown has proven his implication in the killing of Mlle. Morin."

Mr. Justice Hyde found these tactics to be "objectionable and improper". The Crown, he said, was trying to convince the jury that it was their duty to protect society from ideas such as Vallières' and, even though such ideas may constitute some other offense under the Criminal Code, the ideas "in themselves do not constitute the offense for which (Vallières) was being tried."

In addition to changing the charge on his own volition, the trial judge (in the words of Mr. Justice Montgomery) "came dangerously close to advising" the jury to convict Vallières for his ideas. The jury, however, saw the point despite the efforts by the Crown. During their deliberations, they returned to ask the judge if it was of "fundamental importance" that the charge specifically mentioned the H. B. LaGrenade shoe company. Incredibly, the judge replied: "No, this merely indicates the place where the explosion took place . . . . this is a detail." Far from being a mere detail, it was the core of the charge, for to be guilty of murder, Vallières had to be implicated in that particular killing. Given this flagrant misdirection, the jury, which had been intelligent enough to understand the point, could hardly fail to convict. They convicted Vallières of manslaughter, but the Quebec Court of Appeal then ordered a new trial. Vallières was convicted a second time, but sentenced to only 30 months, rather than the life imprisonment he had received at his first trial. When he was released on bail in May, 1970, on appeal from his second conviction, he had already spent three and-a-half years in jail.

The tactics used against Charles Gagnon varied in detail. He faced a number of charges lesser than murder, but the prosecutors chose to bring him to trial first on the lesser charges. Since a murder charge was in abeyance, bail for Gagnon was impossible. At the conclusion of his second murder trial in late 1969, he was acquitted.

The unseemly and illegitimate methods used by the prosecutors and the courts provided a sound factual basis for the view, widely shared by the Quebec leftwing, that Vallières and Gagnon were victims of political oppression. When Vallières was released on bail in May of 1970, it was front page news in *Le Petit Journal*. The tactics of officialdom had indeed been a "trap". Vallières and Gagnon had become folk heroes. They had gained a far wider audience.

Vallières was a figure who could be championed as a victim. More than anything else, he gained a sort of respectability because the government had made his trials a political issue. After his release he was suitable material for interviews in both French and English and in July, 1970, Vallières told Peter Allnutt of the CBC:

"Yes, I am a member of the FLQ. Today, the FLQ represents a real political force in Quebec. It is no longer considered to be a gang of criminals. Its political activity is not just planting bombs. The bombs are only like the tip of the iceberg. The FLQ is working and fighting on many other levels, both underground and publicly.

"The FLQ is necessary in order to meet the violence of the present system with revolutionary violence and to construct a new society, a free society, free from colonialism, exploitation and fear. Revolutionary activity is not only planting bombs or taking up a gun, but working at the same time to radicalize trade unions, citizens committees, student associations etc. The FLQ is working with other political groups in Quebec and outside."

This was a far different picture of the FLQ than that which Vallières had given of a period some five years before. He had said: "For a while we were able to combine our clandestine activity with the organization of fairly widespread para-legal social agitation, particularly among the groups of workers on strike in Montreal. But at the end of 1965 we had to make a definite choice in favor of clandestine action."

From underground, secret work in 1965 to open declarations of "I am a member of the FLQ" in 1970—what had caused the change? The Government of Quebec had in that space of time created an above-ground folk hero and victim in Pierre Vallières.

8 The outlaw organization

"It is common knowledge, Mr. Speaker, that in Canada today there exist many associations and societies developed and organized for the purpose of carrying on a dangerous propaganda, and which, if permitted to pursue their purpose unhindered or unchecked, may ultimately prove a serious menace to our free institutions and to the authority of government in this country."

Hon. Hugh Guthrie, Solicitor-General, speaking on introduction of Section 98 of the Criminal Code outlawing unlawful associations to the Canadian House of Commons on Tuesday, June 10, 1919.

In a smashing election victory on October 23, 1935, the Liberals under Mackenzie King regained power from the Conservative government of R. B. Bennett. Under the firm impression that Canada was again in safe hands and with over 170 seats in the House of Commons, King began to fill his election promises.

High on his list of priorities was the repeal of Section 98 of the Criminal Code. He had promised the Canadian people that this invidious law, which made it a crime to be a member of the Communist party, would be repealed if he was elected. The people had spoken.

Section 98 was a major issue in the election campaign. It was an old issue to the Liberals. As early as 1922, King had twice tried to get rid of it. Although he controlled the government, the Conservative-dominated Senate rejected both attempts. Later the Conservative government rejected the continual Liberal demands for its abolition.

Subsequently, in the 1935 campaign, the Conservatives tried to imply that King was a friend of the Communists because of his stand.

The section had its origins in the "red scare" of post-Russian-revolution North America. Led by the United States, Canada was a willing believer in the evils of Bolshevism and stood by her neighbour's side in the fight to keep it from North America's shores. We even fought harder than our U.S. neighbours in some ways. One of the ways was Section 98.

In June 1917, the U.S. Congress enacted the Espionage Act permitting military and postal censorship. It was amended on May 16, 1918 by a statute commonly referred to as the Sedition Act, creating a number of offenses, the substance of which was criticism of the government and, of course, advocating its overthrow by force. It was so broadly interpreted, especially by the lower courts that merely expressing opposition to war was a crime. Many pacifists were convicted.

Among the more famous of the showcase trials were those which took place in Chicago in May, 1918. The "Wobblies" had been placed on trial all over the United States. But in Chicago there was the grandest trial of all.

There "Wobbly" leader William "Big Bill" Haywood and 92 of his fellow members and officers of the International Workers of the World, were convicted of conspiring to violate the Espionage and Sedition Acts. Like the thousands of lesser known convictions which accompanied it, this was a "war verdict". There were 40,000 pages of typed record, hundreds of exhibits, and scores of witnesses used up weeks of court time. There were 372 separate counts in the indictment. The jury deliberated for less than an hour and convicted on all of them.

The judge promptly sentenced the convicted conspirators to terms of imprisonment ranging from one to twenty years. As they were filing from the courtroom, he asked their counsel if they intended to apply for a new trial. He was told yes, whereupon he recalled the defendants and imposed $20,000 to $30,000 fines on them in addition.

In Wichita Kansas, the trial of the Wobblies was a much slower proposition. There, the defendants had been held for two years without bail in such inhuman jail conditions that the entire affair became a national scandal. The delayed trial was caused by the repeated bringing of indictments against the defendants after successive defence motions to quash them were upheld by the court. In the end, some of the defendants became insane and the rest were convicted.

In Canada, the sedition laws did not have to be specially enacted. They had been in the Criminal Code and in the common law before it for a number of centuries. Under their broad and sweeping provisions it was possible during the first war to obtain convictions against a wide variety of unlikely victims. Faced with a rash of prosecutions the courts began to plead for some sanity. A prime example and typical of the large number of convictions obtained was that of hapless Oscar Felton, a U.S.-born, naturalized British subject and resident of Okotoks, Alberta. Felton had been drinking in a hotel barroom. The evidence of his sobriety was, to say the least, uncertain.

As he ranted about Britain, the old man was overheard by a younger man who didn't want to hit Felton because of his years and instead reported him to the police. In court, it came out that Felton said: "I hope to Christ the Germans cross the Channel and knock out . . . Old England. I am glad the Russians are licked; England put Russia into the war and is letting them get licked."

The Alberta Court of Appeal upheld his conviction

for sedition on the grounds that these were words which supported his seditious intention to "raise disaffection and discontent among His Majesty's subjects." In another case, a remark passed in a small-town drug store on the sinking of the Lusitania—"War is war . . . so they have got her at last have they . . . "—resulted in a man named Trainor being found guilty. On appeal however, the courts indicated they had had enough.

The conviction was reversed and even the one judge who did not agree with the majority verdict wrote: "It is neither necessary, nor wise to rush into court every fool with a wagging tongue and an empty head, because of something which he has said about the war which savours of disloyalty or disaffection."

In Canada, there was no notable use of the sedition laws for the suppression of communism or militant, left-wing trade unionism until the prosecutions which followed the Winnipeg General Strike.

Just before the beginning of the massive Haywood trial, Senator Thomas Walsh of Montana introduced a new kind of bill to Congress. It was popular with the mine owners and industrialists of his home state whose properties and plants had been the scene of bitter Wobbly struggles. The bill outlawed any organization which advocated changes in industry, society or government by the use of force, violence or physical injury to property.

In a country where freedom of assembly and association are constitutionally enshrined rights, such a bill would have been possible only in a time of hysteria. On the eve of the Wobblies' biggest trials, with revolution seemingly imminent, Walsh was able to use the radical labour organization as a target.

"I do not regard the I.W.W. fellows as representatives of the labouring classes at all," he said, "I regard them . . . as public enemies. I have no sympathy with the end they have in view nor the means by which they propose to accomplish their aim. I introduced a bill to outlaw the entire organization, to make it a crime to belong to it, and I believe it ought to be passed."

It almost was. It cleared the Senate without dissent. In the House of Representatives it was blocked by a lone congressman, Meyer London of New York. By various procedural devices he was able to slow it down. Then the Wilson administration, whose Attorney-General, Thomas W. Gregory, was vigorously pressing the Wobbly prosecutions, saw the dangers and began to oppose it. It never passed the House of Representatives. But it was noticed.

On September 25, 1918, just as the Walsh bill was sent into legislative limbo, the Canadian Cabinet adopted the idea and created the concept in law of the outlaw organization. With the armistice still six weeks away and the German menace still in the form of a shooting war, there was no need to go to Parliament. Borden could use the War Measures Act, which was still in force. Under it, however, as its creator, Borden knew its extreme power was limited to times of war. Therefore, in P.C. 2384, he meticulously copied the objective of Senator Walsh's bill, carefully adding to each clause and section the proviso, "while Canada is engaged in war." With those words removed, the law was taken word for word from P.C. 2384 and inserted in the Criminal Code in July of 1919 where it was to remain for 17 years as the infamous Section 98.

No prosecutions were recorded during the short life of P.C. 2384, partly because there was real doubt as to its validity after November 11, 1918—Armistice Day— and partly because Canada was distracted from the Red menace by massive and unsolved problems of reconstruction of a peacetime economy.

In the United States, the reconstruction was not as serious a problem. That country had entered the war late and had committed less of its resources on a per capita basis. When peace came there was still very little to distract it from the Red menace.

In March of 1919, Gregory had been replaced by A. Mitchell Palmer, whose enthusiasm for prosecuting communists knew no bounds. In September of that year, Woodrow Wilson had suffered a nervous collapse in Europe leaving Palmer and the rest of his rudderless cabinet free to do as they would at home. By November, Palmer had set up an anti-radical division of the Department of Justice under J. Edgar Hoover. The notorious Palmer raids began. Hundreds, then thousands, were arrested.

On December 21, 1919, 249 aliens who had committed no offense were deported to Russia. On a single night in January. Palmer's men conducted raids simultaneously in thirty-three cities from coast to coast resulting in the arrest of over 4,000 alleged communists.

Instead of receiving approval, these excesses turned a majority of Americans away from the administration in outraged disgust and, reacting to his plea for "a return to normalcy", the United States elected Warren G. Harding President. In 1921, at the urging of the Harding administration, Congress repealed the Espionage and Sedition Acts.

In Canada, unlike the United States, the government had not balked at expanding the principles of criminal law to include such a political crime as being a member of an unlawful organization. Public opinion in Canada would likely have prevented the resurrection of this idea from the wartime arsenal of regulations had it not been for the Winnipeg General Strike.

Canadians have become comfortable with what happened in Winnipeg in the months of May and June 1919. It is history now. In late 1969, the fiftieth anniversary of the Winnipeg General Strike was marked nationally with some nostalgia and with pride that Canadians could have pulled off something quite so colourful and spectacular.

Then, it was a frightening experience. Many of those involved were radical trade unionists fresh from the Calgary OBU convention. The Bolshevik revolution was just two years old. The imaginary fears of the Canadian establishment were heightened by the return of thousands of soldiers who had little money, almost no prospects of employment and little chance of resuming their normal family lives.

In Ottawa, Parliament was in session and busily engaged in managing the transition from war to peace. The necessary treaties had not yet been finalized and technically, but not in fact, the country was still at war. The War Measures Act was still in force and was being used to justify orders-in-council to establish and regulate such agencies as the Canadian Wheat Board, created after the armistice. The government used its emergency powers to solve the economic problems brought on by the war and the war's end.

Dealing with what occurred in Winnipeg some seven months later, the Chief Justice of Manitoba described the purpose of the strike leaders as "revolution, the overthrow of the existing form of government in Canada and the introduction of a form of Socialistic or Soviet rule in its place. This was to be accomplished by general strikes, force and terror and, if necessary, by bloodshed."

What provoked this judicial description? On May 15, 1919, at 11:00 a.m., 12,000 workers walked off their jobs. Within the day they were joined by a further 15,000. By the third day of the strike, retail trade, including the sale of food, had slowed to a virtual halt. By that time the strikers' numbers had swelled to 35,000 and all activities—industry, transport, banking, finance, postal service, food, water and power supply, fire and police services—if operating at all, were doing so under the authority and with the permission of the Strike Committee.

In fact the entire city was run by the Strike Committee. To fight back, the Winnipeg establishment organized themselves a Citizens Committee. The Committee created a militia-like body of between 3,000 and 5,000 persons.

The Federal government was determined to keep law and order and sent R.C.M.P. personnel in force to Winnipeg. On May 22, General Ketchem, the commander of the Winnipeg Military District sent for more help and got a battalion of troops, some supplies and two Lewis machine guns.

By the week of May 29, the strike wave had gone all the way west, and 60,000 workers were out in sympathy in Vancouver. Thousands left their transport jobs in Edmonton, miners went out in Drumheller and Lethbridge. There were general strikes in Regina, Saskatoon, Prince Albert and Brandon. In Toronto, a general strike was called for May 30, but only 15,000 workers actually left their jobs.

Then during the week of June 5, following demonstrations in favour of the strike by returned servicemen, the Winnipeg authorities dismissed the entire police force and replaced it with 2,000 "specials", sworn in as peace officers for the occasion. On June 9 there was a battle in the streets with the specials, supported by R.C.M.P., charging into a crowd of strikers and ex-servicemen at Main and Portage Streets. There were five injuries.

Borden had sent his Minister of Labour, Gideon Robertson, to Winnipeg as his eyes and ears. On June 13, Robertson suggested that arrests be made. In the early hours of Tuesday June 17, the arrests came. Before dawn, the leaders and many others were whisked away to Stoney Mountain Penitentiary, refused bail, and began the wait for their trial on sedition charges.

Nationwide protests resulted in bail being granted finally on June 20 and on Saturday, June 21, a silent parade was organized to protest the arrests and violence. Predictably the Mayor read the Riot Act; the strikers, their wives and children and the supporting ex-servicemen paraded; and the specials, accompanied by the R.C.M.P., about fifty in number, rode through the crowd. It opened to let them pass and closed up again. On the second charge the riders had their revolvers drawn and began firing into the crowd—leaving two dead and 30 injured. Winnipeg was declared under military control. The strike was broken, and early in July the workers went back to their jobs. The strike leaders were convicted of seditious conspiracy and five were sentenced to one year in jail. One, Robert J.

Russell, was sentenced to two years, the maximum penalty at the time.

The government in Ottawa was essentially the same one which had enacted and operated under the War Measures Act for the nearly five years which preceded the nine tumultuous weeks of the Winnipeg General Strike.

On many of the days when "the events in the west" were being discussed, so was the War Measures Act and regulations made under it. Not once was it suggested that the events in Winnipeg and elsewhere in the country, Bolshevik revolution or not, constituted a state of insurrection within the meaning of that act.

Before the trials began, the government passed stiff amendments to the Immigration Act, forbidding the entry of those inclined to overthrow the government, raised the penalty for seditious conspiracy to a twenty year maximum and gave Canada a peacetime version of P.C. 2384, making it an offense to belong to or support an unlawful association.

An unlawful association was defined as one whose professed purpose or one of whose purposes is to bring about "any governmental, industrial or economic change within Canada by use of force, violence or physical injury to person or property or by threats of such injury, or which teaches, advocates, advises or defends the use of force, violence, terrorism or physical injury to person, property or threats of such injury, in order to accomplish such change, or for any other purpose, or which shall by any means prosecute or pursue such purpose or professed purpose, or shall so teach, advocate, advise or defend."

This section became the infamous Section 98 of the Criminal Code. Section 98 was first discussed in Parliament on June 10, 1919. The Winnipeg General Strike was then in its 26th day and had already caused sympathy strikes as far west as Vancouver and as far east as Toronto. (Senator Walsh was busy in Washington trying to resurrect his stalled legislation. He received some comfort from the fact that the Special Committee on revision of the sedition laws in Canada had recommended that Parliament adopt his idea. But still he was unsuccessful.) On that date, Solicitor General Hugh Guthrie tried to dispel the idea that the government's new package on sedition was being brought in to meet the events in the West. He said neither the increase in penalties from maximums of two to maximums of 20 years, nor the redefining of sedition, nor the provisions of Section 98 (then to be known as Sections 97A and B) were "inspired by, nor are they the result of, the Winnipeg strike."

Perhaps he was correct. The bill which was given Royal Assent on July 7, 1919 did not take effect until October 1—too late to affect the Winnipeg situation. But it was there as a warning to others.

The Harding administration secured the repeal of the Espionage and Sedition laws in 1921: the new administration of Mackenzie King had tried to do its part for the return to normalcy in Canada. They were not to succeed until 1936.

In the meantime, Canada had enjoyed the North American prosperity and benefited from immigration waves of the 1920s. But the Depression was a new kind of pressure, and the law about outlaw organizations was still on the books.

Communism under the skilled and agile leadership of Tim Buck was on the move in Canada. There was no place in 1930 and 1931 to register protest against the desolate conditions which beset the Canadian worker and the Canadian farmer. Buck set out to fill the vacuum.

Using the Workers Unity League, the Communists inspired strikes in the coal mines of Nova Scotia and southern Saskatchewan. In one major strike, led by Tom Ewen of the League, three men were killed. In their anger and despair, the government looked for a way to stop Buck and his followers. They found it in Section 98.

On August 11, 1931, under the direction of Major General V.A.S. Williams, Ontario Police Commissioner, who announced that they were "going to strike a death blow at the Communist Party," the police simultaneously raided the offices of the Communist Party, the Workers Unity League and the homes of various officers of both, resulting in nine arrests. The accused were charged under Section 98 and also with being parties to a seditious conspiracy.

One was acquitted when the Crown was not prepared to prove he was a member of the party, but the convictions of the other eight were foregone conclusions. They never denied their membership and all that remained was to prove the Communist Party an unlawful association under the section. It took the jury just two hours to decide that. Seven, including Buck, were sentenced to five years in jail and the eighth was sentenced to two years.

The highly political trial heightened public concern over the possible threat to political freedom, and the concept of guilt by association inherent in the section resulted in a popular movement for its repeal. The Communists unhesitatingly capitalized on the repeal movement, but even so the cause was acceptable enough for the already-committed Liberals to once again adopt it.

Some of the drama surrounding the Buck case came from a strange occurrence during the tenth month of his sentence at Kingston penitentiary. In October, 1932, the cell blocks were swept by riots and while Buck stood shouting in his cell, two of the prison guards, one with a shotgun and one with a pistol, fired five shots into his cell from a short distance away. It was later clearly established that his cell was the only one fired on in the whole prison.

As the controversy heightened with allegations of attempted assassination, Bennett's government offered the rather lame excuse that it might have been done to frighten or cow him . . . "The situation was serious," said Justice Minister Hugh Guthrie, "and Buck was one who had been encouraging the disorders." Buck was paroled after one-half of his sentence was served and returned to the political wars in the cause now being conducted under a confusing variety of names.

King's Minister of Justice, Ernest Lapointe, who had led the Liberals' earlier attempts at repeal, moved the abolition of Section 98. He referred to the beginnings of this controversial law in 1918 and stated, " . . . we believe it is dangerous to perpetuate in peacetime, enactments which are wartime measures and designed to meet special emergencies due to some extent to the natural panic which exists in time of war. The danger is mainly because of the precedent which it creates. If it can be done, if we can put aside the ordinary rules of law on a matter of this kind, why not put them aside on other matters as well? And this creates a precedent that might be harmful under other circumstances."

With the removal of Section 98, the existing sedition section was also amended, adding in a presumption that, "a person has a seditious intention if he teaches or advocates, or publishes or circulates any writing that advocates the use, without authority of law, of force as a means of accomplishing a governmental change within Canada."

But the law was now clear that no one could be guilty of an offense by reason of mere membership in an organization. A person would only be guilty of a crime by actually committing it, and not by association. The sedition law was further refined in a judicial reaction to the harassment of Jehovah's Witnesses in Quebec. In 1951, in the Boucher Case, the Supreme Court of Canada ruled that sedition was more than merely giving offense to a particular group or government. To be seditious, the conduct must constitute an incitement to illegal conduct by means of the promotion of ill-will or hostility between different classes of people or discontent between the people and the Crown as represented by the government or the administration of justice.

Under P.C. 2384 and its successor, Section 98, unlawful associations were defined. A new twist to outlawing organizations was added in 1939 with the passage of the Defence of Canada Regulations authorized by the War Measures Act. Under the Regulations, the banned organizations were simply declared illegal by order in council.

Along with the Communist Party of Canada, there also appeared, on an ever-expanding list, as the war continued, the Jehovah's Witnesses and its related organizations and Technocracy Inc. While the country accepted a great deal during the war in terms of violation of civil liberties, the most controversial steps taken involved the banning of entire organizations and the subsequent legal consequences to those who remained members. At the war's end the government lost no time in restoring freedom of association to the members of its listed groups, except in some notable cases where it had admitted its error and had revoked its bans earlier. Then came the War Measures regulations on October 16, 1970 and following it, the Public Order Act, passed on December 3.

These laws name their target. "The group of persons or association known as Le Front de Libération du Québec and any successor group or successor organization of the said Le Front de Libération du Québec, or any group of persons or association that advocates the use of force or the commission of crime as a means of or as an aid in accomplishing the same or substantially the same governmental change within Canada as that advocated by the said Le Front de Libération du Québec, is declared to be an unlawful association."

The foregoing is Section 3 of the Public Order Act, which differs slightly from the regulation which it supplants. In the regulation, any group of persons or association advocating the use of force to accomplish any governmental change in Canada was defined as an unlawful association. The later law catches only those trying to achieve separation of Quebec from the rest of Canada by force.

There are striking similarities of language in all of the bills, sharing as they do, the same problems of condemning membership and having to provide special means to prove that membership.

The drafters of the Public Order law obviously drew heavily on the experience of the past.

9 The four-point plan

In the first ten years that Jean Drapeau was mayor of Montreal, Lucien Saulnier was the man who ran the city. While effervescent little Jean Drapeau, more an impresario than a mayor, flew around the country and around the world, bringing to Montreal the World's Fair of 1967, a major league baseball team, a rubber-tired subway and (somewhat to his embarrassment) Charles de Gaulle, the tall, jut-jawed and humorless figure of Lucien Saulnier stayed at City Hall, poring over the thousands of pieces of paper which are needed to get the garbage collected, the snow cleared and the zoning laws properly adjusted in the interests of progress and big buildings.

Every city seeks the regeneration, and the tax revenues, of huge real estate projects, usually referred to as urban renewal and often resulting in the destruction of the homes of the poor and their replacement by office buildings, parking lots, or housing too expensive for the poor to re-enter. This process was more the rule than the exception during the regime of those opposite but well-matched personalities, Jean Drapeau and Lucien Saulnier. Some 2,000 families were moved from their homes in the City's depressed east end in 1964 to make way for the Montreal headquarters of Radio-Canada, with consequent problems of dislocation and disruption which would have become a major social and political problem in any other Canadian city. "We gave everyone $100," Saulnier once said, "we had no problems." Six years after clearance, the site was still vacant.

Once, when asked why Montreal had done so little to correct the scandal of its slums (the city has about 10 per cent as much public housing as Metropolitan Toronto) Saulnier replied: "We have already over 400 dwellings built and occupied and we are engaged in the clearance of 4,500 others . . . " Most of that clearance was for the Trans-Canada highway; only a Saulnier would believe that clearing the slums is the same thing as clearing up their problems.

An area called Victoriatown was razed in 1962 to make way for the Autostade football field and a parking lot, forcing 305 families to find new places to live. Immediately after their relocation, a survey found their housing was costing them 36 per cent more than when they were "rescued" from the slums. Similarly, 62 families displaced by a highway cloverleaf wound up paying 25 per cent more in rent; and "urban renewal" in Côte des Neiges displaced 109 families whose housing costs immediately skyrocketed by 62 per cent.

The structure of the Montreal city government, and the uniquely successful Civic Party which Drapeau and Saulnier founded in 1960, kept to a minimum the political uproar which in other cities would have followed in the path of such efficient city bulldozers. The U.S. real estate entrepreneur who built Place Ville Marie, William Zeckendorf, found much to admire in Saulnier who was, Zeckendorf said, a man "who could look beyond an immediate skirmish to long-term goals and effects," a vision which enabled Saulnier not to mind too much when Zeckendorf's wrecking crews began tearing down Montreal buildings they didn't yet own. At the same time, Saulnier has often been described, and not without reason, as one of the best city managers on the continent. He saved the Place des Arts cultural complex when it was faced with bankruptcy, he reformed the city's purchasing and contracting procedures. In show-business terms, Saulnier was the producer who made possible the stagey, extravagant schemes of the irrepressible Jean Drapeau.

The man who directed all this cold energy toward the efficient, and often 18-hours-a-day, administration of the City of Montreal came from a miserable childhood. Fatherless at seven, he worked after school in his mother's restaurant. He once said, "I can't ever remember playing hockey or baseball as a boy." He had been on the Montreal City Council six years and had two fulltime jobs, one with a successful church magazine, the other as the owner of a clothing store, when he became chairman of the executive committee, and thus chief administrative officer of Montreal, in late 1960. He quit the magazine but kept the store as a sideline, and over the years the strain took its toll. In 1968, he suffered a mental breakdown. His recovery was convincing enough that shortly after his return to City Hall, the newly-elected Prime Minister, Pierre Trudeau, offered him the presidency of Air Canada.

Although Saulnier declined the job, Trudeau's faith in him was obviously undiminished; in the years that followed, Saulnier was frequently able to have private chats with the Prime Minister, on the phone or at Trudeau's official estate, a favor which many of his chief cabinet ministers complained was too much of a rarity for them. Out of this intimacy grew Saulnier's right (although he has never claimed it for himself) to be known as the father of the War Measures Act which was proclaimed into force by Trudeau's government on October 16, 1970.

By his own description, Lucien Saulnier is "somewhat of a liberal." Claude Ryan, the scholarly editor of the morning paper Le Devoir, describes him as a man much given to visions of plots and conspiracies. The political theory, if such it be, behind the Montreal city government is Drapeau's. He calls it Parliamentary Government, the main result of which, in practical terms, is that the executive committee which Saulnier chaired until late 1970 meets always in private. This is similar to the secret meetings of a Parliamentary cabinet, the difference being that cabinet ministers under a Parliamentary system are required to answer the questions thrown at them in public by their political opposition. The members of Montreal's executive committee live under no such restraining rule of examination, nor is there much of an opposition to ask the questions.

The alternate method of dispensing information to the public is the press conference. Saulnier's version of a press conference was to summon reporters to the executive committee chamber, read a prepared statement, and march out again, brooking no questions. This is what he did at 6 p.m. on Saturday, October 11, 1969, a time which was well-designed to catch the lively Montreal Sunday papers, as well as the Monday editions of the Globe and Mail in Toronto, the most influential Canadian newspaper in the English language. The purpose of Saulnier's press statement was to condemn "the clearly subversive activities" of the Company of Young Canadians which, in rough terms, was a federally-funded agency supposed to be doing on the home front what the U.S. Peace Corps was doing overseas, which already had its Canadian equivalent in CUSO (Canadian University Service Overseas). As part of his statement, Saulnier told the press:

152

> *We now know that in Canada, individuals and groups are working actively to implement a plan which has as its objective the destruction of freedom, of our form of democratic Government, and in this plan, the people's will, as expressed in the ballot box, is excluded.*
> *These individuals and groups are inspired and financed in many cases by foreign political powers related to an "Internationale" that does not share our notion of man's fundamental liberties.*

Saulnier's timing in making the announcement on October 11 that foreign funds from the "Internationale" were financing Canadian revolution was certainly no accident. The Montreal civic administration had that week faced its gravest crisis. Angered by their low pay, Montreal's police went on strike and while they were away from their posts, a gang of violent radicals from the Taxi Liberation Movement (MLT) put the torch to the garage of Murray Hill Ltd., which held a transportation monopoly from the Montreal airport.

Curiously, the genesis of official attitudes and official responses to the Quebec crisis of October, 1970 is to be found in the greater violence of almost exactly a year before, when Montreal's 3,700 policemen staged their one-day strike. On the morning of Tuesday, October 7, 1969, the Montreal police radio crackled out a message to all cars: they were to converge on the Paul Sauvé arena for a "study" meeting. The police of Montreal were angry and frustrated. They had given the Drapeau-Saulnier administration three years to come to grips with their grievances but in that time Drapeau had spent his energies campaigning for a $25 million tower at Expo (whose abandonment was said to be his greatest disappointment) for such prestigious and costly projects as an opera company (it was Pierre Laporte who gave the Quebec government's final No to that one.)

In 1969, a first-class constable in Montreal was being paid $7,300 a year, a full $1,800 less than a constable in Metropolitan Toronto, a municipality of approximately the same population and approximately the same-sized police force as the City of Montreal. But the Montreal crime rate, particularly for holdups and violent crime is by far the highest in Canada. The city has more crime than Toronto, Vancouver, Winnipeg and Halifax combined, to say nothing of the special problems created by radical terrorism and a well-entrenched underworld of organized mobsters. In 1966, the Montreal police marched with placards past City Hall and Drapeau put them off with a typical ploy: he referred their grievances to a Provincial commission which was studying the machinery of justice, a study which had absolutely nothing at all to do with how much a policeman should be paid. In 1967, the Police Brotherhood agreed to settle their contract without rancour, in the spirit of Expo. In early 1968, with Montreal tottering from the debts of Expo and the Metro subway, the City suspended its 11 per cent contribution to the police and firemen's pension funds for two years. This would deny no one a pension but as an example of Drapeau-Saulnier cool-headed bookkeeping it was actuarily sound and politically disastrous. By the fall of 1969, the Police Brotherhood had been negotiating with the City for 10 months, and Montreal's policemen were fed-up and militant.

During the morning of Tuesday, October 7, the Paul Sauvé arena filled with policemen, recruited from their cars by the radio calls and from the station houses by the elite mobile squad. At 11:20 a.m., the first bank of the day was robbed of $28,000; before the day was out, five more banks were held up, among a total of 61 robberies for the day.

Drapeau was out of town doing a salesman's job in St. Louis. The policemen in the Paul Sauvé arena learned their pay would be increased in two months to $8,480, still below the $9,112 of the Toronto policemen, and less indeed than the policemen of the quiet, English-speaking Montreal suburb of Westmount, which is completely surrounded by the City of Montreal.

With his boss out of town, Saulnier went to the arena to address the angry policemen, joined now by firemen as well. He told them he would "review" their situation, but their problems would not be solved that afternoon. Drowned out by boos and cries in French of "Drapeau to the gallows" (a typical cry of militant rhetoric in Quebec that should not be taken too seriously) Saulnier retreated with his speech unfinished, hurrying back to City Hall to call upon the Quebec government to bring in the army and the Provincial Police, whose director, lamentably, was in Florida on holidays.

On Tuesday evening, with the police still "studying" at the arena, a snake-march of 75 taxicabs made its way to the Murray Hill garage. A Murray Hill bus was set rolling through the garage doors, then the garage was set afire with gasoline bombs; soon three other buses parked outside were also ablaze. Guards on the garage roof were keeping the demonstrators away with shotgun blasts; from a nearby tenement a rifle replied. Ten persons were hit with shotgun pellets, and one blast of pellets, fired from a 45 degree angle above him, hit Cpl. Robert Dumas in the back. Screaming his pain beside the flames of the burning buses, he died.

The mob moved away from the garage. Joined by others, they roamed in small groups through the downtown hotel and shopping streets of the city, breaking windows in 150 stores, offices and hotels, stealing at least three-quarters of a million dollars in jewels, clothing, stereo sets, even lingerie. Like the carnivals of violence that Newark and Detroit had known before, the looting had little to do with politics, and was not exclusively youthful. Many of those who picked through the broken glass to choose shoes and radios were clearly middle-aged. One man ran gleefully from a store with two fur coats over his arms, announcing, "One for the wife, one for the girl friend." The carnival had largely played itself out by the time the Montreal police came back on the job after midnight. They snapped back immediately to their usual disciplined efficiency, which they displayed again three nights later when a march that *was* political was quickly broken up by the standard technique of dividing crowds with flying motorcycle wedges and chasing the demonstrators up back streets.

Although a police strike, even under the severest provocation, can never be a defensible tactic, the civic administration of Drapeau and Saulnier was clearly in its deepest trouble in almost a decade of rule. In the romantic, hyperbolic world of Montreal politics, it was easy to sympathize with policemen who had been driven to the excess of a sit-down by the City's failure over a long period of time to meet demands which plainly had considerable merit. Saulnier's lacklustre, equivocal speech at the Paul Sauvé arena, entirely lacking in any concrete promises, had not helped, and this was particularly apparent when, less than two weeks later,

Saulnier added another $350 a year to the "binding" award of the arbitrator and, at least as important, offered reasonable compromises to many of the police complaints about on-the-job conditions and harsh discipline.

In the week of the strike, with the political post-mortems being held on the Tuesday night riot, Drapeau and Saulnier were in serious trouble. On Saturday night, Saulnier called in the press and went on the radio to denounce the Company of Young Canadians.

In a week in which roaming street gangs, fire bombs, shotgun fire and the disruption of police work were on everyone's mind, Saulnier's script was a particularly clever and manipulative piece of work. At no time did he blame the CYC or its workers for the riot of four nights before, but the key words which ran through his speech could do little else but leave with the gullible the impression that the "social animators" of the CYC must have had something to do with the terrible events of that week. Saulnier's speech was full of sliding, imprecise innuendo; much of what he said was true in itself, but almost everything he said had no relation whatsoever to the fires and destruction of that week. His charges, among others, were:

> We also find on the premises officially occupied by the Company of Young Canadians and paid for by the Canadian taxpayers, newspapers and pamphlets showing how to fabricate molotov cocktails, paint-bombs, flasks and vials devised to disrupt police work in the maintenance of public order.

The disruption of police work that week had been entirely the result of an illegal police strike, an inflexible—and partly absent—civic administration, and roaming gangs of looters whose radicalism extended to stereo sets and fur coats. While the early targets were clearly political, the Queen Elizabeth Hotel and the Mount Royal Hotel, which is the terminus of the monopoly Murray Hill buses, the Montreal riot quickly became a general free-for-all of smashing and stealing carried out by people of all ages and ethnic groups (an observation made by a University of Montreal sociologist who stationed himself on St. Catherine Street.) The Montreal riot was mainly the work of people whose minds contained not a political thought, nor many of any other kind either. Still, Saulnier's reference to the disruption of police work in the same sentence as the Company of Young Canadians was, to say the least, a skilful diversion.

All this [disruption of police work] is contained in tracts, writing, documents, communiqués which are reproduced on equipment bought or rented by the Company of Young Canadians with our taxes. Its paid or volunteer organizers who define themselves as "social animators" roam the Montreal region in motorcars owned by the Canadian people and use them to sow dissension, panic and to participate in destructive manifestations.

157

Taxpayer-owned cars roaming the streets to engage in destruction could indeed be an electric phrase in the week of Montreal's worst experience of indiscriminate destruction. The government-owned red Volvos used by the CYC had roamed the streets, but not in the riot which took place in the week in which Saulnier spoke. Later evidence was to show the Volvos were used in the *McGill Francais* demonstration (to make McGill University a French-speaking school) certainly an improper use in itself, but none of the cars was abroad on the night which was in everyone's mind as Saulnier spoke; no red Volvos took part in the riots of October 7.

Firearms have been found recently on the premises occupied by the organizers of a Company of Young Canadians project.

Like so much that was contained in Saulnier's statement, this fact was literally true, that is to say, a gun had been found in an office used by, among dozens of other people, some volunteers from the CYC. Saulnier's intention in stating this only four days after there had been open gunfire in front of the Murray Hill garage is abundantly clear. The facts were, however, that everyone injured in that gunfire, and the one policeman killed, were the victims of shotgun fire and no evidence ever put a shotgun in the hands of anyone but the guards who were protecting the Murray Hill garage.

At the time Saulnier spoke, the Company of Young Canadians was already in deep trouble despite its successes, largely unnoticed, in other parts of the country. In north-western Ontario, CYC workers had helped establish an Indian radio station. In Nova Scotia, where raw sewage had once filled the open ditches of a slum, a bright new sewer pipe now carried the waste. Tenants' committees had been formed to pressure landlords to fix up their buildings. All of this had subjected the CYC workers to the charge of being outside agitators, disruptors and so forth. The political norms of many a community had been disrupted as the poor and the disadvantaged began to organize and to use the mere pressure of their existence to gain concessions. When the poor teach themselves how to organize to get a sewer pipe, the end result may be a happy one, but the process of getting there is often painful for the local politicians and administrators, who feel their established ways of doing things are being disturbed and disrupted.

Considering this, Saulnier's final allegation in his press statement of October 11 was particularly contrived and misleading. He said:

> It [the CYC] even has the audacity to publish officially in its report to the responsible minister, Hon. Secretary of State, Gérard Pelletier, in which "social progress" and I quote partially, is defined "as engendering inevitable political disorder."
>
> That should be enough to show that Canada is involved in self-destruction.

Spoken in a week in which Montreal had experienced the worst disorders since Rocket Richard was suspended from the Montreal hockey team (when windows had likewise been smashed along St. Catherine Street) Saulnier's allegation that a federally-financed agency was engaged in "disorder" could hardly have been intended to have any but the most obvious and apparent meaning. When he was asked later how it came about that he decided to attack the CYC in the same week as the police strike and the riots which followed it, Saulnier replied with a straight face: "It is only a coincidence."

The next month, in November of 1969, Saulnier was invited to appear in Ottawa before the House of Commons standing committee on broadcasting, films and assistance to the arts, which was conducting hearings into the CYC. Saulnier brought with him Michel Côté, the testy City Attorney for Montreal, formerly the police department lawyer, known as a "hawk" even at Montreal's City Hall, and the author of the City's anti-demonstration bylaw which was soon thrown out by the courts. The two of them spent one long day, from early morning until after midnight, and the morning of the next day, explaining to the Members of Parliament the imminent danger of revolution. It was at this meeting that the famous "three-point plan" for revolution led by the FLQ was unveiled. It was also at this meeting that Saulnier expressed his fears that the country was ill-prepared for the revolution that was underway and that, consequently, there was an urgent need for a "contingency plan" to be evolved. He also said he had transmitted these fears personally to Trudeau in at least two phone calls, one letter and one personal visit.

In his appearance before the Broadcasting Committee on November 27 and 28, 1969, Saulnier skillfully set forth his theory that the riot and looting of October 7 had been part of an escalating, revolutionary plan to destroy the country. Most observers of the scene had distinguished the Murray Hill riot from the window-breaking and looting on St. Catherine Street. The first had been clearly a political riot, the second had just as clearly been non-political thieving in which persons of all races and ages (not just young French radicals) participated, in a sort of non-liquored drunken saturnalia which has been so frequently observed in American riots. But for Saulnier it was all part of the same conspiracy, as he was to say specifically. A year later, after the kidnappings of Cross and Laporte, Saulnier's theories were to receive much more attention than they did at the time, and he was to be quoted repeatedly (and incorrectly) as the official who brought to light the "three-point plan" (or sometimes a four-point plan) which was the major reason given by Quebec officials, Premier Bourassa included, for seeking from Ottawa the invocation of the War Measures Act.

Saulnier's evidence in November of 1969 is important for the state of mind it reveals, for the frame of reference within which Saulnier saw the two political kidnappings and other events of a year later. His evidence recorded here has been abridged only to remove word repetitions:

"I noticed on October 7 and 8 that when we are faced with emergency situations such as those we had in Montreal the country is not in a position to defend itself adequately.

"On October 7, I had to inform the highest federal authorities of the situation which we were foreseeing for the night of the 7th to the 8th, a situation which I called revolutionary.

"I made a request then that all available troops be sent to Montreal. We noticed that it took more than eight hours to have in Montreal, or near Montreal, a handful of soldiers. And at that time *we had a beginning of a revolution in the streets of our city.* (Emphasis added.)

"I must say that basically I am rather liberal. And before believing that there actually was a plot against the security of our country, I endeavored to satisfy myself. I became rapidly convinced in late September, early October. If I add the escalation I witnessed to the events I saw on October 7 and 8 concerning the defence of our country in emergencies, I felt the time had come for me to inform the Canadian population.

"We have [had] many letters and exchanges of correspondence with the provincial and federal authorities concerned with the security of our country, in most cases at the initiative of the Montreal police department, *to devise a contingency plan of action in these circumstances.* My information is that this has not been very successful." (Emphasis added.)

Saulnier did not elaborate on the "contingency plan of action" he would recommend, but a year later, the Drapeau-Saulnier administration joined with the Quebec government in asking for the extraordinary powers of the War Measures Act and the Montreal police department, although nominally under the direction of the Quebec Police Forces, was the prime instrument in the arrest of almost 500 persons.

Whatever the validity of Saulnier's self-description as "somewhat of a liberal," he repeated several times in his 1969 evidence that he was opposed to the formation of the Company of Young Canadians even if it contained not a single radical or revolutionary. The CYC, Saulnier said, interfered with the smooth administration of civic officials such as himself. There was good communication between the citizens of Montreal and their civic administration. Saulnier was "objecting very, very strongly" to the existence of the CYC in any form.

Saulnier's evidence that the looting of St. Catherine Street had been part of an escalating revolutionary plan was reported at the time and quickly forgotten. The part of his evidence which was to be revived forcefully in the kidnapping crisis of a year later was the "three-point plan" of the FLQ. The leaders of Quebec made it clear that these three steps of escalation, as brought to the Commons committee in 1969, were the primary reason behind the request from Quebec for the War Measures Act.

In a statement to the press on the night the War Measures Act came into force, Raymond Garneau,

Quebec's Minister of Finance, said that the people and the Government of Quebec had been living in a state of false confidence that violent things could not happen here.

He went on to say: "And these things did happen, and taking into account, for example, the different working plans which are well known to the police forces, and which were rendered public by the chairman of the Montreal executive committee [Saulnier] before the House of Commons last year—taking account of this plan, whose first stage was demonstrations, second stage setting bombs, third stage kidnapping—if these three stages had been accomplished, we had every reason to believe that the fourth stage was possible. No responsible government could permit such a thing to happen *and that is the reason for which we took these extreme measures.*" (Emphasis added.)

Later that same Friday night, Premier Bourassa repeated the "three-point plan" to, among others, a CBC English-language radio reporter. "It was well known," Bourassa said, "that there was a plan by a small group of people, perhaps a few hundred, but they were strong enough to create a lot of trouble. They start with meetings. After that they have recourse to bombs, and now the kidnappings. So we have to stop that, because where will it finish? It is not a question of limiting the civil liberties of the people, it is a question of saving democracy. The total population in Quebec and in Canada are for the democratic system, so we have to defend that will of the people."

"You mentioned three points," the radio reporter said, "and earlier today the Minister of Finance mentioned four points—demonstrations, bombing, kidnappings and selected assassination. Are you satisfied these terrorists were prepared to go that far?"

Bourassa answered, and in doing so obviously accepted the three, or four-point, plan as being an established fact. "We had no clear indication that they were prepared to go that far," he said into the reporter's tape recorder, "but obviously, clearly, we have no choice but to take no risks."

Premier Bourassa was even more emphatic about the four-point plan when the Quebec National Assembly held a full debate on the crisis in mid-November. Bourassa explained his reasons for asking for invocation of the War Measures Act in a speech to the Assembly on November 12:

"How long could we force the police to work with one hand tied behind their backs? For days and days they had been ready to exercise the necessary powers in the circumstances, to face up to a form of terrorism without precedent in North America. It was the Quebec government which was holding them back, restricting them by all possible means, once again to avoid any sign of provocation.

"For these reasons, Mr. Speaker, added to others which are already known—the plan which was made public by Mr. Saulnier [was] in four steps: violent demonstrations, bombs, kidnappings, selective assassinations.

"It is true that some people were sceptical. Mr. Saulnier admitted it himself that several Quebeckers could not conceive that such a plan could be applied in Quebec by Quebeckers, with the freedom of expression which we have . . . .

"It couldn't be conceived that anyone should have recourse to violence, to terrorist means, but there, Mr. Speaker, we had three steps which had been accomplished. We had had violent demonstrations, we had had bombs, we had just had kidnappings. What could be the position of the Quebec government? What could be the rational position, the responsible position of the Quebec government in the circumstances? To fold its arms? To wait for other kidnappings? To wait for selective assassinations?

"Our essential responsibility, our first responsibility —it would have been unpardonable not to assume it in the circumstances, Mr. Speaker."

Government leaders were not alone in attaching importance to the four-point plan brought to light by Saulnier. Shortly before Bourassa spoke in the National

Assembly on November 12, the house leader of the Parti Québecois, Dr. Laurin, made this observation: "In the documents seized and which last year convinced Mr. Saulnier of the existence of a major four-step plan, ending with selective assassination, account must be taken, I believe, of the fever, of the megalomania, of the amateurism, and of the very important difference between a project and its execution."

Laurin, whose doctorate is in psychology, was making the point that, as important as the four-point plan might be, governments had to make the distinction between plans concocted by fevered, amateur minds, and plans which were capable of being carried to execution. But of the four-point plan of demonstrations, bombings, kidnappings and selective assassinations, there was no doubt.

A three-point plan for revolution was, indeed, presented to the Commons committee on broadcasting when Saulnier appeared in Ottawa on November 27, 1969. The details of the plan were actually presented by the peppery and determined Michel Côté, the Montreal City Attorney. With considerable pride he told the MPs of the tons of documents, literally tons, which the Montreal police had seized in raids on groups considered to be subversive. He was usually careful to keep to his role of lawyer presenting facts to the MPs but when Philip Givens from Toronto asked incredulously whether the spokesmen from Montreal wanted the CYC disbanded in the whole of Canada, Côté exploded in English that " . . . this would be a very good first step." And when Givens expressed admiration for the kind of case against subversion Côté could prepare if given the time, Côté replied: "I would love to do it." Côté, who seldom appears in public and never gives press interviews was, within the year, to become the important behind-the-scenes figure in pressing Montreal's insistence on invocation of the War Measures Act (according to Brian Stewart, the particularly well-informed City Hall columnist of the Montreal Gazette).

Côté was unusually revealing in his appearance before

the broadcasting committee: thin-skinned on questions he felt touched on his own honor, hard-nosed on questions of what he considered to be subversion. Philip Givens asked whether the delegation was "really being frank with the committee," by which Givens clearly meant that he suspected there was even more evidence of subversion than Saulnier and Côté had brought forth. Côté, believing he'd been accused of lying, exploded to the MP: "Withdraw it and fast!" which is hardly the way most supplicants to Parliament address the hon. members.

Côté mentioned many dozens of times "the plan" which was to emerge a year later with such importance. "There is a revolutionary plan for Canada," he told them. "Canada is now up against a plan for revolution," he said again, and later the same morning he remarked that "as the plan says," the revolutionaries "all get together on certain causes." Côté, in fact, had outlined "the plan" at the very opening of his presentation to the committee.

Côté read to the committee from a pamphlet which he established had been written by the philosopher of the FLQ, Pierre Vallières, who gave it the title: *Revolutionary Strategy and the Role of the Avant-Garde.*

"This war," said Côté quoting from Page 2 of the document, "comprises three major strategic stages.

"The first stage," said Côté still reading directly from the document, "is that of *bringing a radical element into spontaneous social agitation.*" [Emphasis in original.]

"The second point," Côté told the MPs, "appears in the last paragraph, page 2 in the last few lines. It is the second chapter, of three major stages of the war [then quoting, he read]

. . . *the organization of the exploited classes on a vast scale* . . . .

"The third point," Côté continued, " . . . appears on

Page 3, second paragraph [and he read again]

> *The organization of the exploited classes must be brought into effect, when the time comes, with a direct view to popular insurrection which will be characterized by the armed occupation of factories, universities, schools, public services and the national territory.*

"This," Côté said when he had finished reading, "is the third stage of the plan."

That was the three-stage plan as presented to the Members of Parliament by Michel Côté, with Saulnier at his side and Mayor Drapeau sitting in the audience. To restate it, and rephrase it slightly to improve the translation, it consisted of:

1. Radicalizing the already existing examples of spontaneous social agitation (that is to say, implanting a radical message with workers and students who were demonstrating for specific goals).

2. Organizing the exploited classes on a vast scale.

3. Finally, when the time is ripe, popular insurrection with *armed* (it was underlined in the original) occupation of factories, schools and public utilities.

As the Quebec Court of Appeals had already said about other, but similar, writings of Pierre Vallières, this was probably sedition. But where was the four-point plan which consisted of demonstrations, bombings, kidnappings and assassination? It didn't exist. Nowhere in the two days that Côté and Saulnier spent with the MPs in Ottawa was there any mention of kidnappings and assassinations.

Vallières' writing, as presented to the Commons committee by Côté, spoke approvingly of the bombs which had been exploded over a period of years in federal government buildings, in mail boxes and in factories with labor disputes. Vallières wrote in February of 1969:

Since 1963, ever since the explosion of the first FLQ

*bombs, we have been in that first stage of the
revolutionary struggle which will be pursued until
agitation becomes widespread and culminates in a
general political, social and economic crisis. We are
now approaching this crisis very rapidly, and this has
been particularly the case in the past six-months.*

Vallières pictures the six years of Quebec bombings as
part of the first stage of the revolution—part of the
radicalization of protest—not the second stage as
pictured by Garneau, Bourassa and others. Vallières
clearly advocated breaking the law. "Inevitably," he
wrote, "this action must lead to violence and illegality.
It is quite normal that revolutionaries find themselves   167
situated outside the law, since legality is only a legal
justification, imposed by force, of the exploiters' rights."
And Vallières kept returning to his "three-stage plan,"
but it bore no resemblance to the three-stage plan which
was to be stated a year later as being already underway.

*We therefore see [Vallières wrote] that to achieve
these three stages, that is, giving social agitation its
radical character, mass organization, and popular
insurrection with armed occupation of the means of
production . . . .*

Clearly, in Vallières' view, the insurrection was to
occur when masses of armed and organized students and
workers were ready in the thousands to occupy schools
and factories. Vallières' insurrection was to be a true civil
war. Vallières accepted violence and illegality but
nowhere in his writings or in the other pamphlets which
were read to the MPs during Saulnier's visit to Ottawa
was there any mention of kidnappings and assassinations. The concept of "selective assassination" came
from quite another source.

In June of 1970, Montreal broadcaster Pierre Nadeau
was in Jordan making a film on terrorist guerilla training
and quite by accident came upon two men in a camp of
the Popular Democratic Front who, although hooded by

Bedouin scarves, were conspicuous by their conversations in French. They turned out to be a pair of active terrorists from Montreal who readily admitted their part in some 20 acts of violence in Quebec. One, who called himself Salem, had taken part in the Murray Hill firebombing in October, then had left for Algeria, and eventually Jordan.

"We are here to get military training which, though we couldn't receive it in Quebec, we can easily put into practice when we get back," Salem told Nadeau. The two men said that they were the only Québecois who had received such training.

The other Québecois, who called himself Selim, said: "Our training here isn't all that adequate for Quebec, because first of all, the weapons are of Soviet manufacture and difficult to come by in Quebec . . . .

"We are learning more how to kill than how to mobilize popular movements . . . .

"We want to orient our military tactics toward selective assassination. For too long the FLQ has been synonymous with bombs and useless violence. We intend to pick our targets so that the people who are responsible will pay."

An account of Nadeau's interview, with film by Ronald Labelle, appeared in *Perspectives* and in its English-language companion publication, *Weekend.* Nadeau became convinced that the two men he interviewed in the desert were in fact from Montreal and had taken part in previous acts of terrorism; his interview was the first and only source of the concept of "selective assassination." Both Nadeau and Labelle were interviewed by the police when they returned to Canada during the summer. Labelle paid for his knowledge by being carted off to jail the morning the War Measures Act was proclaimed, although he was never charged with anything, but Nadeau, much the better known of the two and the man who had actually conducted the interview, was not detained.

There is, of course, a considerable difference between a preconceived, formulated plan for revolution, of the sort which Michel Côté read into the record from the writings of Vallières, and the violent views of two individuals training in the Jordanian desert because they are disenchanted with the previously "useless violence" of the FLQ. Subsequent statements by Bourassa, Garneau and others combined these two sources into one, claiming that Saulnier had in 1969 revealed a plan of escalation rising from demonstrations, to bombings, to kidnapping to assassination. When Salem and Selim returned to Canada, the country was faced with the police problem of trying to find two men openly bent on murder. But the so-called four-point plan never existed. The threat of "selective assassinations" arose not from any secret plan, but from the open statements of Salem and Selim, a danger which was as real in August or September as in October. The non-existent four-point plan was cited by Quebec's Minister of Finance and by the Premier as a major reason for invoking the War Measures Act, whose main success in this area was in securing behind bars the photographer who had seen Salem and Selim in the desert.

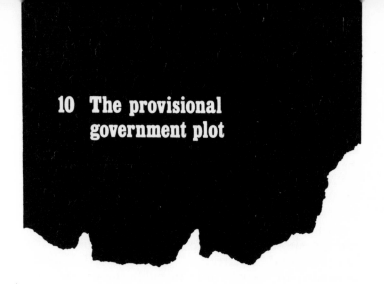

10 The provisional government plot

One week after the invocation of the War Measures Act, the combined police forces operating in Quebec had detained 379 persons, including poets, writers, editors, singers, medical doctors, university professors, trade union organizers and two candidates in the forthcoming Montreal civic elections. In Parliament, two of the opposition parties were filling the Question Period with repeated demands for specific details of what the "apprehended insurrection" really was; the Opposition also wanted more details about the people arrested. Even the bookkeeping was in disarray. After seven days of the War Measures Act, the official police figures showed that 102 persons had been released, 232 still being in custody. Since those figures added up to 334 and left 45 persons unaccounted for, Tommy Douglas of the NDP demanded: "What has happened to these people?"

"I am getting precise information on that," said the Solicitor-General, George McIlraith, obviously unhappy that down below him somewhere there were police officials with a zeal for incarceration but an embarrassing inability to add and subtract.

This confusion over the body-count and the growing suspicion among the opposition that the mood of crisis was being darkened in order to assist in the re-election of Mayor Jean Drapeau of Montreal, resulted, toward the end of the week, in more insistent demands for precise, pin-point replies to the question: why the War Measures Act?

"Surely the people of Canada ... are entitled to know the reasons," Robert Stanfield demanded from the Conservative benches on Thursday.

"A full statement should be made regarding the situation which resulted in the bringing in of the War Measures Act," said John Diefenbaker the same day.

David MacDonald for the Tories wanted "full and concise information as to the exact nature of the apprehended insurrection" and the NDP leader demanded to know, either in public or private, "the basis of the information upon which they took the step they did in determining there was a state of apprehended insurrection."

172

The questing for facts in Parliament was reflected on the best editorial pages of the country. Little of this, at least from the Tories and the press, was intended as criticism of the Government's action. The Civil Liberties Association had demanded "facts not faith" and many of those who had supported the Government were also seeking facts to reinforce their previously-given faith. The Globe and Mail, which is avidly read in Ottawa, asked for "all the facts" on October 24:

> But even those who have supported the Government's action—and we are among them—will want a great many more facts, facts that will justify the trust we have given, as soon as the safety of the country permits. To say that one of the necessary facts in this matter is that Quebec and Montreal requested the awesome powers of the War Measures Act tells us very little. . . .

Into Ottawa in the middle of that week came Peter C. Newman, editor-in-chief of *The Toronto Star*, the author of the two definitive books on the Diefenbaker and Pearson years of government, and although no longer a resident, by far the most important journalistic figure in the capital. The press and the Opposition were demanding facts, facts, and Newman came looking for them. The fame of his books and of the Ottawa column he at one time syndicated to 28 Canadian newspapers was based on the art of the cabinet leak (not that cabinet leaks always come from the cabinet) and it was to the practice of this art that Newman quickly returned. Before the weekend (the weekend on which Mayor Drapeau was re-elected with a stunning 92 per cent of the vote) someone provided Newman with a new set of facts, a set of facts which, if true, not only justified the invocation of the War Measures Act but also provided a picture of even deeper crisis in Quebec, of a government that had been on the brink of total collapse, that had been threatened with a coup d'état.

The resulting article was modestly displayed on the front page of *The Toronto Star* of Monday, October 26 and was anonymously attributed to "our Ottawa bureau" although Newman was in fact the author. The threatened coup d'état, he said, was the final straw which led the Trudeau government to assume the awesome powers of wartime:

> OTTAWA—Top-level sources indicated today that Prime Minister Pierre Trudeau's decision to invoke the War Measures Act was based on something more than fear of the Front de Liberation du Québec . . .
>
> According to these informants, the factor that finally drove the Trudeau government into action was that they became convinced a plan existed to replace the Quebec government of Premier Robert Bourassa. The Trudeau administration believed that a group of influential Quebeckers had set out to see whether they might supplant the legitimately elected provincial government with what they conceived of as an interim administration having enough moral authority to restore public order.
>
> In Ottawa's eyes, such a proposed takeover, no matter how benign or non-violent its perpetrators claimed it would be, *could have ended in the destruction of democracy in Quebec.* (Emphasis added.)

... the federal government seems to have become convinced that Quebec's society was in the kind of convulsion that precedes revolution.

... a number of the province's most influential citizens apparently felt so overwhelmed by events that their only recourse was to replace a government elected just six months ago, with an administration of their own.

Ottawa is understood to have used this information as part of the process to justify in its own mind that "a state of insurrection" did exist.

The story could hardly be more explicit: a group of influential Quebeckers had begun work on a plan to replace a legitimately-elected government, and this was at least part of the insurrection the Trudeau cabinet had put down by its invocation of the War Measures Act. Planning for the story was carried out on Sunday, the day before publication, at a meeting between Beland H. Honderich, publisher of *The Star*; Jake Howard, from *The Star's* law firm of Blake, Cassels & Graydon; and Newman himself. The story was explicit except for one important detail: the names of the "influential Quebeckers" who had hatched the plot. Newman had the names in the story as he originally wrote it, but the lawyer said "You're charging these people with sedition, and you couldn't prove it in court." So the names were taken out before publication.

Names or not, the lawyer's apprehension that the situation amounted to criminal sedition, and the involvement in the planning of publisher Honderich himself, indicated how seriously *The Star* viewed its news report from Ottawa's "top level sources." Another person who took seriously the threat of a coup d'état was Mayor Drapeau, who had let slip some private remarks about the plot three or four days before the Montreal election and then, in his Sunday night election victory speech, told the people of Montreal that their votes had been a way of saying thanks to those who "helped this government to resist not only known revolutionary attacks, but also resisted attempts to set up a provisional government that was to preside over transfer of constitutional powers *to a revolutionary regime.*"

That was a considerably more sensational version of the plot than Newman's, but it was said in the flush of a victory speech, and the next day Mayor Drapeau, while confirming that such a plot had existed, relented to the point of saying that the provisional government could have been "used by the revolutionists." The takeover plot was much in Mayor Drapeau's mind in the few days before the Sunday election, although he mentioned it only privately before his victory. After a Friday night interview on a Montreal radio station, the mayor sat around chatting with the reporters who had come to listen. He told them that without the War Measures Act, the Bourassa government would have collapsed and been replaced by a provisional government made up of the Parti Québecois, the labor unions, and the editor-in-chief of *Le Devoir*, Claude Ryan. Some of this crept into the French press, but coming as off-the-record speculations by a mayor in the midst of an election campaign, it had been reported as interesting rumour rather than hard, front-page fact.

Le Petit Journal said prior to the election that Mayor Drapeau "states that the FLQ had its own provisional government, of which the 'prime minister', according to the mayor, is a well-known editorialist in the metropolis of Canada . . . "

That, of course, meant Claude Ryan, the name that had been singularly lacking in Newman's account in *The Toronto Star.* Sitting in his severely-plain office in the old building which houses *Le Devoir* on Rue Notre Dame, Ryan watched with mounting despair while simple events in which he had participated two weeks before—in fact, one brief conversation on a Sunday afternoon—were now being exploded into plots to overthrow the Quebec government, to install himself as the FLQ prime minister, to replace Bourassa—these desperate plots which (in Newman's version) "could have ended in the destruction of democracy in Quebec."

During the decade of Quebec's emergence from the heirs of Duplessis, during the first years of its uncertain seekings after the election of Jean Lesage in 1960, Claude Ryan was the stern, disciplined spokesman for that moderate nationalism which sought special status for Quebec inside the Canadian Confederation. He became the confidante of every leading Quebec politician of the decade, but friend to none. As an opponent of separatism, he was often the object of fawning, if ill-informed, attention from elsewhere in Canada; a couple of dozen English-speaking universities offered him honorary degrees, all of which he refused. Every Quebec premier of the decade offered him jobs on commissions and inquiries, all of which he also refused. His technique as an editorialist was to consult with everyone he could find, of high and low position, and those in power also consulted him. When Premier Bourassa telephoned Claude Ryan on the very night Pierre Laporte was kidnapped, he did not call him Claude; like most men in power over the years, he still called him Monsieur Ryan.

"It must have been about 12:45 in the morning," Ryan remembered. "I was in bed and getting a lot of calls. The Premier seemed harassed and haggard, obviously a lost man. He was extremely upset by what had happened and was at a loss to decide what to do.

"I told him: 'If I were you, the first thing I would do would be to get in touch with Mr. (Lucien) Saulnier. He is the chief executive officer of Montreal and he has some experience in this kind of situation. I think he could be of tremendous help to you in this situation.'

"And then I added: 'Looking upon the government, I don't feel it is a very strong one to deal with this kind of emergency.' I told him: 'If I were you, I would think of reinforcing the government at the earliest possible date, because you are going to be faced with other similar situations in the future. Don't think this will evaporate.' "

Ryan was already looking ahead, anticipating what would happen to the Quebec government if more cabinet ministers were kidnapped, which seemed on the night of the second kidnapping the most likely escalation. Ryan was aware of the deep divisions within the Bourassa cabinet, where Pierre Laporte himself had joined Jérôme Choquette in the hard line of refusing to negotiate with the Cross kidnappers. Negotiate, Laporte had said, and there will be more kidnappings. Ryan was sympathetic to Bourassa's dilemma, being ground between Ottawa's refusal of concessions and the even tougher line of the Drapeau-Saulnier civic administration in Montreal.

Ryan's newspaper had supported the Bourassa Liberals in the April election (although opposing the Trudeau Liberals two years before) but now Ryan was dismayed at what he considered Bourassa's wavering leadership. Ryan, of course, wanted to influence Bourassa toward a policy of contact with the kidnappers and some form of negotiation. While this was certainly a minority opinion in Canada, it was not an isolated one. René Lévesque had been urging negotiation in his column in *Montréal Matin*, and *The Toronto Star* after the Cross kidnapping had urged the payment of ransom: "Securing the trade commissioner's release, unharmed," it said on October 6, "must take precedence over everything else; (the protection of foreign diplomats in Canada) is an obligation of honor."

"You must remember," Ryan was to recall later, "that from the day that Laporte was kidnapped, a feeling of panic took over in political circles; that is very important. Bourassa was spending the weekend at his country home in Sorel, that's where he was informed of Laporte's kidnapping in the early evening, and I understand he got one or two anonymous calls warning him he was next on the list. He got frightened and decided to flee, and sought refuge on the 20th floor of the Queen Elizabeth Hotel.

"I think if he had been a real leader he would have stayed in Sorel. He would have reinforced the guard around the place and would not have been thrown out of his house by a couple of threatening calls. But this illustrates the kind of reaction that was generated among political leaders by the spectacular kidnappings of Cross and Laporte."

And so, stretched out on his bed at the end of an exhausting Saturday evening, talking to a premier both deferential and distraught, Claude Ryan gave him his advice: "I would think very seriously about this: As long as your government is not a reflection of all the true political forces which are at work in Quebec, we will have this kind of problem. You are going to be shaken by crises like these, that's my reaction." There is an elegant indirection to Ryan's style at times, but his advice to Bourassa early on that Sunday morning was clear enough: Take other people into your cabinet, even those who are antagonistic on other issues, so that in this crisis you can do what you yourself really want to do. The conversation was to assume added importance some two weeks later because, when Bourassa conceded that he had heard of the "provisional government plot" he did not cite this conversation as his source, but an entirely different source. The premier didn't act on the advice he got from Monsieur Ryan, but at least on that Sunday morning he understood that Ryan was trying to reinforce Bourassa as premier, not replace him.

Twelve hours after his conversation with Bourassa, Ryan convened a Sunday afternoon meeting of his editors around the simple table which sits across the room from his own desk. Some of them had been making phone calls on their own to politicians they knew and they agreed with Ryan that the Quebec cabinet was in disarray. As the leading intellectual-nationalist newspaper of the province, Le Devoir is expected by its readers to come up with more than knee-jerk reactions to momentous events. Probably on no newspaper in the world do the editors spend so much time talking to each other, probing the possibilities and coming to a consensus. There are those who believe that this produces signed opinion articles which are soundly-based and thoughtful; there are others who find *Le Devoir's* advice circumloquacious and impenetrably dense. The editors spent three and-a-half hours at their talk, and by 5 p.m. had decided that three possibilities presented themselves, and for each they had prepared their position.

The hard-liners in Ottawa, Montreal and within the Quebec cabinet might quickly win out, bringing the War Measures Act immediately into force. This, in their view, would bestow guiding responsibility on Ottawa, and this they had to oppose.

Increasing levels of terrorism, including more kidnappings, would, in their view, reduce the Bourassa cabinet to impotence. Their answer to that for the short term was a unity government—a provisional government —made up of diverse political elements.

The final possibility was that Bourassa would win out in the struggle (they were all convinced he was personally disposed to a negotiated release of Cross and Laporte) and in that case the Quebec government would emerge strong and self-confident, but it still would benefit from taking outsiders into the cabinet as a sign of Quebec unity. This was essentially what Ryan had personally recommended to Bourassa a few hours before, and to some extent at least Bourassa adopted this idea when, after Laporte's death, he appointed an Opposition member to Laporte's labor ministry.

It is part of Ryan's plodding, time-consuming educative style (education both for himself and others) to talk to all manner of people before making up his mind. With his editors still gathered around the table, Ryan went over to his desk and phoned Lucien Saulnier at home, telling him he had some ideas he would like to discuss. The strait-laced "administrative mayor" of Montreal was no great friend of *Le Devoir*, a newspaper which had often said that Montreal needed more democracy in its government and more opposition on its City Council, but Saulnier had long since accommodated himself to Ryan's reconnaissance missions and the editors of *Le Devoir*, for their part, knew that

Saulnier is always the best-informed man in any local crisis, and that nothing happens in Montreal without Saulnier's consent. Saulnier invited Ryan to stop by the house.

On the way over to Saulnier's house in his car, Ryan learned from the radio of Pierre Laporte's touching letter to the Premier, his *Mon cher Robert* appeal in which he not only asked Bourassa to deal with his captors but also reduced their previous seven demands to only two: an end to police searches and the release of the 23 so-called political prisoners. "You have the power to dispose of my life," Laporte wrote. "Decide on my life or death. I rely on you . . . "

Hearing that, Ryan believed that the Quebec government could be convinced to negotiate for the release of both Cross and Laporte. He had urged negotiations not only because he believed the sanctity of two men's lives was the ultimate consideration but also because of his view that the Trudeau government had so far treated the crisis as entirely a criminal problem; Ryan believed the terrorists had to be contained politically as well as criminally. He was under no illusions that Saulnier would agree. Only a year before, after the insane, two million dollar window smashing and looting riot along St. Catherine Street, Saulnier had proclaimed: "We had a beginning of revolution in the streets of our city," which, he was sure, was financed in part by "international" forces. Others believed that what Montreal had was a one-day strike by its policemen.

When he got inside, Ryan said to Saulnier, "I hope for God's sake that Bourassa will heed that letter from Laporte in the speech he's going to make tonight," and much to his surprise he found that Saulnier had been equally moved by the letter. Ryan then went over the three propositions which he and his editors had worked out that afternoon.

Reaching the proposition that it might be necessary to work for a provisional government, a common front, Ryan phrased the idea along these lines: "Suppose another minister is kidnapped in two or three days, or any other tragedy occurs, will the cabinet ministers have the fibre needed to remain in their jobs? I have my worries about Bourassa himself, he's not proved too strong a man in this crisis.

"If things continue to slip, we may be heading for a situation where Bourassa's government will prove incapable of coping with the situation. We must foresee what might become necessary. There wouldn't be much choice but a unity government, which would have to be made up of the best elements.

"If Bourassa became incapable of continuing to head the government, the man most likely to be capable of doing something might be a man like René Lévesque, because Lévesque was the man who got the highest percentage of French-Canadian votes in the last election after Bourassa. If Bourassa is incapable of continuing, Lévesque is a logical possibility."

The next day, Ryan reported to his editors the response from Saulnier, and he quoted Saulnier as saying: "I don't think we will be driven to that extreme. I think we have to work with the situation as it now is." And Ryan added his own reaction: "I found this very realistic." Ryan's impression was that Saulnier wanted the War Measures Act (its invocation was still five days away) but at the same time was moved by Laporte's plea that his life could be saved only by calling off the police. Otherwise, Laporte had written, there would be "a murderous shoot-out from which I shall certainly not come out alive."

That was the totality of the "Provisional Government Plot," one conversation of an hour or so with the chairman of the Montreal executive committee during which Ryan suggested as one of three proposals that *if* the terrorism escalated and *if* the Government was unable to cope, a leader such as René Lévesque should be installed. Ryan never mentioned it again, and indeed he had no need to, because four hours after he left Saulnier's house, Premier Bourassa made a three-minute appearance on television to offer what appeared at the time to be the start of negotiations.

Claude Ryan pursued his line of urging negotiations with the kidnappers both before and after his meeting with Saulnier of October 11. On October 9, Ryan had written: "The Canadian authorities should seriously consider the possibility of exchanging the liberation of a number of prisoners for Mr. Cross' life." And on October 13 he complimented Bourassa for showing greater "political sensitivity" than his Minister of Justice because, in Ryan's view, "he clearly let people know that (the government) would be open to negotiation over the political prisoners." The Provisional Government Plot was born in the editorial conference of *Le Devoir,* it died when Lucien Saulnier thought the situation was not that bad, it was buried when Premier Bourassa on the same Sunday appeared to choose the course urged by *Le Devoir*, negotiation with the FLQ.

Ryan's technique of surveying the opinions of others before deciding on his own is well known, indeed famous, among Montreal journalists. Gérald Godin, an editor on the union-supported weekly tabloid *Québec Presse*, a man who is about as far left of Ryan as Saulnier is to the Right, told Peter Gzowski of the CBC: "Newspaper men who know how Mr. Ryan works were not very surprised at Mr. Ryan asking as many people as he could what he should write in his newspaper. He does that all the time and that is the proof that he is a good newspaperman. He checks from the taxi driver up to Mr. Bourassa and Mr. Stanfield. I think Mr. Trudeau is the only Quebec politician who doesn't consult with Mr. Ryan, and that may be one of the reasons he doesn't like him. But he is always checking the whole spectrum of opinion before he writes his own in his newspaper. To call that a plot to form a parallel government is sheer baloney."

The importance of the Provisional Government Plot is not its existence—or rather, that it never existed except for a brief academic discussion on a Sunday afternoon. Its importance is that honest men in Ottawa, seeking solutions in a painful crisis, were in such a state of mind as to honestly believe it to be true. The version which appeared in *The Toronto Star*, and in other newspapers as well, two weeks after the "event" was a grotesque contortion of the experience as Ryan lived it, but that version was deadly accurate insofar as it reported what was in the minds of many men in Ottawa as they made the crucial decisions which culminated in the invocation of the War Measures Act. The plot was never discussed at a formal meeting of the cabinet, but some of those who were in the cabinet room convinced Peter Newman that "in Ottawa's eyes" the takeover plot "could have ended in the destruction of democracy in Quebec."

Ottawa's "top-level sources" thoroughly convinced Newman and the editors of *The Toronto Star* of their firm belief in the existence of plans for a coup d'etat. *The Star* checked its version of the takeover plot with Claude Ryan before publication, checked it twice, and in the face of his protestations, ran it anyway.

Ryan first got a phone call on the day before publication from Robert McKenzie of *The Star*'s Quebec bureau, who told Ryan he had been assigned to call him, and would report back his own disbelief in any plot. On Sunday night, after the meeting in *The Star*'s executive suite, publisher Beland Honderich phoned Ryan from his home, and Ryan recounts the conversation as follows:

"Bee phoned me at my home, and he said, 'Claude, what do you say about all these things that are being circulated?'

"And I said: 'For God's sake Bee, tell me what things *you* are going to circulate. We're not in Hitler's Germany, you know, we're in Canada.' "

Honderich summarized the Newman article and Ryan once again explained his brief visit of two Sundays before at the home of Lucien Saulnier.

"And then Bee said: 'I think we must conclude that we are going to publish the story but with no names in it' (a decision which had evidently been made already on the advice of Jake Howard, the lawyer.)

"I said: 'That's not my concept of journalism. As a principle, I repudiate this kind of journalism very, very strongly.' The next morning Newman phoned me and told me he got it from two cabinet ministers."

The story had spread outwards, of course, from Lucien Saulnier. Only those involved know in what terms Saulnier told the story to Mayor Drapeau and Premier Bourassa, but both Drapeau and Bourassa told the story in similar terms when they, in turn, passed on their understanding of it to others. To the friendly reporters gathered around him at the radio station, Mayor Drapeau said a provisional government had been imminent, with a well-known editorialist as its Prime Minister. One of the editors of *Le Devoir*, talking to Bourassa on October 17 reported that: "Bourassa has seen Saulnier and Saulnier told him Ryan was out to form a provisional government."

By some route, the story got to Ottawa, and in precisely the same version as reported by Drapeau and Bourassa. The glittering party held every year at the riverside estate of Bernard and Sylvia Ostry brought together the most knowledgable and articulate leaders of government, the civil service, journalism and the universities on October 24, and the Provisional Government Plot was much discussed. Mme. Gérard Pelletier, wife of the Secretary of State, announced to a number of guests that "Ryan had been out to take over the government." Newman already knew about it, and on the next day returned to Toronto for the Sunday meeting with Honderich, and on Monday published the story with its explicit headline: *Plan to supplant Quebec government caused Ottawa to act.*

Douglas Fisher, the syndicated Ottawa columnist of *The Toronto Telegram* first encountered that headline while sitting in an MP's office listening to the Cassius Clay fight on the radio. His column the next day reflected his goggle-eyed incredulity: "This sounds wild, improbable, fantastic . . . the mind boggles."

But Fisher went out and found his own "top level source" and could hardly contain his amazement that, rather than batting down the take-over plot, his "reliable" friend elaborated on it, and Fisher quoted him directly:

"Why haven't you had some faith in us? If not in Trudeau, in some of the rest of us. Surely, you must have known we wouldn't have taken such extraordinary steps as the War Measures proclamation and sending troops into Quebec unless we were certain the threat was very, very serious.

"We knew what fear and panic were doing in Montreal. We knew the unbelievable strains in Bourassa's cabinet. We learned from unimpeachable sources that such a takeover as Mayor Drapeau referred to was planned. Really big people involved. Trudeau is the last man in this country to panic. We moved because it was that or chaos in the Government of Quebec and among the people."

Although Fisher felt required to hide his emphatic informant behind the usual Ottawa smokescreen, no-one but a member of the cabinet would be in a position to use the royal We with such assurance. And Newman had already said that *two* cabinet ministers provided the information for *his* story.

Other newspapers got around the problem by reporting the takeover plot as an Ottawa rumour, but a rumour that was worth prominent display on their front pages. Victor Mackie in the *Winnipeg Free Press* said the rumours were circulating at Pierre Laporte's funeral the week before Newman's story. Mackie found his own cabinet sources: "They understood some 'moderates' who were prominent citizens in Quebec had proposed that a 'provisional government' be set up . . ."

The rumour story was also on the front page of the *Edmonton Journal.* "The strange thing about the rumours, wild as they are," wrote Arthur Blakely, "is that they haven't yet been met with a hard official denial." Pierre-C. O'Neil, an astute Ottawa correspondent for *La Presse* analyzed the coup d'etat under the headline *Incroyable mais apparemment vrai.*

While arguments over the accuracy of newspaper articles are not ordinarily of much importance beyond

185

the day of delivery, the tortuous adventures of this particular puff-ball raised a number of serious questions, not about the accuracy of newspapers but about the adequacy of government.

Did the Ottawa cabinet ministers have in the back of their minds as they made their decisions on the War Measures Act an honest belief that a coup d'état, an overthrow of Bourassa, was imminent? Did Fisher's (obvious) cabinet minister reflect the quality of judgment and knowledge which led to the decisions in the cabinet room?

When the story was out, such as it was, the Prime Minister told the Commons that the takeover plot had not been among the "reasons" for invoking the War Measures Act, which is not the same thing as an unspoken but substantial influence. Early in the crisis, Justice Minister John Turner had said: "It is my hope that some day the full details of the intelligence upon which the government acted can be made public, because until that day comes, the people of Canada will not be able to fully appreciate the course of action taken by the government." At about the same time, Bryce Mackasey, the Minister of Labour, had urged the Members of Parliament to "read between the lines."

The adventures of the takeover plot finally came to rest on this question: Were members of the Government helping to spread the rumours, caring not about their truth, as a convenient way (1) to discredit Claude Ryan, a leading Trudeau critic in Quebec and (2) to provide a romantic *ex post facto* justification for the War Measures Act?

Trudeau's enmity for Ryan was everywhere apparent. Reading in *Le Devoir* one day Ryan's criticism of journalists who hide behind "top level sources" (Ryan had used the phrase in English) the Prime Minister told the House (in French) "For Mr. Ryan to speak English is evidence enough that he himself is feeling panic," a silly jibe, since Ryan is a frequent speaker in Toronto and other English-speaking cities. Outside the House one day, in an obvious reference to Ryan, the Prime Minister tried a little twist on Lord Acton, passing a remark to reporters that "Lack of absolute power corrupts absolutely."

After the publication of Newman's article, Peter Reilly, the bristly, outspoken Parliament Hill commentator on Ottawa television station CJOH, inquired of Marc Lalonde the Prime Minister's closest advisor, whether—off the record—the rumours were worth pursuing. "I won't tell you anything off the record," Lalonde replied, but I will say this: It's worth investigating." The Prime Minister's press secretary, Romeo LeBlanc, gave the same answer.

"It has not been the government, but rather the opposition and the press gallery that have been launching . . . rumours," Trudeau assured the House, much to the surprise, no doubt, of Messrs. Newman, Fisher and Reilly.

Thoroughly discredited by the end of October, the rumour of the takeover plot ended its days on the fringes of the Liberal Party, like a third-run movie coming around the circuit again. There was "evidence of treason or near-treason of certain intellectuals in the Province of Quebec," Liberal MP Ian Wahn told a Toronto audience in early November. "The object was to destroy the democratically-elected government of Quebec . . . " To the audience, it seemed to have a familiar ring; they booed.

11 The unjudicial process

Even in prison, Robert Lemieux behaves enthusiastically. As he strides down the corridor toward me, the guard escorting him to the interview room has to struggle to keep up the pace. We enter the room and Lemieux settles himself on the client's side of the desk leaving me the lawyer's side, and I feel relief at not having to make an embarrassing choice. He is dressed casually—a loose sweater and jeans, and his finger moves restlessly from object to object on the desk. His hair is long and dark around his strong face, and he has a black drooping moustache. His expression changes rapidly, showing his emotions as he speaks.

As his story unfolds in this Montreal jail, my concern deepens. Lawyers for very unpopular people often take some of the brunt of public hostility, but rarely do they go to jail for their clients. My professional detachment diminishes as Robert Lemieux's conversation reveals that the same circumstances which put him on the client's side of this jailhouse desk, are in the future of every lawyer with a social conscience, a commitment to duty and a controversial clientele.

By the time I leave the building in a grey November drizzle, conscious of my precious freedom, detachment has vanished. In its place is unease, and a very unwelcome feeling of identification with this young, intense and imprisoned lawyer. I recall the well-intentioned judge who, in my second year at the bar, invited me into his chambers and advised me, in kindness, against representing a trade union client which was politically unpopular. "It won't do your career any good to represent such people." he said.

But someone must.

—A.E.G.

Robert Lemieux had been a lawyer for three and one-half eventful years. Fluently bilingual, having been raised in both English and French, he attended McGill Law School and on graduation was employed by an English-speaking law firm whose clientele and associations are Westmount and St. James Street and whose seven-partner name contains no French surname at all.

The firm lent its staff to the legal aid system of the Montreal bar and Lemieux was asked to defend Robert Lévesque, an alleged member of the FLQ. He did, and from there became involved in the defense of Pierre Vallières and Charles Gagnon. A letter from the latter two, addressed to the court, was being prepared in Lemieux's office in January, 1968, when the young lawyer was called before one of the firm's partners and summarily fired. He was handed a cheque for six months pay and told to have his belongings out of the office immediately. One half hour later he was standing on the street with his personal effects in a box beside him, looking for a taxi and wondering about his future.

By this time, his experiences at McGill and his exposure to separatist thinking were leading him to favour a form of Quebec nationalism which would remedy the injustices which he felt had been visited on the French Canadians.

He opened an office and practiced on his own, taking a wide variety of legal work, and becoming established as a lawyer who was not afraid to defend those charged with the bombings and robberies associated with the FLQ.

"I was careful," he said, "to keep away from political speeches or associations with political groups. I was continually being consulted by these groups, but I kept my role to that of a lawyer." In this role he witnessed the police harassment of various organizations, the arrest of leaders on the eve of important events, releasing them later without charge, the seizure of what counsel for the City of Montreal later was to boast, was "tons" of literature.

He attended demonstrations and watched as the police broke them up. When he spoke in public, he spoke about his cases to groups of students.

His enthusiasm and ebullience were to create special problems for him. When James Cross was kidnapped, Robert Lemieux knew immediately that he could help. He had acted for a number of people in jail whose release was being demanded by the kidnappers. He also felt that they would trust him. He bounded into the situation, visited his clients in jail to see if they would accept the exile their release would mean, and was interviewed repeatedly by a news-hungry press.

He urged the Government to make a deal with the kidnappers, a sentiment that was shared by a number of prominent Quebeckers but was still extremely unpopular. On the Sunday morning after Pierre Laporte was kidnapped, Lemieux was arrested, charged with obstructing justice and held without bail and incommunicado until late on Thanksgiving Monday, October 12, when he was visited by Robert Demers, a Montreal lawyer appointed by Premier Robert Bourassa. Demers asked Lemieux to negotiate with him on behalf of the FLQ. He showed Lemieux the communique in which the FLQ had indicated that it wished for him to represent them. Lemieux agreed and was promised his release. At noon on Tuesday, October 13, Lemieux was released on his own bail. His files, including confidential, clients' papers, which had been seized and examined at the time of his arrest, were returned to him.

"I felt that Demers had made my position official," he said. "I was worried that I might be considered to be on the FLQ side. I felt the government should do something to prevent these lives from being lost." The press conferences he was using to communicate with the kidnappers quickly became a shambles. The government was using the "negotiations" to buy time, and Lemieux was being relentlessly sucked into that oldest of lawyers' problems, public identification with his clients. He had already been jailed once and this experience drove him further into his clients' cause. On Thursday evening, October 15, he found himself standing on the stage of the Paul Sauvé arena—not as a bystander or legal observer—but as a participant, cheering the speakers and shouting slogans.

When the War Measures Act was proclaimed, one of the first to be arrested was Robert Lemieux. Wakened from his sleep at the Nelson Hotel where he had resided, he was escorted by five policemen in two cars. They took the same files and clients' papers they had taken the Thanksgiving weekend before.

In his enthusiasm to participate, Lemieux had not pulled the lawyer's protective cloak over himself. No matter how he saw himself, he became whatever the press chose to label him, "FLQ spokesman", or "FLQ lawyer". In this unique situation, a frustrated Government and a frustrated public became increasingly angry at Lemieux who had made himself a visible and real target. He was subjected to the same legal violence as his fellow prisoners. But to a legally-trained mind, the deprivation of counsel, bail, the absence of a charge, and being held incommunicado, even from the other prisoners, was exquisite torture. Part of the process to which he was subjected was the denial of a preliminary hearing and therefore he could only speculate, and then not very well, as to what the evidence against him would be.

Most trial lawyers have to teach themselves not to "go to jail with their clients." This professional detachment makes a cool, clinical approach possible. As the demands of certain situations, especially those with explosive political content, require more and more involvement from the lawyer, he becomes more and more vulnerable to attack for becoming a part of his client's cause. Given the tensions of the Cross and Laporte kidnappings and being put in Lemieux's position, many lawyers who would now claim to be wiser, might have found themselves in the same position. The protective colouration of only being a lawyer, "doing his job" loses its effectiveness as the lawyer gets drawn closer and closer to his client's position. Differences in background help, but very often, in political situations, similarities are more obvious than differences. The sedate, detached lawyer is a luxury which a political defense cannot afford.

Lemieux's English background and his marriage to the daughter of a prominent English-Canadian New Brunswick family should have helped him, but it worked in reverse. At the time when his political views were being formed, he was living the life of a typical undergraduate of English-speaking McGill University. But his experiences at McGill and in the old-line English law firm exposed him to the prejudice that submersion in the French milieu would have spared him. His reaction to those experiences influenced his life style and brought him more strongly into public identification with his clients.

Lawyers are treated with great deference at the Centre de Prevention, the Quebec provincial lockup occupying the top three floors of 1701 Parthenais St., near downtown and not far from Montreal's Champlain Bridge.

The guards are friendly and courteous. Special interview rooms are provided where counsel and client can meet across an imitation walnut desk, seated on soft office-type chairs. The closed door ensures privacy and provides the only window, used periodically by a guard who peers discreetly in.

The pass issued after the lawyer's identification is established names the clients who will be brought to the room. It must be signed by the lawyer, who thereby agrees to submit to search and to abide by the various prison rules. But the privacy of counsel's briefcase is respected and no files are looked into in the perfunctory glance which completes the procedure.

The building also contains the headquarters for the Quebec Police Forces and a fourth floor lockup which serves as a transfer point to and from the courts. Here there is no search. The lawyer states his business and can speak to his client through a metal grill in a glass wall so ingeniously devised that it is hard to imagine even the voice passing through.

For two weeks following the early morning of October 16, the interview rooms were being used, not by lawyers but by teams of police officers who were interviewing detainees. The interviews could not, for the most part, be described as interrogations. They were friendly, often pointless, and for the most part based on a questionnaire which bore detailed questions on the identity of relatives, job histories, education etc.

A child could have evaded the bald questions asked. "Are you a member of the FLQ?" "No." "Did you kidnap James Cross?" None had.

Some were incriminated. They could not know that making statements in support of the FLQ, even to a police officer in a friendly chat about "politics and that sort of thing," could be used in court as proof that they were guilty of the crime of belonging to the FLQ, which was defined in a law of which they were not allowed to be aware, as "the unlawful association."

The question "Do you agree with the FLQ Manifesto" could be answered "yes" with innocence by social reformers with revolutionary zeal but who either held an active dislike for terrorism or who thought the FLQ was engaging in very stupid tactics, however these persons may have admired the objectives and shared many of the sentiments expressed in the manifesto, which was read over the CBC on October 8.

They could not have known that their statement would incriminate them. The students, writers, technicians, office boys, civil servants who were picked up in the massive sweep, even the lawyers who were arrested, could not have known of the new law which made innocent views and associations on October 15, a crime on the very next morning.

A person who feels he is innocent of any wrongdoing will succumb to the desire to engage in human communication—we like to talk. It calms tensions and anxieties. Perhaps it will encourage a response from the questioner so that one can find out what is happening.

Even lawyer Robert Lemieux, one of the first to be plucked from his bed in the before-dawn raids, talked. The best advice he could have given himself would have been to exercise his right to remain completely silent. His answers, however, are unlikely to be used against him.

"I told them nothing," he recounted. "They filled up exactly one half a page. They asked me if I was in favour of making social changes by violence. My answer was that I recognize the government of Peking as the Government of China."

Some, like Michel Chartrand, used the interrogation to relieve themselves of their feelings at being caged up without knowing the charge on which they were arrested. Characteristically, Chartrand blasted his questioners with a stream of language from which even the cleverest police officer could draw only embarrassment.

It is a traditional requirement of the law that a person arrested is entitled to be informed forthwith of the reason for his arrest. Most of the detainees asked and were told something vague about the War Measures Act. Some were told it was martial law. The reason for an arrest must be that the person arrested has committed an offense. Under the regulations passed by the Cabinet in pre-dawn secrecy, an arrest could be made if the authorities had reason to suspect that the person being arrested was a member of the FLQ or any other group advocating the use of force or crime to accomplish governmental change, or that he professed to be a member or had reason to suspect "has committed, is committing *or is about to commit*" any act in support of the FLQ or such other group.

This crime, hitherto unknown, was so complex and incapable of definition that the police were either unwilling or unable to explain it to their prisoners. If there was enough evidence to arrest, there must also have been enough evidence to lay a charge. Under the regulation the police were entitled to wait for seven days, which period could be and was extended to 21 days, before laying their charges. But they were *not* prevented from bringing their prisoners before the courts the very same day or the next, if they wished. But then, the prisoners would have heard the charges against them, could have received the advice of counsel and the protection of the court from other abuses. They could not have been released on bail without the agreement of the Attorney-General of Quebec. However, if they were to be denied their freedom before trial they would at least have been guaranteed their right to know the charge they faced.

Pains were taken to ensure that the prisoners were kept in the dark about the law under which they were being held. Their cells had piped music, taken from a radio station in Montreal. The news broadcasts came every hour and during that period, the imprisoned listeners heard only silence and speculated.

Virtually all of the 103 released in the first seven days learned the precise reason for their detention only afterwards.

In Montreal, where all but a few of those arrested were detained, lawyers played virtually no role in securing the release of their clients. The detainees were simply not charged, and then they were permitted to go home on some date before the 21 days were up.

The entire process of their arrest, imprisonment and release was accomplished by administrative action. The special powers for which the police asked and which they got made the judicial process irrelevant for approximately 90% of those affected.

The Canadian Bill of Rights protects the "right to retain and instruct counsel without delay," along with the right to be informed promptly of the reason for an arrest and detention. The author of that Bill was thoroughly familiar with the need for such protection. In 1945 John Diefenbaker defended a client named Hicks who had refused to answer questions, in the absence of his lawyers, put to him by excise tax investigators. As Prime Minister in 1960, Diefenbaker made sure that the right to counsel he had won for Hicks was assured for all Canadians in his Bill of Rights.

The Bill of Rights was inapplicable to the detentions under the authority of the War Measures Act. Even so, the continued denial of counsel was not authorized by the War Measures regulations and was a clear abuse of these wide powers which had been given to the Attorney-General of the Province of Quebec. His conduct was a distinct embarrassment to Justice Minister Turner.

By October 22, 369 persons had been arrested, 103 had been released and none had been charged. Still, no counsel had been permitted to see any of those held. Under fire from NDP leader Tommy Douglas, Turner expressed confidence that the Attorney-General "recognized that the arrested persons had the right to instruct counsel on their behalf," after "discussions" which had been held between them.

Choquette had issued a statement in Montreal the previous day, presumably after the "discussions", which made it very clear that Crown counsel were hard at work, a group of investigators having "been set up to study the record of each of those detained as promptly as possible, in order to determine whether they are to be indicted and brought before the courts or released because of lack of evidence."

As to counsel for the defense, the statement was a little less certain. "The minister," it stated, "has also announced that he recognizes the right of the individuals detained to retain services of counsel, but here again there are administrative problems, which are being overcome." A few days later counsel found their way past the guards to the consulting rooms for a first meeting with their clients. It took 10 days for the detainees and their lawyers to come together. The detainees had already been interrogated.

After the revelations of former Soviet cipher clerk Igor Gouzenko, Justices Robert Taschereau and Roy L. Kellock of the Supreme Court of Canada were appointed Commissioners to enquire into the facts and to examine upon oath those who had been detained by regulations made under the War Measures Act in great secrecy and urgency. Despite the elements of national security involved in the inquiry and the fact that the entire proceedings were held in secret, each person called to testify was allowed counsel of his choosing upon request. Counsel were required to undertake not to communicate any of the facts they learned or any other matter relating to the subject of the inquiry.

In 1954, the Toronto police arrested two persons at a football game. When a lawyer retained to act for the men asked to see them, permission was refused. The advice to refuse was given by a Crown Attorney of many years experience who assured the officer in charge that until the police investigation was finished and complete, no person could see them. In a subsequent judicial inquiry into the event, it came out that the main reason for refusing permission was so that the prisoners wouldn't have a chance to be told not to say anything. The police told the inquiry they regarded such advice as "definite obstruction".

Mr. Justice Roach reported to the Attorney-General that the two prisoners were improperly denied the right to consult with their counsel and that they were detained for an undue length of time at the police station. He termed the idea that the refusal was justified, "a most shocking one" and observed that . . . "there can never be any justification for holding a prisoner incommunicado."

The War Measures regulations permitted the Attorney-General to arbitrarily refuse bail. He did. It was not until three women were released from custody on Thursday, December 10, that any consents were given at all. The right to deny bail was important to support the detention impact of the regulations. Of what use would be the ability to arrest FLQ suspects so-called, if they could be bailed out immediately?

But once a charge is laid, different considerations apply. Then the detainee becomes an accused. He is before the court and, in normal circumstances, the court is entitled to secure his attendance at trial by means of bail instead of by holding him in custody.

The factors to be considered are the roots the accused has in the community, the severity of the penalty likely on conviction (the five-year maximum under the regulations is relatively light, compared to many criminal charges on which bail is normally allowed) and the likelihood that the accused will commit further offenses. The last factor is the only one inconsistent with the well-known presumption of innocence. Bail is very important and its right is enshrined in the Canadian Bill of Rights.

Most of the accused charged under this sudden and unusual law remained in custody on the orders of the Crown, their adversary in the trials to come. The courts were powerless to intervene, until December 28 when, as a result of negotiations leading to the capture of the Roses and Simard, the Justice Minister finally agreed to let the courts resume their function of deciding bail.

Professor Martin L. Friedland of the University of Toronto Law School did the definitive study of bail practices; the information gained became the basis of subsequent federal law reform. In his book, *Detention Before Trial*, he makes the key point, "Custody during the period before trial not only affects the mental, social, and physical life of the accused and his family, but also may have a substantial impact on the trial itself. The law should abhor any unnecessary deprivation of liberty and positive steps should be taken to ensure that detention before trial is kept to a minimum."

On November 9, in desperation, imprisoned lawyer Robert Lemieux wrote a letter to the Bâtonnier of the Quebec Bar. In it, he described the events which led to his arrest and pointed to the arbitrary manner in which he was being kept in custody. He asked for the Bâtonnier's intervention with his fellow member of the bar, Jérôme Choquette, to secure his consent to bail.

The letter, an open one, was widely publicized in Montreal as having been "smuggled" from jail. But the

Note: M. Lemieux's letter appears in full on page 293.

real question, as in the controversy which developed over a recording of Messrs. Lemieux and Chartrand made in prison and played at a union meeting, was whether their right to communicate their ideas and to make their complaints in person, was not being wrongly withheld from them.

Then, in desperation, on Thursday, November 26, Lemieux appeared before Mr. Justice Mackay of the Quebec Superior Court and applied for bail. To do so, he had to attack the validity of the law under which he was being held. If the law was valid, it was Mr. Choquette who would make the all-important decision about his bail and not the judge. In a 12-page written brief he attacked the constitutional validity of the Public Order regulation and the factual basis on which the Government acted. He quoted Trudeau, the Universal Declaration of Human Rights and a number of legal precedents.

It was all to no avail. His request, like those of Vallières, Gagnon and Chartrand, was refused. The Court ruled that the act was valid and that it had therefore no jurisdiction to consider bail. The power of the Crown to imprison, at least until the trial was over, was absolute.

After the arrest of Paul and Jacques Rose and Francis Simard, taken from a cold wet tunnel leading from an abandoned farmhouse in St. Luc, the Attorney-General no longer blocked bail applications, but permitted the courts to decide them upon their merits. Mr. Choquette maintained that he had intended to permit this anyway, but the three fugitives negotiated this concession in exchange for not offering violent resistance to their capture, which took place in the early morning hours of December 28. In the rush of bail applications which followed, many of those imprisoned, including some of the more prominent prisoners, were released.

Choquette's Ministry of Justice had to make the decision to release or lay a charge within 21 days of each detainee's imprisonment. Three crown attorneys from the District of Montreal staff began to review the "records" pertaining to each detainee. This material was all supplied by the police, reporting on their interviews and forwarding other police information. No legal requirements applied to this evidence and the facts on which these very important decisions were being made were not communicated to the prisoners; they were thus unable to rebut falsehoods or raise defenses.

Soon swamped by the sheer numbers of those arrested, the Crown attorneys were replaced by specially-appointed counsel, drawn from the best available legal talent in Montreal. Six lawyers, all in private practice and experienced in criminal law, took over the job. Most detainees were then released but some were kept in jail and later charged. The first court appearances were on the 20th day after the first arrests. On that day 26 men and four women learned for the first time what crimes they were alleged to have committed.

Their fate was now in the hands of the courts, and the adversary system was allowed to come into play— almost.

As the screening process went on, so did the arrests. After the first two weeks, prisoners began to see their lawyers, but until the decision was made by the staff of Crown counsel as to whether the detentions would continue or be terminated, there was little that the lawyers could do.

In normal cases under the criminal law, the decision to charge an offence is almost simultaneous with the decision to take the accused into custody. In approximately 10% of the cases, the Crown, either through more senior police or Crown counsel, will decide not to proceed. This decision is also made without the accused present—but there is a substantial difference. He is entitled to counsel immediately, he must be brought before a court and he can be released on bail.

Of the October arrests, about 10% were proceeded with. The remaining 90% were held in custody, without charge, without bail and in most cases for most of the time without counsel, while the decision to release them was being made.

Imprisonment is punishment. It is inconsistent with the concept that an accused person should be proven guilty before being punished that he be imprisoned without hope of bail before being tried. Justice Minister John Turner early in 1970 had committed himself to reform of the nation's bail system through amendments to the Criminal Code which would establish the right to freedom until guilt is proven. The purpose of pre-trial imprisonment is only to secure the attendance of the person charged at his trial.

The 435 persons who were released without being charged after periods of imprisonment ranging up to 21 days—according to figures released by Turner in February, 1971—were punished. They had been placed at the worst possible legal disadvantage, denied information on what was alleged against them, denied counsel, interrogated and then "tried" in someone's office in their absence.

The regulations under the War Measures Act did not require this treatment, they merely permitted it. The decision by the police and the Quebec Attorney-General to take full advantage of the "rights" given to them, was theirs alone.

As of December 3, there were 49 persons charged under the regulations, of whom 15 were also charged with seditious conspiracy.

The first convicted was François Mercier, a 27-year-old music teacher in Granby. He was allowed to plead guilty on November 5 before a lower court judge in Cowansville, Quebec. He was sentenced to 15 months imprisonment on the charge that he was a member of the FLQ.

Those before the courts did not find that their position had improved much. They could now consult counsel and they had heard the charges read against them. But the decision as to their freedom pending trial was still not one the courts were permitted to make. The regulation provided that persons arrested under it would be detained in custody without bail pending trial "unless the Attorney General . . . consent to the release of that person on bail."

In Montreal the Crown decided to take advantage of a little-used procedure which effectively prevented the defense from examining and testing the evidence to be used against them prior to trial.

When a person is charged with an indictable offense in Canada, he is first charged on an information in the lower courts and a preliminary hearing is held. If the judge or magistrate believes there is sufficient evidence to commit for trial, he will do so. The Crown calls its witnesses and the defense may cross-examine them. Even if the accused is not discharged at this stage, he has had an opportunity to examine the Crown's evidence in detail and then make important decisions concerning his defense. The procedure ensures that there will be an adequate opportunity to make a full answer and defense to the charges and that there will not be a trial "by surprise".

While the ordinary procedure was used in prosecutions commenced in Rimouski, Sherbrooke and Quebec City, the Government chose to prefer indictments directly in the Superior Court at Montreal by-passing the preliminary hearing.

Among the rights usually available to a person charged with an indictable offense is the right to elect trial before the lower court judge or before a higher court judge with or without a jury. The right to trial by judge alone, which usually ensures a speedier trial, can be very important to an accused person who has been denied bail and who believes that freedom awaits him at the end of his trial.

On November 5, the problem of speedy trial was raised and Crown counsel sent a letter to defense counsel offering to facilitate trial by judge alone in the Superior Court. Later, the Crown took the position that it had been mistaken in law, and the court was told that the offer had been withdrawn. That right to a speedy trial was no longer available.

On December 1, Judge Jacques Trahan, sitting as a

coroner and presiding over the inquest which had commenced November 6 into the death of Pierre Laporte, sentenced a reluctant witness to six months imprisonment for contempt of court. Lise Rose, 25, was detained under the War Measures regulations and charged with being a member of an unlawful association. She was arraigned with the first group of 24 at Montreal on November 5.

On November 24, she was called from her cell and taken into the room where the inquest was being held. The police were already searching for her brothers, Jacques and Paul, believed responsible for the kidnap and murder of Laporte. Such knowledge as she may have had of the circumstances of his death would have either been to the detriment of her brothers or possibly herself, or have been of no value at all.

Lise Rose was not alone in this problem. Before her, a number of witnesses, among them Lise Balcer, François and Francine Belisle, Richard and Colette Therrien, and Bernard Lortie, a friend of the Roses who was in the kidnappers' house before Laporte's death, had added to the facts by identifying themselves with the events in small but significant ways. None of them could refuse to testify even though their evidence might tend to incriminate them. They were all subsequently charged.

Section 23 of the Quebec Coroner's Act provides that "A witness cannot refuse to answer for the reason that his reply might tend to incriminate him or to expose him to a proceeding of any kind; but his replies cannot be used against him in any subsequent criminal proceedings, except for perjury."

Most criminal systems of justice permit brothers and sisters, parents and children and other closely related persons to be required to testify against each other. The line is drawn, even in Canada, at husbands and wives who cannot be compelled to testify against one another.

However the privilege against self-incrimination has been enshrined in the English Common law since Edmund Campion refused to incriminate himself in an investigation into plots against Queen Elizabeth in the

16th Century. He was tortured for his silence and his hands were so mutilated that he could not lift them to take the oath at his trial.

This and other grisly stories of the ancestors of the "confession" have left us extremely wary of them. The methods of protecting ourselves from abuse have taken the form of requiring the prosecution to be able to prove its case against an accused without his evidence. He is not to be compelled to testify against himself although he is free to testify if he wishes. That is the law in Canada.

However, there are instances in the legal system where a person may incriminate himself other than at his trial. In the United States the protection against self-incrimination extends to every place a person may be made to testify. It is enshrined in the famous Fifth Amendment of the United States Constitution.

In England, the rule is a common one, expressed most often in Latin *Nemo tenetur seipsum accusare*, no man shall be required to incriminate himself. While the English judges and ours have praised it as "a maxim of our law as settled, as important and as wise as almost any other in it," various provincial and federal governments have done their best over the years to circumscribe it.

They have succeeded quite well. Section 5 of the Canada Evidence Act, which covers all serious crime, permits any person to be called as a witness and forced to answer any question.

It states: "No witness shall be excused from answering any question upon the ground that the answer to such question may tend to incriminate him, or may tend to establish his liability to a civil proceeding at the instance of the Crown or of any person." Thus, the whole community including prospective jurors may be treated to a detailed and verbatim confession or something similar, the Crown and police may use the evidence so given to build a case against the accused, but he cannot refuse to testify.

The second subsection of Section 5 protects the

witness' evidence from being used against him in any subsequent criminal proceeding if he would have been entitled to claim the common law protection against self-incrimination and he objects to answering the question. With proper procedures, therefore, the incriminating statement can be kept from being used as a confession—but that is all. That situation arises in cases where the trial of another person is being held, or at any judicial inquiry or, where a death has occurred, at the inquest. The only requirement is that the evidence sought is relevant.

The inquest has been a popular method of pumping suspects since the Barnes case was decided by the Ontario Court of Appeal in 1921. That decision confirmed the Crown's right to call anyone as a witness before an inquest, even though that person was already charged with the crime in the criminal courts. That decision was considered good law until 1965 when the Supreme Court of Canada held in the Batary case that the Barnes case "was wrongly decided and ought not to be followed." Writing the majority judgment, Mr. Justice Cartwright said, "It would be a strange inconsistency if the law, which carefully protects an accused from being compelled to make any statement at a preliminary inquiry, should permit that inquiry to be adjourned in order that the prosecution be permitted to take the accused before a coroner and submit him against his will to examination and cross-examination as to his supposed guilt. In the absence of clear words in an Act of Parliament or other compelling authority, I am unable to agree that that is the state of the law."

Obviously relying upon the distinction that those being called before the courts were not yet actually charged with any crime relating to the death of Pierre Laporte, counsel on behalf of the Quebec Attorney-General ignored the Batary decision and called witnesses ranging from Bernard Lortie, who stated: "I want to tell all I know, even if I'm involving myself," to Lise Rose whose accusations that she had been beaten and stripped naked by the police as they interrogated her were not sufficient to deter the authorities from pressing her into the witness stand. Her refusal to testify was in protest of her treatment. It was obvious that she had no desire to give information, either under beatings or under oath. She was sentenced to six months in jail for contempt of court.

Those who were described by Lortie as occupying the Queen Mary Road apartment in which the Rose brothers and Francis Simard later hid, Francine Belisle, Colette Therrien and her brother, Richard, were called to testify at the inquest. They were later charged with giving assistance to their visitors under Section 5 of the War Measures regulations.

Conspiracy to commit an offense is a broad charge. Any person who does anything for the purpose of aiding any person to commit an offense, or who sets out to carry out an unlawful purpose with another person who commits an offense which the first person ought to have known would be a probable consequence, is equally guilty of the offense. An accessory after the fact is also guilty of a crime and includes anyone not married to the person trying to escape who, knowing of the offense, "receives, comforts or assists him for the purpose of enabling him to escape." It is a separate crime to be an accessory after the fact.

In the excitement of the events of the fall of 1970, it was forgotten that the privilege against self-incrimination is a right enshrined in centuries of Western law. The systematic calling as witnesses of a number of persons certain to be charged as accessories posed a serious challenge to the principles which had been asserted in the Batary case. That principle was circumvented by the mere device of delaying the charges until after their testimony was taken.

Bernard Lortie had already testified before the coroner's inquest, implicating the Rose brothers and Simard in the death of Laporte. When the three men were finally arrested they were held on coroner's warrants and, on January 4, 1971, were paraded into the hearing room before Judge Trahan. Both refused to testify, claiming that they were prisoners of war. They gave the numbers which appeared under their mug shots taken by police on their arrest. Jacques Rose even invoked the Geneva convention concerning war prisoners. Not to be deterred, the Crown called a Quebec Provincial Police corporal who proceeded to intone into the record a confession which he said Simard had made but refused to sign on the day of his arrest. No one challenged the authenticity of the statement and the usual guarantees of a *voir dire*, in which the question of its voluntariness is determined, were missing. Only at the forthcoming trial would the question of whether or not it was proper evidence be decided. There is a clear Government policy against premature release of statements made by persons accused of crimes. It is illegal for a newspaper to publish such a statement if admitted at a preliminary hearing, for example. Even the other evidence may be withheld from publication, by means of an order of the court, which is usually easy to obtain.

This was an inquest and no actual law existed to bar the broad publicity given to Simard's unsigned confession. For all the world to know, including of course, all the prospective jurors who would be empanelled at Simard's trial, it was quoted verbatim in radio, television and newspapers. The statement was a clear admission of guilt. "The next day, at about 6 p.m., all three of us, Paul, Jacques and myself, strangled Laporte with the chain he was wearing since we kidnapped him. All three are responsible, we all knew what we were doing and the political act was done."

The same day, Judge Trahan delivered his verdict and closed the inquest. "After hearing testimony from the medico-legal experts, we are satisfied," he said, "that Mr. Laporte died a violent death and we are convinced that Paul Rose, Jacques Rose, Francis Simard and Bernard Lortie should be held criminally responsible for the death."

The law on the interpretation of statutes, especially penal statutes, is clear. No law shall be interpreted as creating an offense before the date it was enacted, unless it specifically states that it is retroactive. In one case in Whitby, Ontario, during the Second War, the defense was successful when it established that the Defense of Canada regulation under which a man had been charged had not, at the time of the offense, been advertised or published in the Canada Gazette. The Regulations Act, which also applied to the 1970 regulations, provides for the same requirement: no man shall be convicted of breach of a law of which he could not have been aware.

Under the regulation there could not have been a conviction for the offense of being a member of the FLQ prior to the time the War Measures regulations were announced in the House of Commons, at eleven o'clock in the morning. The hundreds who were rounded up under the authority of this law could not be assumed to have committed their crime while asleep. Even after being awakened by the police in the early morning, the detainees could not gain precise knowledge of the offenses, and hundreds were in jail before the text of the regulations was tabled in the House of Commons. Even Robert Stanfield didn't know until 10 a.m.

While there was no retroactive language in the War Measures regulations, the Government attempted in the subsequent Public Order Act to make evidence of conduct prior to October 16 admissible. It was still not an offense to have been a member or to have supported the FLQ prior to that date—this the Government dared not do.

The Federal Government, in spite of its repeated denials, was creating a retroactive crime under the guise of permitting retroactive evidence in order to establish guilt after the date of proclamation for acts which were legal when performed.

The best available defense would have to be that the accused resigned in his sleep.

12 The cause is always noble

"History shows that governments bent on a crusade or officials filled with ambitions have usually been inclined to take short cuts. The cause being a noble one (for it always is), the people being filled with alarm (for they usually are), the Government being motivated by worthy aims (as it always professes), the demand for quick and easy justice mounts. These short cuts are not as flagrant perhaps as a lynching, but the ends they produce are cumulative, and if they continue unabated they can silently re-write even the fundamental law of the nation."

Justice William O. Douglas,
Supreme Court of the United States.

There have been many crises in Canadian history involving domestic upheaval and government reaction: the Fenian raids, an invasion from the United States, the Mackenzie Rebellion, the Riel Rebellion, the conscription riots, and the Winnipeg General Strike. Those occasions which most disturbed the national conscience in later years were those in which we were unable to reconcile our reactions of the time with our later knowledge of the real state of events. Our disturbance is increased with the severity of the measures taken.

What proclamations would be made, what emergency powers would be taken, if a latter-day Riel appeared from the ranks of the undernourished Métis living in their tarpaper shacks in Northern Saskatchewan, raiding armouries and Hudson's Bay posts?

Had it been intended to be used in peacetime, the War Measures Act certainly would have been used by the Borden government—which had passed it five years earlier—to settle the Winnipeg General Strike. It was clearly not intended to be a peacetime measure. It would certainly have been considered an abuse of its intended purpose if it had been used on the strikers massed on the streets of the Manitoba capital.

The Winnipeg strike is another of those Canadian events which was the object of hysteria at the time, and became an object of affection later. The civil libertarian looking back 50 years sees the refusal of the employers to recognize the unions of their employees, the use of armed vigilantes by the city government and their assistance by the R.C.M.P., with the resulting loss of life, and the trials and convictions for sedition against leaders whose crime was their rhetoric in the defence of the right to organize.

The hysteria of the time was enough to secure the passage of the infamous Section 98 of the Criminal Code as well as restrictive amendments to the Immigration Act. In 1919, no voice was raised against Section 98. Only two years later, attempts were already underway to secure its repeal, and they were continuously repeated with major public support until 1936 when a Liberal government finally got the House of Commons and the Senate to agree.

Now the Winnipeg General Strike is regarded as an exciting part of Canadian history. And Section 98 is regarded as an historical and legal aberration which we regret and wish good riddance.

Our second world war experiences with government by regulation in a time of unequalled national tension, are barely old enough to enable us to take an historical perspective. At the time, the country conceded that the government's measures were wise and necessary. It was unpatriotic to think otherwise. Each regulation had its reason and each prosecution, detention, censorship or deprivation of the right to meet, assemble, worship or even live in one's own home was regarded as necessary and wise. We are a nation which has always placed trust in its leaders.

The history of the use of the War Measures Act, even during an emergency as great as World War Two, is that in granting broad powers and discretion, the price for achieving efficiency is abuse. We have also learned that temporary legislation can have permanent effects. When it ceases to operate, potential new victims of its arbitrary power needn't worry. But what of those it has already affected? Does the job the detainee lost suddenly reappear? Does the stigma of being suspected of such unpopular conduct ever disappear? Can vanished property rights ever be fully reinstated? Most important, when a person living in the security of a free society sees that security destroyed, can his attitude toward that society and those who allowed it to happen ever be restored? The deprivation of freedoms, even temporarily, creates permanent change.

Torazo Iwasaki is an example. His problems did not begin when Japan attacked Pearl Harbour on Sunday, December 7, 1941. He had suffered the prejudice of the west coast from his arrival in Canada in 1901. And when that fateful attack came he lived in a country which was ready, aye, eager to exercise its arbitrary power over him.

The objection is not that the removal of Iwasaki and 21,000 of his fellow Japanese-Canadians was done by administrative fiat and secretly—under the War Measures Act. Given the mood of the country and the prejudice which existed, it could have as easily been accomplished by an act of Parliament. The government accurately assessed the mood of the country toward those citizens and residents it described as "of the Japanese race". We wanted to do our bit for the "boys over there" and to show "them" that "they" couldn't treat our prisoners like that.

The thoughtlessness which allowed national loyalty to be confused with "race" could only have come from prejudice, incubated and nurtured on the west coast since the first Japanese arrived there in 1877. They followed the Chinese who arrived 19 years earlier to provide cheap labour in the Fraser River gold rush and on the railroad construction gangs. By 1884 there was agitation to limit their immigration. Such action was the result of increasing alarm that Orientals were prepared to sell their labour more cheaply, and that their birth-rate was sufficiently higher than the European community to threaten the ambition the whites had to fill the province with British immigrants.

The western provinces, led by British Columbia, were able eventually to secure legislation to restrict Chinese Immigration, but they were prevented from prohibiting the Japanese by reason of existing treaties with Japan which were binding on the Dominion government. Although frustrated, the British Columbia government, supported by its white majority, made life as difficult as possible for its non-Caucasian inhabitants. It prohibited them from voting in provincial and municipal elections, from employing white women in their businesses and from working on provincial Crown property (mainly logging camps). Attempts to bar them from working in the coal mines and to restrict their occupations were struck down by the Privy Council which, however, upheld the voting restrictions and the prohibition on employing white women.

Torazo Iwasaki and his wife Fuku survived the prejudice and the public attitude toward their race which made the restrictive laws possible. He worked as a fisherman and saved as much as he could. He bought a parcel of 640 acres on Salt Spring Island in the Strait of Georgia, paying a good price in the post World War One market of $3,950. By 1940 he had paid off the mortgage. The land contained sea frontage and approximately 4,250,000 board feet of timber. He sold a part of the timber rights, worked his land and fished.

Just 56 years old, Mr. Iwasaki was not yet thinking of retirement; his land was his security for that. Then came Pearl Harbour. The couple had to register as persons of the Japanese race, a minor indignity compared with what was to follow. As a "person of the Japanese race" he, like the owners and crews of approximately 1,100 fishing boats on the West Coast, was prohibited from earning his livelihood. Their boats were impounded and eventually sold by a committee to non-Japanese owners under the authority of order-in-council P.C. 288 which condescendingly recited that, "The owners of these vessels, though being of Japanese origin, are Canadian citizens whose productive power, by virtue of this ownership, contributed significantly to the fishing industry."

Then came the cruelest blow of all. Without regard to national loyalty, citizenship or to the terrible tragedy thus created, the government ordered, under the authority of orders-in-council, the evacuation of all persons of the Japanese race from their homes and what was left of their communities. This followed an unsuccessful attempt to remove the males from 18 to 45 years of age. They didn't want to leave their families, Ottawa didn't want to apply too much force and the British Columbian prejudices were not satisfied.

The Japanese were herded into Vancouver's Hastings Park, sleeping in the exhibition buildings, carrying all they could with them in the maximum two suitcases allowed per person. Gradually they were dispersed, but with considerable difficulty as community after community in the interior rejected the idea of the camps being placed there. Finally, the specially-created British Columbia Security Commission chose ghost towns in the interior, which were fixed up for the stay of the evacuees. Others were sent to the sugar-beet farms of Southern Alberta and to the Winnipeg area. Many refused to leave the familiar west and stayed on the side of the Rockies they knew as home.

Ironically, so that the displaced Japanese-Canadians

could work at the timber-cutting which was necessary for the war effort, something had to be done about the racist law which existed in British Columbia preventing them from working on Crown lands. So that the men in the camps could work, Ottawa passed P.C. 1422 setting aside the restriction on persons of Asiatic racial origin "for the duration of the emergency created by the present war."

Meanwhile, lands owned by the Japanese had been vested in the Custodian of Enemy Alien Property. He was given such broad powers to deal with the land by the regulations that the courts later found that he could not even be considered a trustee in law. This was to be important to Torazo Iwasaki.

On May 23, 1943, the Custodian took control of his land and although there was no evidence of what made it necessary to sell it, it was included in a catalogue listing all the seized land for sale. Beside each piece of land, there was the name of the agent appointed by the Custodian to sell the property. Beside the properties on Salt Spring Island there appeared the name, Gavin C. Mouat, of Ganges, B.C.

In addition to his duties as agent for the Custodian, Gavin C. Mouat found time to be a director and 20% shareholder in a company called Salt Spring Lands Ltd. That company offered to buy the land and so did a Captain Smith. The Custodian replied that he required an independent valuation. It came in at $5,000. Salt Spring Lands Ltd. then offered $5,250 and was allowed to purchase the property on March 1, 1945. At the time, the true owner was in the Greenwood Detention Camp in the B.C. interior and powerless to interfere.

On May 23, 1945, the Custodian informed Mr. Iwasaki that he had $4,838.54 for him. That sum represented the purchase price less commission! Mr. Iwasaki refused to accept this sum and the matter was eventually referred to a Commission established to investigate the considerable number of complaints which arose from the sale of similar property. The Commissioner, Mr. Justice Bird, of the British Columbia

Supreme Court found, on the basis of the evidence before him, that a true valuation on the date of sale was $12,000, or 140% more than had been paid. In exchange for a cheque, he released the Crown and the Custodian from future claims.

Unlike some of his disillusioned brethren, Mr. Iwasaki declined the "offer" of deportation to Japan at the end of the war. This, too, was accomplished by order-in-council. But Mr. Iwasaki stayed. He became a Canadian citizen on June 19, 1951. In 1967 he petitioned the Exchequer Court of Canada for relief, claiming the land was now worth $1,500,000, and pointing to the irregularities in the sale made while he was a virtual prisoner in the interior. The Exchequer Court denied his claim, partly on the ground that the Custodian was not a trustee, partly on the ground that the subsequent owners were not in the action, which was against the Crown which had taken his land away, and partly on the basis of the release which he had signed. The Supreme Court of Canada rejected an appeal against this decision on the basis that the release he signed was valid and binding.

The Japanese Canadians do not discuss the days of the Second World War very much. Those who lived through it would like to forget. But they know of the indignity, the hardship, the shattering of lifelong dreams and the torture of impossible explanations having to be attempted to bewildered children. In homes in Japan, former Canadians remember landing in a foreign land where they could not speak the language and where their only identification was their similarity of appearance. The regulations all expired or were repealed before 1950. But the land, the fishing boats and the dreams are still gone.

As British Columbian prejudices were catered to in the West, Quebec's were met in the East. The Japanese-Canadians of Quebec were the Jehovah's Witnesses. Largely because of their virulent attacks on the Roman Catholic Church and their boldness in spreading their views, they were, for a number of years before the second world war, the object of whatever means the Quebec establishment could find to harass them.

The unlikely employment of the Defence of Canada Regulations to outlaw the Jehovah's Witnesses, along with the Canadian Union of Fascists and the Communist Party of Canada, fits well into the pattern of harassment although it did not begin there, nor did it end there. In fact, there were 1,665 reported prosecutions of Jehovah's Witnesses in the Province of Quebec alone, from the war's end to 1953. Although centred there, there were incidents and prosecutions involving them in the other provinces of Canada, both before, during and after the war.

During the war, the power to declare organizations illegal was given to the Cabinet under the War Measures Act. And it was used, both on the Witnesses and their related organizations and on Technocracy Inc., a proselytizing organization with semi-religious and authoritarian overtones.

Prime Minister King defended the move as best he could. The declaration which was announced on July 4, 1940 was made because, "The literature of Jehovah's Witnesses discloses, in effect, that man-made authority or law should not be recognized if it conflicts with the Jehovah's Witnesses' interpretation of the Bible; that they refuse to salute the flag of any nation or to hail any man; and, that they oppose war. The general effect of this literature is, amongst other things, to undermine the ordinary responsibilities of citizens, particularly in time of war."

Repeated objections to the treatment of the Witnesses as subversives under the regulations were raised in the House. In 1942, a special committee of the House of Commons met to consider the Defence of Canada regulations and recommended that the Jehovah's Witnesses be taken from the list of illegal organizations. A year later they were still being prosecuted under the regulations. The government's answer was that while it was true that the committee had made that recommendation, the report had not yet been formally made.

Finally, in late 1943, the government, without the benefit of a vote of the House, rescinded the order-in-council on the same authority that it had made it, the War Measures Act.

In the meantime, the Witnesses felt the sting of outlawry. They did not stop their prayer meetings and they continued to practice their religion. As they came to the attention of the authorities, they were arrested, charged and convicted of being members. While it was not an offense to attend a prayer meeting, it was an offense to "act as a member". Prosecutions took place all across Canada, with the majority in Quebec. In Ontario, the Custodian of Enemy Property tried unsuccessfully to convince a Court that property left by will to the also-banned Watch Tower Bible and Tract Society, related to the Witnesses, should not go to the other beneficiaries but should be given to him. The will had been made in 1931. The other beneficiaries won.

A Manitoba Witness who wrote a letter to the chairman of his school board protesting the expulsion of his children from school for refusing to sing the national anthem and salute the flag was charged with publishing a letter containing statements intended or likely to be prejudicial to the efficient prosecution of the war, contrary to the regulations. The letter quoted his religious beliefs that it was contrary to the covenant of his faith to salute the flag or sing the national anthem. He was convicted at trial but acquitted on appeal on the grounds that he had a right to address private correspondence to the chairman of his school board.

In Hamilton, Ontario, Robert Donald had to resort to a lawsuit, which was finally successful on appeal, to get his children, who had been suspended for the same reason as those in Manitoba, reinstated to their classes.

It was difficult at times to decide whether some of the prosecutions were savage or just plain silly. On November 13, 1940, George Burt, then an organizer and later the Canadian Director of the United Auto Workers, led a picket line at the No. 2 plant of Chrysler Corporation of Canada in Windsor. The pickets were orderly and their purpose was conceded to be to persuade workers entering the plant to join a strike.

Under the general heading of "Espionage and Acts likely to assist the enemy," there was a prohibition against loitering in the vicinity of a protected place. A protected place was one where essential services were being performed. The purpose of the regulation, according to the court, was protection against espionage.

The police told the union men that the government had declared the Chrysler plant an industry of essential services and asked them to leave. The pickets left and announced they would return at noon, which they did. They were arrested and charged with violating the regulation. Notwithstanding that this conduct was clearly labour picketing, Mr. Justice Hogg confirmed the conviction on the ground that it constituted loitering.

The labour movement found that it had much to fear from the Defence of Canada regulations. Charles Millard, then a major force in the United Steelworkers, was charged in Timmins in the early months of the War for stating that we should have democracy in Canada before we go to Europe to fight for it. As part of a general speech on unionism, he said that there is "not a great deal of sense in going to Europe to fight Hitlerism when we have Hitlerism right here, and men join the army to be sure of eating regularly."

John A. (Pat) Sullivan was interned on June 18, 1940 under a detention order signed by the Minister of Justice the day before. He was the president of the Canadian Seamens' Union. The sole reason given him when he took advantage of the objection procedure to a special committee was: "Your detention has been deemed necessary in the interests of the State because representations have been made that you are a member of the Communist Party of Canada, a subversive organization which is opposed to the interests of

Canada. In view of this it would appear that you are disloyal to Canada."

His counsel protested to the Ontario Supreme Court that it was impossible to defend him on those allegations since they were general, quoted unnamed sources and did not contain all of the facts on which the Crown relied.

The court held that there was no obligation to show him more. An appeal to the Court of Appeal, in which his counsel was joined by John L. Cartwright K.C., later to become Chief Justice of Canada, was denied and he continued in custody.

In May, 1941, James A. Murphy, a C.B.C. employee and president of the radio division of the Association of Technical Employees, was taken into custody and detained under the regulations as he returned from a meeting at the Department of Labour in Ottawa, where he was attempting to set up a conciliation board. He was denied the right to see his counsel and his wife was not permitted to visit him.

The statement that he was suspected of having made some radio equipment for the communists did not overcome the suspicion that he was in his dilemma because he had proved troublesome in his bargaining role. As the result of the matter being raised by C.C.F. Leader M. J. Coldwell, his wife was allowed to see him on Monday, May 26, the arrangements being that "she be not restricted to the usual three-minute interview."

There were wholesale internments during the war, based on Section 21 of the Defence of Canada regulations which required only that the Minister of Justice be "satisfied" that it is necessary to "detain" the person with a view to preventing him from acting in any manner prejudicial to the public safety or the safety of the state.

A person detained was not permitted to consult a lawyer until he decided to object to his detention. Such objection was then heard before a committee, usually of one person, who could make a recommendation. The procedure was usually the same as that described in the

Sullivan case. Often the Minister of Justice did not release a detainee when the committee recommended it. There was never a trial and the detention was deemed by law to be legal and habeas corpus was consistently refused. By 1944, 80% of those detained had been released.

Historians may never be able to analyse the existence of just cause for these detentions since everything about them was kept strictly secret. Only those cases which found their way into parliamentary debates or the courts were ever discussed, and then the evidence was still not known—even to the detainee.

Similarly, cases under the sections of the regulations prohibiting statements or publications containing statements harmful to recruiting, relations with friendly powers, the safety of the State or the prosecution of the war were widely publicized at the beginning of the war. However, censorship regulations were eventually applied in such a way that it became impossible to know for what statements persons were being convicted. A civil liberties column in the Canadian Forum began publishing such details in December of 1939, but ceased completely 13 months later.

Political opponents threatened the use of the regulations upon one another. In November 1939, a Conservative M.P., T. A. Thompson (Lanark) told his audience, "J. S. Woodsworth and his henchman M. J. Coldwell should be interned for unpatriotic statements in the House." And the C.C.F. was warned by B.C. Premier Pattullo that to oppose an expeditionary force was an offence under the regulations. George Drew, Ontario Conservative Leader, was charged because of his criticism of the handling of the Hong Kong Expeditionary Force. The charges were later withdrawn.

Dorise Nielsen, who represented North Battleford for the C.C.F. in the wartime Parliament, made a speech in the 1940 Budget debate which was reprinted in a pamphlet entitled, "Why I Opposed the Budget" and widely distributed in Western Canada. Reports reached her that the R.C.M.P. and other police forces were systematically searching for the pamphlet and removing it when they found it. It was disconcerting to her supporters, to say the least, to be visited by the police and to be asked for copies of the document. She raised it in the House, and some time later, Ernest Lapointe, the Minister of Justice, lamely explained that the investigation, which produced nothing by way of charges, concerned the pamphlet reprinted by a printing house, and not her speech.

It was suggested that something had been added to Mrs. Nielsen's pamphlet—but even that did not make it censorable or the proper subject matter of a charge. The police visits were merely an investigation, he asserted. No explanation was given as to why it continued long after the pamphlet had been examined by the authorities.

Then came the punch line. "I should not like to say anything that might offend the hon. member in any way," he said, proceeding to do so. "If, however, the police have searched for those leaflets, of which search she complained so strongly, it is because my hon. friend keeps bad company, very bad company indeed." After some interjections, he continued, " . . . But were I at liberty to say what there is in the files of the Royal Canadian Mounted Police!"

Samuel Levine was a young geophysicist who returned to the University of Toronto in October 1939. His Ph.D. was good enough only for a research fellowship and $1,500 per year. He rented a small house for $40 per month and to balance the budget, he rented a room to a total stranger named Stern. Stern said he was a writer. He brought a typewriter with him and he wrote—not a book about Spain as he told the Levines— but what later was proved in court to be subversive literature. He had been allowed to use the dining-room table when the Levines weren't there and when the police raided two weeks later they discovered a wrapped package full of papers on that table. Mr. Stern had disappeared.

Levine was charged with being in possession of

literature contrary to the regulations, convicted, dismissed from his university position and sentenced to six months in jail. Efforts to secure his release on appeal and by civil liberties groups failed and he served his time.

But the story does not end with his sentence. The efforts to release him had to be continued for a considerable time afterwards because, on his release, he was picked up at the prison and taken to an internment camp where he spent the next two years.

The change in atmosphere by 1943 was remarkable. Russia was on the side of the Allies. No longer were Communists to be distrusted. What had been done now could be undone. But it wasn't easy.

In July, 1943, the House of Commons was presented with some very embarrassing affidavits which established that some of the property seized from the Ukrainian Labour-Farmer-Temple Association in Edmonton was turned over to a rival organization which was reputed to have pro-fascist tendencies. There were very few neutrals among the Ukrainians.

They also disclosed some highly repulsive incidents of book-burning. The affidavit of Steve Solonynka reads in part,

"3. I was formerly employed by the Pullan Paper Stock Ltd. at Trinity and Parliament Streets, in the said City of Toronto and was employed by the said firm for about five years until about six months ago.

"4. I remember distinctly in the early part of 1941 a load of books, containing about five tons, was brought to the yard of the said company, and the said books were torn and destroyed by the workmen of the said company. These books bore the stamp of the Ukrainian Labour-Farmer-Temple Association.

"5. Many of these books were in the Ukrainian language but many others were in the Russian and English languages.

"6. I remember definitely seeing the following books printed in the English language: works of Victor Hugo, Anatole France, Robert Burns, William Shakespeare,

Jack London, Upton Sinclair, Karl Marx, W. Lenin and the History of Canada.

"7. I also remember seeing books printed in the Russian language by Leo Tolstoy, Turgeniev, Maxim Gorki, Pushkin, and books in the Ukrainian language by the following authors: Taras Shevchenko, Ivan Franko, Olga Kobylianska, Kulish, Wasil Stefanyk.

"8. While these books were being destroyed by the workmen of the said company, the destruction of same was being supervised by plainclothes police officers of either the Dominion or Provincial government."

The affidavit of Mike Andrichuk, a Ford worker who had moved to Windsor from Edmonton, where he had been employed as a janitor of the Ukrainian Labour-Farmer-Temple Association Hall at 10628 9th St. until April 1, 1941, was also filed. That organization was the same as the one in Toronto. Both had been declared illegal organizations by Federal cabinet order.

He swore: "2. In the said hall at the time of my said employment was a library belonging to the said Ukrainian Labour-Farmer-Temple Association consisting of approximately 1,000 library books some of which were used in a schoolroom and some of which were used for general library purposes amongst the membership of the said association. Amongst the said books were works of Gorki, Marx, Tolstoy and other great Russian writers as well as works in English by Shakespeare, Burns and Winston Churchill. There were also works by Shevchenko, the Ukrainian national poet and by Jack London.

"3. In or about the month of April, 1941, the said hall was sold by the Custodian of Enemy Property to the Ukrainian National Federation, a pro-fascist organization. By instructions given to me by a Mr. Wenspir and a Mr. Hamilton, representatives of the said Custodian. I was ordered to burn, and did burn approximately 500 of the said books in the furnace in the basement of the said hall.

"4. The said burning took place about one month prior to the sale of the said building and I was further ordered by the said Wenspir and Hamilton to assist in loading the balance of the said books into a truck and the said books were taken by the said truck to the said garbage disposal plant of the city of Edmonton and there destroyed. At the time of the destruction of the said books the same were in good, usable condition. The said Wenspir and Hamilton or an auctioneer were present with me in the basement of the said hall when I began to burn the said 500 of the said books in the basement furnace according to their instructions."

While Canadian Communists were languishing in internment camps, being prosecuted and having their publications and organizations banned, Prime Minister King and a number of dignitaries attended various functions designed to change public feeling about our ally, Russia. On June 22, 1943, he addressed a gathering called "Salute to Russia" at Toronto's Maple Leaf Gardens.

"Apart altogether from our comradeship-in-arms there are many reasons why friendship between our two countries should be particularly close," he said. Furthermore the promotion of such understanding and friendship were, in his words, "the beginnings of the new world order."

All of this caused the Toronto Globe and Mail to wonder editorially. On the same day as he spoke, his Minister of Justice had explained that he still regarded the Communist party of Canada as an illegal organization, and had no intention of lifting the ban on it. Pointing out that the Soviet Union had not given up communism, the Globe said, "We hope that Mr. Feodor Gousev, the Russian minister, has a strong sense of humour and can laugh at the farcical coincidence of our Prime Minister's elaborate eulogies of communist Russia and his Minister of Justice's reiteration of his determination to keep the Canadian Communist Party suppressed."

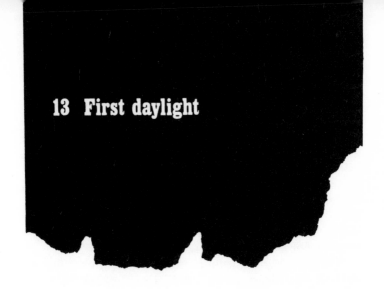

13 First daylight

The architecture of Montreal presented a distinct disadvantage to the kidnappers of Jasper Cross. Many residential buildings are divided into two or three flats, with access, in the European manner, by way of circular metal stairways on the outside. The kidnappers of Cross had decided not to risk a long drive outside of Montreal and therefore they needed an apartment in a neighborhood where they had not lived before and at a price they could afford. They could hardly take the risk of ushering a man wearing a blacked-out gas mask up the winding, difficult steps of an outside staircase. The house at 10945 Avenue des Recollets provided the answer. It had been built, unlike most of its neighbors, after the Second World War and offered an inside entry from the basement garage to the main-floor flat. In an area of modest, French-speaking wage-earners, a 1962 Chrysler would not be out of place.

The house was the only investment of Tom Sasso, which was a risk in itself, but unlike many such landlords, he was not nosey or officious about his property. In the month before, Jacques Cossette-Trudel, with his wife Louise, had rented the house from Sasso, giving the name of Paul Tremblay and paying one month's rent of $140 in advance.

The front windows of the first-floor apartment were covered by heavy drapes, but the new tenants caused no stir among the neighbours. On one occasion, Cossette-Trudel asked the elderly lady who lived upstairs not to be shy if she heard any unusual noises coming from the apartment below. She assured him she did not, and he asked her to tell them if she did. Mrs. René Charbonneau did hear a loud noise one evening, as if someone had dropped something heavy. Her grandson, seven-year old Fredo, staying with her and her husband said, "Maybe they're trying to blow us up." She dismissed it as childish nonsense.

As Mrs. Charbonneau worked in her kitchen at the rear of her apartment, Jasper Cross could hear her footsteps. He was handcuffed and lying on a mattress placed on the floor of the rear bedroom immediately below her. His place of confinement was a small bedroom, next to the bathroom which separated it from the kitchen, also at the rear. A hall divided the apartment, with the living and dining rooms on the left of the front entrance and two other bedrooms on the right. Cross's room was behind the living room.

When Cross arrived, the gas mask was removed and replaced by a cloth hood through which a slit had been cut at the mouth to permit him to breathe. The handcuffs were removed, his arms placed in front of him, and then handcuffs put on again. He was forced to lie down on the mattress.

The room contained a table, a chair and a television set. Unable to see his kidnappers, he talked in French with the faceless voices about what they had done. They read him the communiqué and their FLQ manifesto. Excitement filled the room as news bulletins reported the kidnapping and government reaction to it.

Each of the men involved in the kidnapping had a face mask, but in their nervousness at Cross' home, they forgot to put them on. In the apartment the masks came in handy when Cross was permitted to wash or shower. His armed guard would don a mask completely hiding his face and Cross was permitted to remove his. When he was asked to look at anything, such as television or a letter he was being required to write, his mask was

228

transformed into a hood, with the pieces at the side placed in such a way as to prevent any vision except straight ahead. It was like wearing blinkers.

In this personal darkness, listening to the excited voices around him, Cross began to assess his position. Obviously his life was in jeopardy. He decided that escape was impossible. The only practical alternative was to co-operate as much as possible and to try to survive each 24 hour day as it arrived.

He asked for and was granted permission to write a reassuring letter to his wife. It was delivered along with a message from the kidnappers to radio station CKAC at 10:00 p.m. on the Tuesday night. The message con-tained a threat to Cross's life: "Let it be clear that when the deadline has passed we will not hesitate to do away with J. Cross . . . because the life and freedom of the political prisoners and the boys from Lapalme are well worth hundreds of diplomats dedicated only to the financial interests of the Anglo-Saxon and American big bosses."

By Wednesday noon, the 48 hour deadline set out in the first message had passed. In another message boldly delivered to the switchboard operator at radio station CKLM, the kidnappers announced that they had given the authorities a further 24 hours to prove their good faith by broadcasting the entire text of the FLQ manifesto on the CBC and by immediately halting all police searches. Cross had been forced to write out a note asking "the authorities to respond favourably to demands of the FLQ" and, to relieve a cause of earlier concern, he assured everyone of the fact that he was receiving medication for his high blood-pressure and was being treated well.

At dawn on Wednesday, the police made a number of coordinated raids on what they considered to be FLQ haunts and arrested thirty persons. Later in the day, police took Mrs. Cross and Mrs. Santos, the maid, to police headquarters to view those arrested through one-way glass. None of the suspects was identified and they were all released. But an examination of a large number of photographs paid off with the identification of Jacques Lanctôt. It came as no great surprise, since Lanctôt's brother was already in custody awaiting trial in the aborted attempt to kidnap the U.S. consul, and a warrant had been issued in that case for Jacques Lanctôt himself. (It was curious that, having uncovered plots on the American and Israeli consuls, the police did not, apparently, deduce which "exploiting" nationality would be next on the list.)

In the first few days, it was easy to conclude that only short-term captivity had been planned for Cross. The routine seemed too uncomfortable to be sustained for long. The kidnappers' careful concealment of their identity from Cross would make it easy to release him unharmed. When the governments did not capitulate quickly, the kidnappers became increasingly frustrated. The Thursday noon deadline passed and a new message was sent, this time to Pierre Pascau, a Hot Line host at radio station CKLM. It invited further negotiations by asking the government to specify which demands it found unreasonable, turned down the suggestion made earlier by Mitchell Sharp that a mediator be appointed, and again insisted on the cessation of police activity and the broadcast of the FLQ manifesto. The CBC announced that it would broadcast the text in full at 10:30 that evening.

That afternoon, Cross was permitted the luxury of sitting in a chair at a table in the corner of the room, still handcuffed. The hood was adjusted so he could see straight ahead and he was able, at times, to see the television set in the other corner. Cross talked with the persons guarding him. They were careful to stay behind him and he found it difficult and tiring to use a language he had learned only after coming to Montreal, and to carry on a continuous conversation, not knowing to whom he was speaking or when his listeners had changed. He discussed their political objectives with them, asking them what they hoped to achieve and the reasons for his kidnapping. The answers were full of political rhetoric. They watched the FLQ manifesto being read.

Cross went to sleep dreaming about having been freed and walking across Westminster Bridge. In other rooms the radios played, the stations being turned from newscast to newscast as Carbonneau, Lanctôt, his brother-in-law Cossette-Trudel and Pierre Seguin, later identified as Yves Langlois, and the two women listened in vain for the indications that their plan would work. They had calculated that the government would accept their demands within four or five days. As those days passed, new reasons were found to explain the unexpected refusal of both governments to deal with them. Lanctôt's theory was that the government did not want to let the kidnap tactics succeed in North America because the Americans would then have similar problems with the Black Panthers and Weathermen. He speculated that Washington had already advised Trudeau not to give in.

As the tensions built up, the kidnappers and Cross were careful to maintain as much courtesy as possible. They called each other "monsieur" and while there was nothing resembling a personal relationship, their conversations were amicable. Cross got the impression that they were capable of violence and had decided to establish a revolutionary state in Quebec by means of violence. They were, he thought, typical revolutionaries in that they would be prepared to go to any ends, including their deaths, for their cause.

Then, on Friday morning, they heard a Quebec Government appeal for more time. In the afternoon, through Pierre Pascau of CKLM, Justice Minister Choquette asked them to supply proof that Cross was still alive by sending a letter from him including the words, "It is now five days since I left and I want you to know, darling, that I miss you every minute."

At about the same time that the broadcast appeal was being made, the kidnappers were delivering their own communiqué, although it was not found. Then in reply to Choquette, they wrote back giving a fifth and "final" deadline for six p.m. Saturday. They said this was to be their last communiqué and that no one would find Cross again if their demands were not met. A letter from Cross containing the requested words was enclosed together with a copy of the earlier communiqué which had not been delivered. The entire bundle was located by CKLM reporters acting on a telephone tip.

The occupants of the apartment were adjusting to the routine and making do as best they could. Cross was being fed cheese and toast for breakfast with rice and spaghetti dishes making up the bulk of the other meals. Occasionally, Chinese food was brought in and from this he chose the minute quantities of meat which were all he saw during his captivity.

On Saturday, October 10, Choquette was preparing his reply. The deadline was drawing near and there was a tenseness in the air as Cross and the six with him listened for some word. The Justice Minister was not ready until 5:30—one half hour before the deadline. He refused to meet the demands of the kidnappers. He announced that the Federal Government had offered safe conduct for them in exchange for the release of Cross unharmed. He also promised clemency toward the prisoners whose release was being sought, a reference to the possibility of early parole. In his reply, Choquette emphasized that the government could not permit its decisions or the decisions of the courts to be erased by blackmail, "because this signifies the end of all social order."

Cross, watching on television, asked the faceless voices behind him what they were going to do with him. They would continue to hold him for a few days, they said, just to taunt the police, and then they would let him go. Lanctôt, whose identity had already been established, and who was being widely publicized as a man wanted for the kidnapping, had the insurance he needed in the offer of safe conduct. The kidnappers kept open Cross' chance to live by the great care they took not to be identified by him.

In their communications, the group always referred to themselves as the Liberation Cell. Cross had never been given any indication that there was any coordination, up to this time, with anyone else, let alone another cell of the FLQ. When the television set in Cross' room revealed the Laporte kidnapping, it came as a complete surprise to them all, and it complicated the plan to release Cross after the police had been sufficiently humiliated.

As they watched the details of the Laporte kidnapping unfold during Saturday evening and Sunday morning, Cross began to feel a kinship with the other man whom he had never met. The Chenier cell, responsible for the second kidnapping, was demanding the fulfillment of the first demands made by Cross' kidnappers by 10 p.m. Sunday night. Through the day two more communiqués came from the Chenier cell, repeating the death threat to Laporte. Here was a new complication. As Bourassa broadcast his message asking for negotiations, but insisting first on machinery which would ensure the safety of the two hostages, the small group gathered at Des Recollets decided to keep going. Their "final" communiqué of the Friday before was not to be their final communiqué at all. Cross was required to write a letter expressing full confidence that the FLQ would release him if its demands were met and thanking Premier Bourassa "for saving my life and that of Mr. Laporte." In the message accompanying the letter, Carbonneau and Lanctôt demanded the fulfillment of their demands for the release of the "political prisoners" and their safe conduct to Algeria or Cuba and a halt to police activities. It suggested Robert Lemieux as an intermediary.

Lemieux, the Montreal lawyer who had represented a number of those whose freedom the kidnappers were seeking, had been loudly discussing the merits of the various government positions taken during the past week with any reporter who would listen. Earlier on that Thanksgiving weekend, he had been arrested and held without bail on a charge of obstructing police.

A telephone call directed reporters from another radio station, CKAC, to a trash can in a subway station near Place des Arts where Laporte's kidnappers, the Chenier cell, had placed a message to the authorities insisting on all their demands, accompanied by a letter from their victim. Laporte's letter, obviously dictated, indicated that he was well, and supported the demands. The Chenier cell, too, indicated that it wished Lemieux to negotiate on their behalf.

The government, like the public, was relieved that the two men were still alive, and to establish the appearance of negotiations and to buy as much time as possible, appointed their own negotiator, a young Montreal lawyer, Robert Demers. Demers knew where to find Lemieux, in Parthenais St. jail. The two met Monday night and Demers showed Lemieux the FLQ communiqués naming him as their negotiator. Lemieux agreed to negotiate and his release on his personal bail was to be obtained by the government. For some unexplained reason, the release of Lemieux was not obtained until noon on Tuesday.

By this time, Cross was engaged in a friendly but cool dialogue with his captors, living from day to day with the tension of uncertainty. During the second week he could feel the hostility of Lanctôt, Carbonneau, the Trudels and Seguin increase as news speculation that he was sending coded messages appeared in the papers. His letters to his wife had been rewritten on the direction of his guards to prevent a code and those which he had written to the authorities were dictated. He had no idea where he was. He could not see out of the blinded window and only the television and casual inquiries gave him the time. He was later to complain of the danger of this sort of speculation: "There's been a lot of talk about journalistic responsibility. But people have responsibility to the kidnapped, to the chap in there, he's the loneliest man in the world. And speculation about what he's trying to do may cost him his life."

Lemieux met with Demers at the Quebec Hydro building on Dorchester Street on Tuesday afternoon.

The government demanded counter-hostages from the FLQ to be held until Cross and Laporte had been released. Lemieux said he had no instructions to agree to this. Since his only indication of what the FLQ was prepared to do came from the communiqués which Demers had shown him, he needed a further mandate. This announcement was made at a press conference in the Nelson Hotel where Lemieux lived below City Hall in the Bonsecours market area of Old Montreal. The press conference became a rally with the presence of Pierre Vallières, Charles Gagnon and Michel Chartrand. The latter, President of the Montreal Council of the Confederation of National Trade Unions, stated that he supported the FLQ manifesto. They were watching at 10945 Avenue des Recollets.

At 5 a.m. Wednesday, the next morning, radio station CKLM was notified that it would find a message under a carpet at 391 St. Joseph Boulevard West. For the first time, and unknown to Cross, there was an indication that the kidnappers of both men had been in contact. Lanctôt and company, who sent the message, indicated that its contents had been approved by the Chenier cell. The message rejected the idea of counter hostages. It suggested that the country of refuge would detain the released prisoners as well as the money until Cross and Laporte were freed. Lemieux again met with Demers that afternoon, and in the evening, René Levesque and Claude Ryan held their press conference, together with the labor representatives (they had never even considered including Michel Chartrand) and leaders from the teachers' federations and the credit unions.

On Thursday, things seemed quiet in the hideout and the news was minimal. Lemieux had briefly talked with Demers but there was little more that could be said by either man. Quietly, preparations were being made for the exercise of emergency powers by the police. At 9 p.m. Bourassa made a short statement repeating the government offer of safe conduct out of Canada. The government also promised to recommend parole for five eligible prisoners out of the 23 whom the FLQ wanted freed. The FLQ was given until 3 a.m. to respond.

There was only the silence of before, broken by the dramatic 4 a.m. announcement of the proclamation by the Federal Government of a state of apprehended insurrection and the approval of regulations giving to the police, and the armed forces assisting them, powers of search, arrest and detention unprecedented in peacetime.

The mass arrests which followed did not result in any change in the way that Cross and his captors carried on their day-to-day lives. Their attention was fixed on the events swirling about them in the city but they could have been hundreds or thousands of miles away. The arrests and searches did not result in any visits to their door. The hostility brought about by the suggestion that Cross was sending out coded messages lifted when the lack of their discovery made it obvious that the suggestion in the press was untrue.

Cross, struggling to keep his mental equilibrium, sensed by this time that`there had been communication between Laporte's kidnappers and his. He later felt that they knew of Laporte's death before it was announced on the radio, but when it was announced at about 12:30 on the morning of Sunday, October 18, it was a complete shock to him. Shortly afterward Cross, whose constant source of strength was to think of his wife and daughter, was wrenched by the announcement that his body had been found at Rawdon, north of Montreal. He was overcome by the horror of his wife watching the news at home. In fact, she was asleep.

On Sunday, Cross wrote a letter to his wife which was placed in the Church of St. Jean Baptiste de la Salle on Pie IX Boulevard. Another letter, intended for the authorities, was picked up by police at Beaubien St. and Pie IX Boulevard, in a telephone booth after a phone call had been received by radio station CKLM. As it was dictated, Cross wrote, "The only danger for my life is if the police find out where I am and want to intervene. The FLQ will not give up and I will be the first dead. My life is not menaced at present."

236

Marc Carbonneau, still in the apartment, learned that his name had been released by the police as another prime suspect in the kidnappings. Still, Cross noted no change in the attitude of his captors.

It was Cross who changed. On hearing of the death of Laporte he decided that he didn't want to talk to them too much. Their relations remained amicable, but limited. "We lived in two solitudes," he recalled later, "mine, me in my little chair, and them in the rest of the house, and we occasionally would talk about something. We would, of course, discuss the communiqués when they wanted to send a communiqué. We might discuss something that happened on television, something on the news, but these were not conversations of long duration."

Cross began a long wait. The occupants of the apartment came and went with little apparent concern for the manhunt which was being conducted for them. The Trudels engaged in neighbourly conversations with the Charbonneaus upstairs and Lanctôt was known as a friendly man by neighbours on the street. Sometime toward the end of October, Cross was asked to take off his blinker-like hood and was placed on a box with another one in front of it, and photographed playing solitaire. All of the photographs were signed by Cross on the back and, after some threats from the police, later withdrawn, the photographs appeared in the press.

Cross tried to keep his sanity by thinking of his past and exercising his mind as much as possible. He was losing weight because of the skimpy diet. With the exception of the bitchiness of Louise Cossette-Trudel who, accusing him of not keeping his head turned away, would interrupt his shaving half-done, there was no mistreatment. His courage was obvious to his captors and there was grudging personal, if not political, respect for him.

Sometimes Cross lost a day in his reckoning, and as one day slipped into the next he found their similarity obliterated them from his memory. He whiled away the time watching innumerable French movies and hoping and wondering about freedom. He was permitted to write another letter to his wife which was found with another one for the authorities, obviously dictated to him, in which he assured them he was "in good health and being well treated."

" . . . time drags heavily after six weeks of imprisonment," he wrote. "They consider me as a political prisoner (spelled prisonner) and they will keep me in captivity as long as the authorities do not accept their demands." Cross deliberately misspelled the word "prisonner" to tell the police that the letter had been dictated to him and that he had translated it into English and written it out.

With no alternative before them but the safe conduct offer, the Liberation cell of the FLQ sat back and waited. The result was almost inevitable, but it took six weeks after the enactment of the emergency measures for the police to find them.

Elsewhere in the city, other men hid whose option of exile had been killed with their hostage. On the Sunday morning after Laporte's body was found, police issued a bulletin describing Paul Rose, the 27-year-old former teacher, officially making him a wanted man. Rose had been seen on the streets of Montreal and was followed by teams of Montreal city police while Laporte was still alive. Noticing that he was being followed, he succeeded in losing them. When his photograph was published, it resulted in neighbours of the small white frame bungalow at 5630 Armstrong Street, in the South Shore suburb of St. Hubert, recognizing the man who had lived there under the name of Alain Blais. Rose's fingerprint turned up on one of the early communiqués from the so-called Chenier cell.

Paul's brother, Jacques, had a girl friend Colette Therrien, who lived in Apartment 12 at 3720 Queen Mary Road. The building is part of a large block of similar buildings past which tourist buses travel daily on their way to show the passengers peering from the windows the wonders of St. Joseph's Oratory and Montreal's Wax Museum nearby. Her brother, Richard, a law student at the Université de Montréal, and Françine Belisle also lived there. When Françine's brother, François, 19, came from their home town of Victoriaville to work for an uncle as a carpenter's apprentice, he was allowed to stay with his sister. François Belisle was to learn a great deal more than big city ways.

On Tuesday, October 13, Paul Rose called Lortie at the bungalow where Laporte was being held and told him that he was being shadowed. Then, with two men in a blue Volkswagen following him, he arrived, unannounced at the home of Roger Venne in Longeuil, across the St. Lawrence River from Montreal. It was noon. Venne and his wife Thérèse had not seen Rose for a year and he was asked to stay for the afternoon, to watch a world series baseball game and have supper.

During the afternoon he asked the Venne's 14-year-old son René to go to the corner on his bicycle and see if the blue Volkswagen was still parked there. It was, and René reported to Paul that two men were seated in it. After supper, at his request, the Vennes and two of their children left in their car along with Rose who left his dark coat behind. They drove him to a street in east end Montreal and left him. The police stayed at the corner in their little car waiting for Rose to emerge.

On Friday, with wholesale arrests being made in the city, Paul Rose met Lortie at the cavernous Berri de Montigny subway station where Lortie told him of Laporte's attempted escape and of his injuries. The next evening Rose arrived at the Queen Mary Road apartment just before supper. Shortly after, at about seven o'clock, Jacques Rose arrived with Francis Simard. Lortie stayed elsewhere. Later that evening the discovery of Laporte's body was announced on television and through the next day as the radio blared the news, including the discovery of the St. Hubert hideout, the three devised a plan.

On Monday, Jacques asked François Belisle, Françine's young brother, to buy some Gyproc and wood, cut to measurements which he gave. Colette Therrien, Jacques' girlfriend, went with him. When they returned they found Jacques removing clothes from the cupboard. He began to work with the materials the two had brought back. At noon on Tuesday, Colette and François brought in more wood and Francis Simard and Jacques' brother Paul helped him cut the wood and place it to make an additional small enclosure at the back of the closet. With some wallpaper purchased nearby, they finished the interior of the cupboard, painting the woodwork to hide their removable panel. As a temporary hideaway, the tiny, hidden enclosure would be adequate. But the way it was at 6 p.m. Tuesday, it was useless as a place to stay any substantial length of time. It was altered by Jacques in a move which was later to give them extra weeks of freedom.

Jacques spent Wednesday afternoon and evening building an air vent for the tiny enclosure and he made a long seat out of a precut piece of plywood, purchased at his request by Colette's brother, Richard. From then on, the three practiced hiding quickly behind the false wall. They disappeared at every knock on the door, but later on, to avoid unnecessary hasty exits, they devised a code of six knocks which was used by the occupants of the apartment.

On Friday, October 23, the police announced that they were looking for Jacques Rose, Francis Simard and Bernard Lortie. The occupants of the apartment watched and listened on Saturday morning to news reports that Bernard Lortie had been picked up in Hull, Quebec during the night. As the story of the unfortunate University of Ottawa student who bore the same name and was the same age as the wanted man began to unfold, their concern turned to amusement. Lortie, of Ottawa, heard the news bulletins that the other Lortie was wanted and, fearing possible confusion, called the Hull police to tell them he was the same age, had the same name but was not the same person. This precaution brought a visit from Quebec Provincial Police detectives to his residence in a rooming house near the university in the middle of the night. They searched his room, took some books about communism and hustled the bewildered first year arts student into a cell at Hull headquarters. The Saturday papers announced his arrest. He was taken, protesting, to the Parthenais St. headquarters of the Quebec Police Forces in Montreal and lodged on the fourth floor next to the "important" detainees, Pierre Vallières, Charles Gagnon, Robert Lemieux and Michel Chartrand. He was questioned by successive teams of investigators, convincing each in turn that he was not the wanted man, only to face further questioning by others who did not seem to know that his innocence had been established or that Lortie himself had phoned in order to prevent exactly this confusion.

Saturday afternoon he was paraded before the wanted Lortie's brother-in-law who told police they had the wrong man. They issued a statement announcing that "Bernard Lortie of Bourget, Ontario, who lives at Ottawa, is not the same Bernard Lortie sought for conspiracy in the kidnappings of the Minister, Pierre Laporte." That was what Lortie had said all along. He was told that he would be released, but he wasn't. On Sunday, he was visited by two inspectors who apparently did not know he had been cleared. On Monday, his father attempted unsuccessfully to visit him. He was told his son would be released. Instead he was taken back to Hull, still in custody, questioned again and released Tuesday morning.

On the Sunday following, the fugitive Bernard Lortie knocked on the door to Apartment 12, at 3720 Queen Mary Road, sending three men scurrying into the closet. Richard Therrien opened the door. He did not recognize Lortie who had changed his appearance from the month before. When he finally recognized him, he called the others from their hiding place and there was a general reunion.

Lortie was shown the hidden cubicle behind the closet and the days of the four passed in casual love-making with the girls, uneventful discussions of their plans, and watching the ever present television. The police had not checked this apartment of Paul

Rose's girlfriend. They had been engaged in massive searches of selected areas and systematic checking of likely hideouts, such as abandoned houses and other suspicious or unusual places. One of the officers at the house in St. Hubert where Laporte had been kept noticed a scrap of paper with a phone number on it. After a lapse of 19 days, the police visited the apartment. (On this evidence the police could have obtained a search warrant but, as they preferred to do since the new powers to search had been given them, they relied on their right to enter without one.)

The knock sent the four wanted men into the cupboard, but the panel was closed before Lortie could get through. He was discovered as police opened the door, surrendered without a struggle, and stood by as a systematic search was made of the entire apartment. Colette Therrien and Françine Belisle were arrested and taken to Parthenais Street. Lortie was questioned overnight, found to be co-operative and the next morning, Saturday, November 7, he testified as to his participation in the Laporte kidnapping before a coroner's inquest. On subsequent days, the other occupants were called to tell all they knew under oath before an Acting Coroner, Judge Jacques Trahan.

From their ventilated hiding place the Rose brothers and Simard listened as police investigators continued to work in the apartment through the night and all day Saturday. Two guards were left after the detectives departed. When the guards went for their supper, the three opened the panel and walked out the back door to freedom. A week later Paul Rose sent a communiqué, using the name Information Viger Cell, mocking the police and describing their escape in detail.

Michael Viger, thirty years of age, the son of a Longeuil insurance agent and a well-known separatist, was among the hundreds arrested in the first wave after the October 16 proclamation. He was questioned and subsequently released without being charged. The month before, Viger had rented a picturesque farmhouse near the village of St. Luc, 20 miles southeast of

Montreal. Surrounded by fields on three sides and L'Acadie River on the fourth, the house is 500 feet back from a sideroad which, in turn, runs one-half mile to the highway into St. Luc. It is out of sight to passing traffic and shielded from the neighbouring house by a bend in the road and a cluster of pine trees. It was a perfect hideout.

St. Luc is a small village at the intersections of Highways 7 and 35, on the way from Montreal to the U.S. border. Its Chief of Police, Alain Dufresne, a former R.C.M.P. officer, thought it would make a perfect hideout too. In a small place like St. Luc, all things were noticed and Dufresne wondered one night about the lights he saw in what he thought was an abandoned farmhouse. He had read the directive of Quebec Police director, Maurice St. Pierre, asking local forces to think of any good hideouts in their areas. He had thought immediately of the abandoned house, now owned by the South Shore Credit Corporation. On the Sunday following the discovery of Laporte's body, a truck stolen from a St. Hubert grocery store was found about a mile away from the house. Only the food was missing. He reported the occurrence to the Quebec police detachment at nearby St. Jean but was told that the force was too busy to worry about stolen trucks.

The lights were the final inducement. Dufresne notified his superiors of his suspicions and on Friday October 23, the R.C.M.P. joined the Quebec Provincial Police in a search of the house. They found power tools in the garage, a shovel with fresh earth on it, a minimum of furniture and no signs of life. One officer noticed a hole in the basement floor next to the furnace, but observed that it did not lead anywhere.

After police left, Dufresne wondered why such an obvious break-in as the police raid would not be reported by the occupants. Viger was in no position to complain. He was in custody in Montreal. When Dufresne got his name from the local municipal office, it meant nothing to him. He was asked by the R.C.M.P. to keep the house under surveillance but not to enter it.

Viger, released, was observed leaving the farm in his car and this fact was duly reported through the chain of command. A couple more visits were made to the farm but no one was found and no new suspicions were aroused.

In the middle of November, Paul and Jacques Rose and Francis Simard, were spirited from a farm hideaway to finish preparing a new one—at the farm rented by Viger. Working without attracting the attention of either neighbours or the watching police, they finished the tunnel which extended down from the rear of the furnace in the basement and then out approximately 25 feet. They shored up the side and roof with two-by-four beams and chicken wire. A hand-operated sump pump was inadequate to keep the chilling water out, but it was kept to a level of three or four inches. Concrete slabs which could be lifted from underneath concealed the hole in the floor behind the furnace.

There they remained hidden, sneaking into the house when they needed food, or to relieve themselves, or to escape from the dampness. This dismal hiding hole could not compare with the comforts and companionship of the Queen Mary Road apartment, nor for that matter with the place where James Cross was still being held prisoner on Avenue des Recollets. But then, the three had no captive as a bargaining weapon. Their wait was for arrest and they knew it.

On December 2, two R.C.M.P. officers visited the Charbonneau's apartment, upstairs from the Cross hideout on Des Recollets, asking them to move temporarily, explaining that it was "a very serious matter," but offering no further information. The Charbonneaus moved. That was at 2 p.m. At approximately 7:30, Jacques and Louise Cossette-Trudel left the apartment to shop at a nearby store. As they walked out of sight of the apartment, they were arrested. The police confirmed their suspicions. When the Cossette-Trudels failed to return, the remaining Lanctôt and Carbonneau suspected the end of their wait had come. It was ten o'clock.

They came to Cross and put the handcuffs on him, explaining that the police knew where he was. He was permitted to remain on the mattress, wide awake and alert until 2 a.m. when he was taken into the corridor and seated on the floor, handcuffed to a doorknob. He remained there for the next five hours, uncomfortable with his arm held upraised, waiting and wondering what would happen next. His hood was removed and he saw the faces of both men for the first time since his capture. The light and heat had been cut off as a sign from the police that the place was surrounded but there would be no shootout. As two policemen approached the front of the house to try to cut off the water, Lanctôt appeared at the front bedroom window, and they withdrew. Inside, they painted FLQ on the blinds in the front windows as an act of defiance. Then, at 4 a.m. a lead pipe containing a note was hurled out of the front window. The police rushed in, recovered it and read, "If you try anything (gas, guns etc.) Mr. J. Cross will be the first to die . . . We have a number of sticks of dynamite fused. If you want to negotiate, send us a journalist from *Québec Presse* or *Le Devoir* and Mr. B. Mergler. We will win. FLQ."

As daylight broke, busloads of troops cordoned off the entire area. Helicopters began ferrying in additional soldiers, landing at a nearby school, whose pupils were delighted to find that it was closed for the day. Police took up positions throughout the area surrounding the house. A building opposite was taken as a command headquarters.

Lawyer Bernard Mergler arrived in his office on St. Phillips Square that morning without knowing anything of the activity at the other end of the city. He had been retained to act for a great many of those who had been charged under the War Measures regulations and the strain of the additional load to his busy practice had taken its toll in fatigue. He answered the telephone call from Chief Inspector Paul Benoit in a slow and deliberate voice. Benoit arranged to meet him at a north end police station and by the time the conversation had ended, a senior officer had arrived to drive the puzzled lawyer to the rendezvous.

He was briefed by Robert Demers, who would represent the government in the negotiations to follow. Together they proceeded to Avenue Des Recollets where Mergler entered the house at 11 a.m. He met Lanctôt and Carbonneau and was taken to where Cross was now lying, freed from his handcuffs, with a blanket over him. "Are you all right?" asked Mergler. "Oh, I'm fine," Cross answered smiling, "considering the circumstances."

Mergler recognized Cross from photographs right away, but following police instructions to make doubly sure, he asked Cross the name of the bull terrier he had had when he was posted to Delhi. "Garm" was the correct answer. Mergler explained the terms of the offer of safe conduct to the two men and reassured them that the police did not intend to ambush them.

Mergler left and reported to Demers and Benoit, in the house across the street. They decided to proceed to the Canadian Pavilion at the former Expo grounds on St. Helen's Island, declared to be Cuban soil for the occasion. They would use Carbonneau's old Chrysler.

When Mergler returned, a third man, Langlois, who had been in the house, was with them. Cross was handcuffed and led to the car in the garage below. With their luggage packed in the trunk, they tried to add a television set. It wouldn't fit, and it was placed in the back seat between Cross and the door.

A police escort sped the car through the streets of Montreal, barricaded at every intersection along the route. Inside, at the wheel, Carbonneau maintained the 50 mile per hour speed and smiled broadly. Next to him, holding a machine gun, was Langlois and on the outside front seat, Mergler, trying in this setting, unique for a lawyer, to remain imperturbable. In the back, with his handcuffs removed, Cross was trying to hang on to Lanctôt as the car swerved. Lanctôt was holding the door, which wouldn't close properly.

At the Canadian pavilion of Expo, the Cuban Consul was in charge, according to an arrangement reached at the request of the Canadian Government some weeks before in preparation for the bargain of safe conduct. The Consul kept away the Minister of Justice, Jérôme Choquette. Cross was taken to an office in the pavilion and the kidnappers were taken to another to await the Cossette-Trudels and Lanctôt's wife and child. In the evening, a helicopter took them to Dorval airport, where a Canadian Forces transport plane had been waiting all day to fly them to Cuba.

Cross was served French fries, a club sandwich and coffee. He had lost 22 pounds, as the result of his meagre diet but had otherwise suffered no medical problems. He remained on the island until the kidnappers reached Cuba, then he was rushed to the Jewish General Hospital for a complete checkup. His first act at the pavilion was to phone his wife, anxiously awaiting in Switzerland at the home of friends. After that call was complete, he reached Peter Hayman, the British High Commissioner to Canada, at his Ottawa office. His opening words were, "Cross here, reporting for duty."

Quebec police picked Viger up for questioning in Montreal on December 23. They released him and visited the St. Luc farmhouse on Christmas Day, noticing a sleeping bag on the main floor. Posing as snowmobilers, skiers and in a variety of other disguises the police maintained their vigil. When a light went on the night of December 27, they moved in, waking Viger who was sleeping upstairs and convincing him to reveal the hideout. As police poured into the house carrying an arsenal of weapons, including sub-machine guns, Viger led Captain Pierre Viau, in charge of the operation, down the basement stairs to the trap door in the floor.

Viau was fearful of a shootout and when the men threatened that they were prepared to die rather than surrender, discussions through the concrete slab began. The trapped men wanted a mediator, but they rejected Viau's suggestion that it be Jacques Hébert, a Montreal publisher and President of the Human Rights League, equivalent of the Civil Liberties Association. Police rejected their choice of Dr. Serge Mongeau, leader of the Movement for the Defense of Political Prisoners. Finally a compromise choice was reached. They agreed on Dr. Jacques Ferron, medical doctor, author, and a man much praised as a true humanitarian by Pierre Vallières.

Ferron was contacted by special Crown counsel Jacques Ducros who convinced the physician to agree by pleading that "There has been one death too many in this affair already." He arrived in the basement and quietly, through the concrete hatch, negotiated for the peaceful surrender. The terms were that the government would no longer automatically oppose bail for all those already in custody.

Handcuffed and awaiting transportation back to Montreal, Simard's only remark was that it was cold underground. The Roses were more political. They were, Paul said, part of the lost generation. They handed over their "arsenal". It consisted of one rusty shotgun, a starter's pistol and a clip of .22 calibre ammunition.

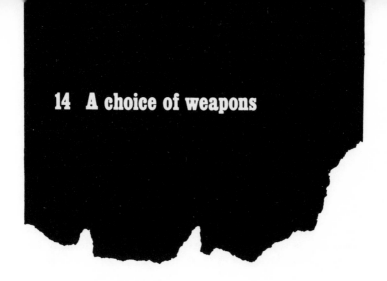

14 A choice of weapons

"The democratic left," Laurier LaPierre wrote in the *Toronto Daily Star* on Saturday, October 24, "the non-violent, democratic left, is being assassinated." The McGill University history professor, supporter of the New Democratic Party and sometime television "personality", wrote his essay in the first two weeks of the War Measures Act. The arrests of hundreds of persons, accused not of terrorism but of wrong-headed political beliefs, were reaching their apogee. The knock on the door in the pre-dawn darkness, the police trooping in with the inevitable green garbage bags, hauling away mountains of books and pamphlets, the detention at Parthenais Street and other jails of the Province of Quebec, some for three months, but most for one week or three weeks—with releases as wholesale as the arrests themselves—these were the terrors of the moment which seized one thoughtful, if dramatic, French-Canadian intellectual.

"You can't help wondering," said LaPierre, describing himself as only a marginal activist, "if you are going to be the next one, if the police will come in the middle of the night and take you away without word for 90 days."

"More and more of our people are losing faith in the system," LaPierre wrote. "We are told every day that our democratic system is flexible and responsive enough to meet any emergency, any deed, any aspiration." And yet, he went on to say, the Montreal, civic elections would proceed on the following Sunday, amid soldiers with guns and bayonets and with candidates for legal political parties in jail and their organization maligned as a front for the FLQ by a very important politician, Jean Marchand.

Any society needs and develops the mechanisms to defeat a threat to its peaceful existence, as the body's "white army" of corpuscles surrounds and isolates the threatening intruder. Society's protection ordinarily lies in the criminal law. On October 16, 1970, the Governments of Quebec and Canada and—according to the Gallup Poll, the vast majority of Canadians—believed that the existing law was insufficient to challenge the criminal event of two kidnappings and the uncertain threats of greater violence. Those, like Laurier LaPierre and distressingly few others, who believed the therapy was a greater threat than the disease, were usually cast into the invidious position of being in favor of cancer. They were not. They were opposed to decapitation, amputation, mutilation, as the prescribed therapy to save democracy.

Of the Western democracies, only two kept their wartime emergency powers legislation in reserve for use in peacetime: Ireland and Canada. Of the two, Canada was the first actually to use the powers of a wartime government in a time of external peace. Considering the problems of many of the nations whose company Canada seeks, considering Canada's own comparatively placid history, few persons anywhere, given an advance opportunity to guess, would have chosen Canada as the holder of this dubious record.

The semantics of the situation were, however, largely irrelevant. It matters little whether it was the *War* Measures Act that provided the instrument; it might as easily have been some other instrument under some other name produced by some other method than 4 a.m. executive fiat. The 90-day detention laws of South Africa do not escape the censure of civilized society merely because they have been passed by a Parliament and bear some other legislative title than "War". Irrespective of the formal title of *War* Measures Act, the moral dilemma for thoughtful Canadians was contained in these questions. Were the extraordinary powers assumed by the state necessary and honestly motivated? Were the powers, if necessary, successful? Were they less a threat to the society they sought to serve than the danger they sought to exorcise?

The fact that the police asked, or were encouraged to ask, for such extraordinary power is in itself a mechanism, not a reason. The regulations proclaimed on October 16 outlawed the FLQ, made membership or support a crime, and gave the police the power to search and detain without warrant and to imprison without charge, trial, or opportunity for bail. Whether these powers were "necessary" depends, of course, on the objectives they were meant to fulfil.

The first objective was to find James Cross, Pierre Laporte and their kidnappers. This meant raids not only on suspected hideouts but also on the homes of those who may have had guilty knowledge or may have acted as accessories or may, indeed, have had third or fourth-hand information. The existing search warrant was certainly adequate to fill these needs; it is largely a *pro-forma* document in Canada, rarely challenged and even more rarely refused.

Anonymous stories appeared in the press alleging that justices in Montreal had refused to sign search warrants out of fear of reprisals. Since the highest level of genuine fear appeared in Montreal after the proclamation of the War Measures Act, these stories, coming invariably from unnamed police sources, bore the suspicious stamp of *ex post facto* justification. All the diligent reporters in Montreal failed to produce any specific incident of a specific refusal; and if one justice did demur one night, was he the only one available in a city of 2.4 million? On the fifth day after the Cross kidnapping, the police announced they had on that Friday night conducted their one thousand and first raid—it happened to be on the south shore opposite

Montreal. An average of some 200 raids a day does not sound realistically like a police force hampered and impeded by cumbersome legal machinery.

In addition to the search warrant, easily obtained, a number of other instruments were available to the police. The principle of "fresh pursuit" permits the police in Canada to bash down any door behind which a fugitive has recently vanished. Thus, a suspect seen to re-enter a house anytime after the kidnappings could have been pursued inside. In practice, however, no policeman would do anything so foolish, since a headlong raid would serve only to imperil the lives of the captives. When Pierre Laporte spoke of the shoot-out and bloodbath which would ensue, everyone suspected he spoke only the truth. There would inevitably be long negotiations to pry loose the fugitives, as there were in fact in the discovery of Cross and in the arrest of the Rose group at St. Luc. The search warrant was never an impediment to effective police action and in the final episodes in both kidnappings it was an entirely irrelevant issue.

The arrest warrant is similarly unimportant. Any police officer may arrest without warrant anyone he reasonably believes has committed, is committing, or is about to commit an indictable offense. Aiding a fugitive is an indictable offense. The courts have never been overly strict in their interpretation of "reasonable". A leading case says that the police, when looking for a burglar long-vanished, should not arrest a boy wearing running shoes. That is the dividing line, and inside that slight restriction the police were able within the first five days to take into custody for varying periods of questioning, some 44 persons. All were released. The lack of success in that first week did not stem from a lack of power, but from a lack of suspects. And when those who were implicated in the crimes did become suspects, it was not through the emergency powers, but entirely as a result of ordinary diligent and competent police work.

The request, purportedly from the police, that they

needed the War Measures Act did scant credit to their outstanding record of previous successes. Some 135 persons had been sentenced since the first acts of political terrorism in 1963; hardly a major outrage had gone unsolved, the rate of success was far higher than with ordinary crime.

There were a number of factors which assisted an already effective police force. As criminals, most FLQ adherents were amateurs. No seasoned bandit would have pulled the trigger inside the International Firearms Co. in 1964. That ended the holdup, and also ended that "generation" of the FLQ, all of whose members were either convicted or discovered. There were, in addition, a number of defections, which are usually more likely in political crimes than in others. When Serge Demers blew up a 16-year-old boy, he stopped making bombs. The discovery of the FLQ hideout at Prevost in 1970, with the Harrison Burgess ransom note, was obviously the work of an informer. This discovery was the essential element which, within a few days of the Cross kidnapping, enabled the police to identify Jacques Lanctôt as a suspect. Political criminals, furthermore, need to communicate—ordinary bandits do not send notes to radio stations—and it was the act of communication which helped solve both cases: the similarity of the Burgess communiqué in the first case, and a fingerprint among other clues, on one of the Laporte communiqués in the second. The police had not only the benefit of ordinary competence but also the additional advantages inherent in the pursuit of politically-motivated criminals.

All this presupposes, of course, that the invocation of the War Measures Act was honestly motivated by a desire to pursue criminals and, at the same time, to suppress political activity which so endangered the existence of the state as to be criminal, i.e. the "apprehended insurrection". It is here that we encounter the elegant and complex mind of Pierre Trudeau who, in his writings published on the eve of his entry into federal politics, found it difficult, indeed impossible, to make a distinction between separatism and criminal violence. In one of his most famous essays *Separatist Counter-Revolutionaries*, published in *Cité libre* in May of 1964, Trudeau wrote:

"The fact is that, at bottom, the Separatists despair of ever being able to convince the public of the rightness of their ideas. That long work of education and persuasion among the masses undertaken by the unions for many decades, done by the Social Crediters themselves for thirty years—for this the Separatists have neither the courage, nor the means, nor especially that respect for the other man's freedom which is essential in undertaking it and leading it to success.

254 "So they want to abolish freedom and impose a dictatorship of their minority. They are in sole possession of the truth, so others need only get into line. And when things don't go fast enough they take to illegality and violence. On top of everything, they claim to be persecuted. Imagine that, the poor little souls. There are numbers of them in the editorial rooms of our newspapers; they swarm at the C.B.C. and the National Film Board; they press with all their weight on the mass media, but still they find the place given them in this society unfair.

"Because a few of their people have been bothered because of their ideas (so they say) they want to be done with peaceful and constitutional methods. They proclaim to the newspapers that from now on they will go underground. These terrorized terrorists will be led by a Mr. X. And, in courageous anonymity, they will sow their ideas while waiting to set off their bombs."

Read in later years after the successful formation of the Parti Québecois, the words take on a frightening significance: "*And when things don't go fast enough, they take to illegality and violence.*" The words were written in 1964 and chosen by the author for republication in 1968, the first occasion being on the eve of his entry into federal politics, the second occasion on the eve of his entry into federal leadership. They are sentiments, obviously, to which Trudeau owes an abiding allegiance. After he wrote them, the Parti Québecois was formed, an ordinary, legitimate and unexceptional political party, organized in the traditional way into constituency and regional groups, possessing a fund-raising, press-clipping, speech-writing and propaganda apparatus, posturing somewhat to the left of the New Democratic Party but obviously attracting legions of voters who, if such a party existed in any real sense in Quebec, would be voting for the NDP.

Whatever Trudeau may have believed in 1970, the vast majority of English-speaking Canadians outside of Quebec—being functionally illiterate in Quebec politics—accepted his ideas, without needing to read them, as an accurate, current philosophy: separatism *means* terrorism and violence.

An interesting outgrowth of this was the great difficulty the English-language press experienced in finding the correct words to describe the process of detention and the qualities of those detained under the emergency regulations. They were usually described as having been "arrested". Arrest means detention. But no one can ordinarily be arrested in Canada except on a specific charge. Almost 500 Quebec citizens were detained under the War Measures Act and 435 were released after periods of one to three weeks without being charged with anything, not even under the imprecise offenses of the emergency regulations. The word "arrest" seemed, perhaps, the only one available but ordinary men understand that "arrest" implicitly means detention on some specific complaint. For some 400 Quebec citizens, no such complaint was ever produced.

The perfectly good English word for detention without arrest, that is, in the absence of a specific complaint, is internment. The press universally avoided this word because it carries the pejorative implication of the detention of persons by class, i.e. of enemy aliens during the two world wars. It is undoubtedly true that the vast majority of English-speaking Canadians understood the process to be internment, and accepted and supported it as such, although the word was never used. Those detained *seemed* like enemy aliens to English Canada, and English Canada accepted their internment, as it accepted the internment of persons during two world wars by reason only of their race or citizenship.

English Canada had been prepared for this by many influences, first of all by Trudeau's early writings which equated separatism with violence. Premier John Robarts of Ontario had prepared the country a few days before the invocation of the War Measures Act when he went out of his way to declare that, "this is total war." After the invocation of the War Measures Act, Judge Redmond Roche made a speech in the English-speaking Montreal suburb of Westmount, emphasizing, with approval, that the situation in Quebec was parallel to the situation in Canada at the outbreak of World War II. As a description of the mood of the country, it was entirely accurate.

Given this preparatory mood-setting, much of the coverage in the English-language press became ludicrous because, although technically accurate, it came from an unreal world. The *Toronto Daily Star*, an extremely sophisticated newspaper with an ample supply of bilingual reporters and managed by the most able and knowledgable editors in the country, declared in the first paragraph of its main story on the day of the War Measures Act, that the police in Montreal were busy "rounding up *known separatist sympathizers.*" This was literally true, and for 7/8ths of those detained that was *all* they were, known separatist sympathizers; if they had been terrorists, or supporters or advocates of terrorism, they could easily have been charged under the emergency regulations, but they were not.

Since fully 23 per cent of the voting population of the Province of Quebec consisted in 1970 of "separatist sympathizers", the roundup and internment of known separatist sympathizers should have caused an upheaval of opposition among the libertarian leadership of English Canada. It did not, because English Canada had been conditioned to believe that separatism meant violence and terror, and the conditioning was completed in October of 1970. English Canadians did not have to face the issue that the War Measures Act was invoked only in small part to fight violence, and in larger part to suppress a legitimate political movement, because they had come to believe that that political movement was inherently, necessarily violent. The lasting, irreparable damage done to mutual understanding between the founding races would inevitably affect Canadians in the future. How could French and English ever again disagree rationally?

Whatever the depth of Prime Minister Trudeau's 1964 conviction that separatism means violence, not even two politically-sensitive kidnappings in the supposed cause of radical separatism could in themselves cause him to shed his sincere civil libertarian beliefs. The pivot on which the emergency powers decision turned was a political one. Bourassa not only had the police on his back, he had the accumulated emotions of a cabinet of strong men. There was more than one occasion when resignations were offered and withdrawn. Claude Ryan recognized the need for solidarity and unity at such a time and made his now famous suggestion, first to Bourassa, and then to Saulnier, after conferring with his own editorial colleagues.

Trudeau, too, saw the need for solidarity. In the Bourassa Government he had invested much prestige and considerable electoral support, and he hoped to reap more vindication in the future for the concept of Federalism in Quebec. His dark references to "the parallel power" meant not only the FLQ, but also the Ryan suggestion, taken far out of context and given excessive significance in the tense atmosphere of Quebec and Ottawa. The term "erosion of the public will to resist," used by a knowledgable Liberal MP, was also a reference to Ryan and those others who joined in the plea to the Quebec Government to negotiate with the kidnappers.

Trudeau was adamant that the Government must

appear to refuse to negotiate, and he deeply resented the Ryan suggestion. The employment of a new and powerful weapon would put an end to this process of "erosion", would strengthen Bourassa's hand within his divided cabinet by giving him a new reason not to negotiate, and would provide new hope that the victims could be recovered alive.

Trudeau is a man of compassion and humanitarian motives and there is every reason to believe that he was always motivated to do everything possible to save Cross and Laporte. He was entitled to take the political considerations into account so long as nothing was done that detracted from the primary purpose of saving lives.

There were many good arguments on both sides of the question of negotiation. Those who urged that there was a better chance to save the lives by really negotiating had no guarantees, although the chances seemed better. The others looked to the future and saw the likelihood of repeated kidnappings and blackmail as success became more likely. Trudeau made a popular choice but still wanted very much to save the lives involved. He still faced the problem of escalation of kidnappings—his strategy contained no guarantees either.

The choice not to negotiate over the "political prisoners" was one Trudeau could enforce since the prisoners whose release was sought were in Federal custody. His decision, and the fact that he had the means to enforce it, gave him a separate interest, similar to Bourassa's, but distinct, in finding a weapon to replace negotiation. Trudeau had to anticipate growing public sentiment to save the lives just as Bourassa had to deal with such a bloc of thinking in his cabinet. From his answers in the House of Commons, Trudeau appeared to be tortured by the decision. He was sincere and appeared concerned when he asked former Prime Minister John Diefenbaker for his advice when the subject came up in the House of Commons on Thursday, October 15. But the anguish of decision was later denied by Trudeau in an interview with Tom Buckley of the *New York Times* on November 10,

1970. To Buckley, he said that it had not been a difficult decision to make. "Neither emotionally nor intellectually was there a great struggle . . . The question of timing was very important, and I won't say we didn't discuss this a fair amount. It wasn't a question of whether we were doing something basically objectionable in our consciences in invoking this measure. In my own mind, the importance of democratic movements not fearing to take extraordinary measures to preserve democracy—this importance has always been established."

The decision to fight back was natural and the choice to escalate was necessary for political reasons. The real quarrel rests with the choice of weapons. The War Measures Act provides a broad range of powers to a government proclaiming it into force. Under its provisions in the past there have been massive reorganizations of the economy, with control of prices, rents and the movement of commodities. In war, the Federal Government had taken powers usually exercisable only by the provinces. On one occasion during the second world war, it set aside British Columbia legislation which prohibited Asiatics from working on Crown land so that interned Japanese might help the war effort by felling trees. That legislation had been previously upheld by the highest courts in the land. It was ended by the War Measures Act.

If the Government had reason to proclaim the War Measures Act, it could also have employed the great economic powers contained in it to defuse the complaints of the FLQ and those who supported them. It could have provided for equality of opportunity in employment for French Canadians and could have passed regulations with real teeth—such as are expected in time of war. But the object of the Government was not the overall solution of these massive problems. The object of the Government was to rescue Cross and Laporte, rescue Bourassa, and deal a blow to the philosophy of separatism.

The weapon they chose from the War Measures

arsenal was the weapon of arbitrary police power. The exercise of the arbitrary police power was based on the outlawing of the FLQ and similar organizations. The use of the War Measures Act exposed a number of major weaknesses in the Canadian constitution. There is, for one thing, no defence against the abuse of government power. The courts are largely precluded from dealing with an executive decision to invoke these powers because of wartime decisions which gave Parliament (most likely controlled by the same government whose decision is in question) the exclusive right to review the wisdom of the decision. This was reinforced when the Bill of Rights of 1960 created a right of review by Parliament on the petition of ten members of the House of Commons.

All the opposition could do in the House of Commons was to try to expose to the country the sham of stretching what had happened in Quebec into a "state of apprehended insurrection." The Government had a carefully prepared three part answer giving reasons for proclaiming the Act. Amid speculation induced by statements made by members of his own cabinet that there were more facts which could not be made public, that there had been a plot to establish a provisional government, with hints of a 3,000-member FLQ, Trudeau repeated the three points again and again.

His clearest and most concise explanation was on October 26: "They are very clear facts. First, we had from the authorities of the Province of Quebec and of the city of Montreal a clear statement that they apprehended insurrection.

"Second there had been the abduction of two very important citizens in the province of Quebec, with an intention to murder them if the Government did not give in to ransom.

"The third fact was circumstantial, if you wish, that approximately two tons of dynamite had been stolen in the province of Quebec this year, as well as a sizeable number of small arms and other ammunition.

"Also, there was such a state of confusion and threats

of violence in the province of Quebec, we decided to act on these facts as we interpreted them, and on this the Government will stand or fall."

Taking these arguments in reverse order, we find that:

The state of confusion can refer only to the disarray in the Quebec cabinet, the divisions and the threats of resignation, together with the comic opera rumours of the Claude Ryan "provisional government". It is arguable, to say the least, whether police-state powers never used before in peacetime can properly be used to restore political order—in a democracy that is usually considered to be a function of the ballot-box.

The dynamite plot kept reappearing. It was mentioned by many Liberal leaders, the Prime Minister included. He emphasized the point not only in the House, but also in his briefing of party leaders on October 15. Perhaps it matters little whether the FLQ had "two tons" of dynamite or two pounds—any amount was too much, and one stick can kill a man. But two tons of dynamite translates into 8,000 sticks, which was not the amount stolen in Quebec "this year", but in fact was more than had been stolen in two years, a great deal of which had either been recovered (650 pounds of it on the previous June 21) or had deteriorated from amateur storage.

The "two tons" of dymanite was a figure which inspired fear. But the FLQ could not conceivably have had two tons of dynamite. Whatever amount it had, its use would be to blow up public buildings, which were guarded by troops, a precaution to which absolutely no responsible commentator objected. In any event, the War Measures Act was not required to locate dynamite or guns nor to prosecute for their possession; the Criminal Code was quite adequate.

Surprisingly, Canadians did not appreciate at that time that the supposed possession by the FLQ of huge armouries of rifles and small arms was inconsistent with the supposed next step of "selective assassination" as outlined by, among others, Premier Bourassa. If the next step had been "selective assassination" (which it wasn't) the simultaneous use of two guns, or four, could have brought the country to its knees. If the FLQ had a huge storehouse of weapons, how was it going to use the weapons—in a march from the Laurentian hills like Castro marching on Havana? Such a march needs friendly villagers, and there were no friendly villagers for the FLQ.

No special laws were needed to enforce the strict Canadian laws on possession of firearms. (In the end, the largest cache of guns to fall into the hands of the police during the FLQ crisis in the fall of 1970 was voluntarily turned in by a millionaire gun collector in Ontario named Clinton Duke.) As for the abductions "with an intention to murder", the War Measures Act could not, and in the end result did not, assist in the pursuit of these crimes because the emergency regulations, while giving the police the power to intern innocent but (presumably) politically wrong-headed persons, did not offer the police in practical terms any useful powers of search, seizure or arrest they did not already possess under the existing criminal law. While some of those whose capture assisted the police (Jacques Lanctôt's sister-in-law in Montreal North and the tenant of the St. Luc farmhouse) may technically have been held briefly under the War Measures Act, they could equally have been arrested under the Criminal Code.

That leaves only the Prime Minister's opening point, that the Governments of Quebec and Montreal made "a clear statement that they apprehended insurrection." At no time did the Federal Government ever state on its own authority that there existed a feared or discovered insurrection in Quebec. The motion introduced by the Prime Minister in the House of Commons on October 16 said the powers of the War Measures Act were needed, "to meet the state of apprehended insurrection in the province of Quebec as communicated to the Prime Minister by the Government of Quebec and the civic authorities of Montreal . . . . "

Of all the reasons given by the Prime Minister, the

crimes, the dynamite, the confusion, only the reason of "apprehended insurrection" was valid for invoking the War Measures Act, because "apprehended insurrection" was the operative phrase in the act itself. It cannot be invoked to fight "crime" no matter how serious. And the "apprehended insurrection" was the only reason which the Federal Government consistently avoided stating on its own authority—it was always stated on the authority of the Governments of Quebec and Montreal.

The Government of Montreal means Jean Drapeau, the mayor; Lucien Saulnier, then the chairman of the executive committee; and Michel Côté, the city attorney and former lawyer for the police department. Only a year before, the three of them had come to Ottawa to state that during the police-strike riots of October, 1969, 'we had revolution in our streets'. The MPs who listened took seriously their description of criminal disorder and federal involvement in the funding of the Company of Young Canadians; but their notion of "revolution in the streets" had been quietly laughed out of town. Yet the Federal Government acted, so it said, at the urging of these same people who had cried 'revolution" the year before.

The weapon selected was a combined package of police powers which included the right to enter any place and seize anything or anyone without warrant, and the right to detain without charge, court appearance or bail, for substantial periods of time. For 21 days, it amounted to internment, which is the technique of democratic nations at war and of dictatorships at any time.

The Government decided to resurrect the concept of outlaw organizations, so long discredited in Canadian legal history. The FLQ was a prime target since it was so clearly, in its methods, a danger to the Canadian peace and tranquillity by its criminality. There is, however, no lack of laws for the apprehension, prosecution and punishment of criminal conspiracies. As for the outlawing of political parties, the history of the Communist Party offers a useful parallel.

The western democracies have for the most part ceased their attempts begun 50 years ago to outlaw it as an organization. Attempts to banish the Communist Party have been found to be ineffective, the source of much unfairness and, in the American phrase, counter-productive. The Communist Party was, at least, an organization which had to have membership lists: it needed membership lists to know who to expel. The unhappy and unsuccessful experience of vainly attempting to outlaw the Communist Party should have provided the historical precedent to discourage the Government from the same attempt with the FLQ, if only because "membership" in the FLQ does not exist and "membership" is achieved by the voluntary act of entering into a criminal conspiracy, to bomb or to kidnap or whatever, actions for which there is no lack of existing criminal sanction.

The history of prosecutions against the Communist Party is littered with the liberal victims, misguided or otherwise, who insisted that adequate standards of proof and a fair trial on substantial allegations are standards which ought to be applied to Communists no less than to bandits. Since the FLQ lacked any membership standards, when does a man become a member, supporter or advocate? Does he become an advocate of the FLQ by insisting that Pierre Vallières and Charles Gagnon deserve a fair trial? Does he become a "member" by going to a meeting? By cheering and shouting at some statements at the meeting, does he become a co-conspirator in every action implied by the speakers? The futilities of the past should have provided some guidelines for present caution.

All this presupposes, of course, that the intention of the Government in proclaiming the emergency regulations was in fact the intention stated by the regulations, that is, to outlaw the FLQ organization. The police forces operating in Quebec took, in round figures, 490 persons into custody, of whom 435 were released after periods of one to three weeks, with no charges being laid, not even under the vague standards of the regulations. No police force can possibly be so inept as to need to arrest eight times as many persons as it can, in due course, find evidence against. The inescapable conclusion is that a major intention of the Government was precisely what happened, the detention of hundreds of persons who could not be accused even of advocating the policies of the FLQ, but who certainly could be accused of opposing the Government's policies toward the FLQ. There were no standards at all for the detentions (at least in wartime a person had to *look* Japanese) and persons could be detained quite literally for being in the wrong bed at the wrong time, or for having rented the wrong apartment, which, with women particularly, is what happened.

The standard of the criminal law that a man is responsible for the reasonable and probable consequences of his actions applies with equal validity to the Federal Government. Its chief ministers had all reached their political maturity in the Province of Quebec (including, but not limited to, Trudeau, Marchand, Turner, Pelletier and Mackasey.) They gave the police forces of Quebec the power to detain anyone without accountability to a court or any other forum. They might as well have given matches to a child and denied responsibility for the subsequent fire.

A decision on whether the invocation of the regulations under the War Measures Act was necessary depends, therefore, on the real intentions of the Government. If the intention was to outlaw the FLQ, then some legislative enactment was certainly required. But a secret, middle-of-the-night enactment was not required to outlaw the FLQ: it could not be said that a Parliamentary debate would drive the FLQ underground; it was already underground. But if the intention of the Government was to ensure the events which did ensue—the internment of 400 persons guilty of nothing— then the 4 a.m. proclamation of emergency powers certainly *was* "necessary", because no Parliament would for a moment have granted any such mandate. All of the members of the cabinet may not have understood that the jailing of 400 persons guilty of nothing was a reasonable and probable consequence of their action. But they are responsible for the result nonetheless.

Surely Trudeau must have remembered that it was in his province that Canadian civil liberties have suffered the most. It was Trudeau who contemptuously wrote of his fellow Quebeckers in 1962, "What French-Canadians now in their twenties will find hard to forgive in people of my generation a few years from now is the complacency with which we have watched the rebirth of separatism and nationalism. Because by then they will have realized how appallingly backward French Canada is in all fields of endeavour . . . What! They will say to the judges and lawyers, civil liberties having survived in the province of Quebec thanks only to the Communists, the trade unions, and the Jehovah's Witnesses, and to English and Jewish lawyers and the judges of the Supreme Court in Ottawa, and you had nothing better to do than cheer on the coming of a sovereign state for French Canadians?"

As abuse piled upon abuse, as counsel was denied to the detainees, as bail was uniformly denied, as persons were held incommunicado, these complaints made their way into the question period in the House of Commons. There they were met by the stock answer that the administration of justice in this matter is a question only for the province of Quebec. Trudeau, the strict constitutional constructionist, was able to slough off the abuses his government had specifically permitted to happen—'Ask Mr. Choquette'.

While prosecutions were in the hands of provincial governments during the Second World War, the right to detain, and the right to review these detentions never left federal hands. The problems which were referred to Mr. Choquette were problems more closely related to the problems of detention than the problems of organizing and conducting prosecutions. It would clearly have been possible to place the use of these extraordinary powers in federal hands, under precisely the same authority by which the Federal Government created them. The state of apprehended insurrection can be met in more than one way and the power to keep in federal hands the administration of this special and temporary law would have been undeniable.

It can happen again. And in this simple fact Canada is a changed nation. Nothing short of the repeal of the 1914 War Measures Act, or its redefinition to prevent its use of times of peace, would be sufficient. The use of the War Measures Act was in itself an abuse. If it was politically motivated, then the abuse becomes aggravated into a transgression of trust which cannot be tolerated in a Parliamentary system. Under a majority government, the Parliamentary system provides only at election time any real check against arbitrary power. Elections are too distant a remedy for the arbitrary jailing of hundreds of innocent persons.

The actions of the FLQ, as assumed in the legislation, would have constituted for the individuals involved, the offenses of seditious conspiracy or treason, certainly kidnapping for those involved, and other offenses such as theft, robbery and the unlawful possession of firearms. The police had ample jurisdiction under the Criminal Code and could have arrested anyone they had reasonable and probable grounds to believe had committed or was about to commit the offenses which already were in existence. It must be repeated that this could have been done without warrant.

Neither the War Measures regulations nor the Public Order Act would improve the investigative quality of the Montreal or the Quebec Police Forces. Neither act could put more men on the case and neither act could motivate the kidnappers to free their victims. The regulation had, however, one very real effect. It created the FLQ as an entity. This was probably the first terrorist organization in legal history to be incorporated by a special act of Parliament.

By calling these largely unrelated groups of violent agitators an organization, the government created it, as surely as if it had decided to give it a constitution. Up to October 16 the government knew, or surely ought to have known, that the FLQ was a collection of three letters which, like a popular song, was repeated whenever an appropriate occasion arose. To some, it was the expression of a violent philosophy. Any two or more would-be adventurers merely had to drop a parcel of dynamite, spraypaint the letters on a nearby brick wall, and when the bombs went off, voila! The FLQ has struck again.

The conduct of the varied groups, from disgruntled Gaspé fishermen who fire on the deep-water fishing-boats taking their livelihood, to the taxi drivers who vented their fury on Montreal's Murray Hill Limousine Company after facing years of frustrating monopoly, shows remarkable variety. A few students, anxious to act out their rage at some real or fancied grievance, or a few young punks, anxious to do the same, decide to heighten the disturbance they will cause by placing the initials on the wall or in a communiqué. When the police sent undercover men to join this new terrorist organization, they couldn't find it. They were looking for the clubrooms and the membership cards. All that the diverse workers shared was a deep sense of injustice and their willingness to do something illegal to express it.

The police had been under some fire from politicians for having been unable to infiltrate these terrorist organizations. Having never before tried to infiltrate an organization that did not exist, they could only explain that they were unable to join because the cells demanded that a newcomer participate in some crime as a sign of his good faith. This they could not do. They seemed not to understand that the act to be performed was in reality all that "membership" consisted of.

Police theory assumed a hierarchy. But there is not only no evidence of a hierarchy in the so-called FLQ, there is pathetic evidence that there is not even the slightest coordination.

It is possible to give the events credit for exposing another myth. The "fund-raising cell" which had recently stolen $35,000 was, however, unable to finance the operation of the "Chenier financing cell" which kidnapped Pierre Laporte, and that cell had to use the

$60 in Laporte's pocket to buy themselves food. The relationships which existed in these so-called cells indicate that being a relative or good friend is more important than having been ordered by Mr. Big. Perhaps James Cross was not in the best position to tell, but after 60 days in their custody, this bilingual diplomat observed, "It was a case of six kids trying to make a revolution."

Anyone who has been in police custody is familiar with the Mutt-and-Jeff technique of interrogation. The first policeman takes an aggressive, antagonistic stance, he is belligerent and insulting. The second policeman is reasonable and understanding; we all have our problems and perhaps we can work this out. To save himself from the implied excesses of "Mutt", the prisoner forms an unspoken alliance with "Jeff", whereupon both Mutt and Jeff get what they want.

The Canadian people were subjected to a particularly effective variant of the Mutt and Jeff technique in the days following October 16. Jean Marchand said the FLQ had infiltrated to the highest levels of public life in Quebec; "some pessimists" said their number was 3,000; the anti-Drapeau party in Montreal was a "front" for the FLQ. Another minister, George McIlraith, presented to the House of Commons as a statement of settled fact, that a woman across the river from Ottawa had been kidnapped and the initials FLQ carved upon her belly. Unnamed ministers told their favorite correspondents that "really big people" in Quebec were involved in a plot to over-throw the Government. The Prime Minister's closest advisors said: "It's worth investigating." The Minister of Justice said he hoped that someday the Canadian people could be told the full nature of the threat they had faced.

None of this speculation ever crossed the lips of the Prime Minister. His was always the voice of concern and reason. The Government hated doing what it had to do, but what other choice was there? The assumption of such extraordinary powers might, indeed, be a trap, he said, but Opposition leaders would be consulted, and the powers would be withdrawn as soon as possible. The Canadian people were given a choice: they could join in the war-whoops of Marchand or they could choose the reasoned concern of the Prime Minister. Either way, it added up to the same thing: the invocation of the War Measures Act was necessary to suppress an "apprehended insurrection", to the existence of which the Prime Minister at no time attached his own unequivocal testament; it was always "as reported" from the Province of Quebec.

In judgments made almost contemporaneously with the events, it is only possible to decide if there were motives for the invocation of the War Measures Act other than those stated publicly by examining the words spoken by those men who made the decision. George McIlraith, whose position at the time was to report to Parliament for the Royal Canadian Mounted Police, told the story of the woman carved by the FLQ on the day after the proclamation. McIlraith, who must have known as much as there was to know in Ottawa at that time, did not feel the slightest need to question this demented tale that cried out not for the strictures of the War Measures Act but for the mercy of the Mental Hospitals Act. The importance of the story is not that it was false, but that the Solicitor-General of Canada immediately accepted as true the notion that Canadian citizens were being tortured by a revolutionary force virtually within the shadow of Parliament Hill.

Jean Marchand became famous for his demagogic remark that the anti-Drapeau party in Montreal was a "front" for the FLQ. His explanation that he was confused between the French and English meanings of the word became something of a national joke. Perhaps the most significant part of the episode was that Marchand expressed his view for a Vancouver radio station, whose listeners, he could hardly fail to realize, were the least informed and the furthest removed from the facts. If Marchand was speaking in English but thinking in French, his meaning was even more bizarre since, instead of accusing the anti-Drapeau party of being a clandestine supporter of the FLQ, he was accusing it of an open and public alliance. And when Marchand warned that the FLQ—perhaps 3,000 strong—had infiltrated to the highest levels of Quebec life, he was guilty of another revealing slip. He obviously meant not the FLQ, but separatists.

Just as the English-language press found it difficult, indeed impossible, to distinguish between criminal terrorists and "known separatist sympathizers", federal cabinet ministers engaged in the same blurred thinking—including Marchand and the two cabinet ministers who informed Peter Newman and the one minister who informed Douglas Fisher of the Provisional Government Plot. Whether or not it was a conscious intention to smear the cause of separatism with the label of criminal terrorism, that, inescapably, was one of the results. English-language Canadians, curiously enough, find it possible to discuss with equanimity the problem of whether Newfoundland should have joined the United States, or whether British Columbia should now; they find it possible to discuss the various structural changes often raised in the Prairie Provinces and in northwestern Ontario, but they find it pathologically impossible to regard the separation of Quebec as a political, rather than as a criminal, problem. Their ability at rational analysis was further diminished by the invocation of the War Measures Act.

A number of equally dangerous precedents were implanted in the Canadian political consciousness by the use of the War Measures Act. One was the notion that peaceful opposition to government policies should, and can, be suppressed by internment. Another was that in times of stress the law should be used like a club. Another was the notion that the legal machinery of the courts, what lawyers call procedural guarantees, constitutes an impediment to democracy, rather than its bulwark. In addition, the War Measures regulations defied the ancient tradition that a man must be given an opportunity to know what the law is and to remedy his actions: by the time the regulations were tabled in the

House of Commons, some 200 persons were in jail. Most dangerous of all, the Federal Government sought to establish a retroactive crime. Several dozen persons were charged with membership in or advocacy of the FLQ, but were not charged with sedition; despite government disavowals, these persons were charged with "crimes" which were legal when performed.

In the same way that prohibiting the Communist Party led to burning Shakespeare and Tolstoy and the destruction of ethnic communities, in the same way that transporting the Japanese from the West Coast led to outrageous profiteering by white men, the danger of the War Measures abuses lies not only in themselves but also in the course they set for the future. Such abuses have a habit of happening the second time in a cause slightly less noble than the first, the third time in a cause slightly less noble than the second.

Even if the abuses were never repeated, they remained objectionable in themselves. One of the primary safeguards against arbitrary imprisonment is the guarantee that justice shall be dispensed in public. It begins with the guarantee that an accused person shall be brought before the first court of competent jurisdiction. The absence of this procedural guarantee permitted the Province of Quebec to keep secret the names of those detained for periods up to 21 days and then released without charge. If any terrorists were in this group, their absence could hardly be a secret from their colleagues—and the names of the better-known detainees, Pauline Julien, Henri Bellemare and the others, soon appeared in print—so that the only effect of the secrecy was to hide the identity of the Government's more obscure mistakes.

The War Measures regulations created an offense of membership in, or advocacy of the FLQ, provided for arrest and then for the laying of a charge within no less than 21 days. Eight times as many persons were arrested and detained as were eventually charged with anything, and since no police force can conceivably be that incompetent, it is clear that with the vast majority of arrests, there was no intention or likelihood of any charges being laid. The purpose was clearly for short-term internment, and not even internment for advocacy of the FLQ, since, had that been found, charges could have been laid. The purpose was for internment on grounds *other* than those stated in the War Measures regulations. In the majority of cases, these grounds were radicalism, objectionable to some but legal nonetheless, and opposition to Government policies.

More than half the arrests were completed in the first 12 hours after the proclamation at 4 a.m , a clear indication of advance preparation. Policemen have to be scheduled, divided up into teams, given lists of names and addresses, briefed on what to do. The federal cabinet must have known the way in which the powers it granted would be used in the province of Quebec, to assume otherwise is to assume the mindless signing of a blank cheque. The federal cabinet therefore bears the responsibility, as the grantor of the power, for the wholesale jailing of Canadian citizens for no other reason than their political beliefs, and those beliefs, even under the most restrictive sanctions ever imposed in peacetime, were legally unobjectionable. There is only one kind of country in which people go to jail without suspicion of crime.

The Canadian Bill of Rights specifically exempts the War Measures Act from its protections. It is clear from the Canadian experience of 1970 that if such an exemption is to continue, it should be amended to provide that Bill of Rights protections will not apply to the War Measures Act *only when used in wartime.* The Bill of Rights, being merely another act of Parliament, can be changed in a wink by any succeeding Parliament. The experience of 1970 should have convinced Canadians of the need for a *constitutionally-entrenched* Bill of Rights, changeable only after a broad consensus is achieved in the nation. This is the concept Pierre Trudeau advocated as Minister of Justice and which he continued to advocate as Prime Minister. Taken together, these two provisions might not deter a future government intent on arbitrary and abusive action. They would, however, guarantee any citizen a right of access to that place where his liberty ought to be decided, a court of law. Denial of access to the courts stands as the clearest indictment of the decision made at 4 a.m on October 16, 1970.

Appendices

Appendix A

The FLQ Manifesto

On the evening of October 8, in partial fulfillment of demands
made by the kidnappers of Jasper Cross, a so-called manifesto of
the FLQ was read over the radio and television network of
Radio-Canada, the French language service of the Canadian
Broadcasting Corporation. The text follows.

The Front de Libération du Québec is not a messiah, nor a modern-day Robin Hood. It is a group of Quebec workers who have decided to use all means to make sure that the people of Quebec take control of their destiny.

The Front de Libération du Québec wants the total independence of Quebeckers, united in a free society, purged forever of the clique of voracious sharks, the patronizing "big bosses" and their henchmen who have made Quebec their hunting preserve for "cheap labor" and unscrupulous exploitation.

The Front de Libération du Québec is not a movement of aggression organized by high finance and the puppet governments in Ottawa and Quebec (the Brinks "show," Bill 63, the electoral map, the so-called social progress tax, Power Corporation, "doctors insurance," the Lapalme boys . . .)

The Front de Libération du Québec is self-financed by "voluntary taxes" taken from the same enterprises that exploit the workers (banks, finance companies, etc. . . . .)

"The money power of the status quo, the majority of the traditional teachers of our people, have obtained the reaction they hoped for: A backward step rather than the change for which we have worked as never before, for which we will continue to work."—*René Lévesque, April 29, 1970.*

We once believed that perhaps it would be worth it to channel our energy and our impatience, as René Lévesque said so well, in the Parti Québecois, but the Liberal victory showed us clearly that that which we call democracy in Quebec is nothing but the democracy of the rich. The Liberal party's victory was nothing but the victory of the election riggers, Simard-Cotroni.

As a result, the British parliamentary system is finished and the Front de Libération du Québec will never allow itself to be distracted by the pseudo-election that the Anglo-Saxon capitalists toss to the people of Quebec every four years.

A number of Quebeckers have understood and will act. In the coming year, (Premier) Bourassa will have to face reality: 100,000 revolutionary workers, armed and organized.

Yes, there are reasons for the Liberal victory. Yes, there are reasons for poverty, unemployment, misery and for the fact that you, Mr. Bergeron of Visitation St., and you, Mr. Legendre of Laval who earn $10,000 a year, will not feel free in our country of Quebec.

Yes, there are reasons, and the guys at Lord know them, the fishermen of the Gaspé, the workers of the North Shore, the miners for the Iron Ore Co., Quebec Cartier Mining and Noranda, also know these reasons. And the brave workers in Cabano know all the reasons.

Yes, there are reasons that you, Mr. Tremblay of Panet St., and you, Mr. Cloutier, who work in construction in St. Jerome, that you cannot pay for "vaisseaux d'or" with all the "zizique" and the 'fling-flang' as does Drapeau the aristocrat—who is so concerned with slums that he puts colored billboards in front of them to hide our misery from the tourists.

Yes, there are reasons that you, Mrs. Lemay of St. Hyacinthe, can't pay for little trips to Florida like our dirty judges and parliamentary members do with our money.

The brave workers for Vickers and Davie Ship who were thrown out and not given a reason know these reasons. And the Murdochville men, who were attacked for the simple and sole reason that they wanted to organize a union and who were forced to pay $2,000,000 by the dirty judges simply because they tried to exercise this basic right—they know justice and they know the reasons.

Yes, there are reasons that you, Mr. Lachance of St. Marguerite St., must go and drown your sorrows in a bottle of that dog's beer, Molson. And you, Lachance's son, with your marijuana cigarettes.

Yes, there are reasons that you, the welfare recipients, are kept from generation to generation on social welfare, yes, there are all sorts of reasons, and the Domtar workers in East Angus and Windsor know them well.

And the workers at Squibb and Ayers, and the men at the Liquor Board and those at Seven Up and Victoria Precision, and the blue collar workers in Laval and Montreal and the Lapalme boys know those reasons well.

The Dupont of Canada workers know them as well, even if soon they will only be able to express them in English (thus assimilated, they will enlarge the number of immigrants and neo-Quebeckers, favored children of Bill 63).

And the Montreal policemen, those strongarms of the system, should understand these reasons—they should have been able to see we live in a terrorized society because without their force, without their violence, nothing could work. Oct. 7.

We have had our fill of Canadian federalism which penalizes the Quebec milk producers to satisfy the needs of the Anglo-Saxons of the Commonwealth; the system which keeps the gallant Montreal taxi drivers in a state of semi-slavery to shamefully protect the exclusive monopoly of the nauseating Murray Hill and its assassin-owner Charles Hershorn, and his son, Paul, who on several occasions on the night of Oct. 7, seized from the hands of his employees a .12 calibre rifle in order to fire on the taxi drivers and to kill Cpl. Dumas.

We have had our fill of the system which exercises a policy of heavy importation while turning out into the street the low wage earners in the textile and shoe manufacturing trades in order to provide profits for a clutch of damned money-makers in their Cadillacs who rate the Quebec nation on the same level as other ethnic minorities in Canada.

We have had our fill, as have more and more Quebeckers, of a government which performs a thousand and one acrobatics to charm American millionaires into investing in Quebec, La Belle Province, where thousands and thousands of square miles of forests, full of game and well-stocked lakes, are the exclusive preserve of the powerful 20th century seigneurs.

We have had our fill of the hypocrite Bourassa who reinforces himself with Brinks armor, the veritable symbol of the foreign occupation of Quebec, to keep the poor natives of Quebec in the fear of misery and unemployment in which they are accustomed to living.

We have had our fill of taxes which the Ottawa representative to Quebec wants to give to the Anglophone bosses to incite them to speak French, to negotiate in French. Repeat after me: cheap labor means manpower in a healthy market.

We have had our fill of promises of jobs and prosperity while we always remain the cowering servants and boot lickers of the big shots who live in Westmount, Town of Mount Royal, Hampstead and Outremont, all the fortresses of high finance on St. James and Wall St., while we, the Quebeckers, have to use all our means, including arms and dynamite, to rid ourselves of these economic and political bosses who continue to oppress us.

We live in a society of terrorized slaves, terrorized by the large owners like Steinberg, Clark, Bronfman, Smith, Neapole, Timmins, Geoffrion, J. L. Levesque, Hershorn, Thompson, Nesbitt, Desmarais, Kierans. Beside them Remi Popol, the gasket, Drapeau, the dog, Bourassa, the sidekick of the Simards, and Trudeau, the queer, are peanuts.

We are terrorized by the capitalist Roman Church, even though this seems to be diminishing (who owns the property on which the stock exchange stands?); by the payments to reimburse Household Finance; by the publicity of the grand masters of consumption like Eaton, Simpson, Morgan, Steinberg and General Motors.

We are terrorized by the closed circles of science and culture which are the universities and by their monkey directors like Gaudry and Dorais and by the sub-monkey, Robert Shaw.

The sub-monkey numbers of those who are realizing the oppression of this terrorist society are growing and the day will come when all the Westmounts will disappear from the map.

Production workers, miners, foresters, teachers, students and unemployed workers, take what belongs to you: your jobs, your determination and your liberty. And you, workers of General Electric, it's you who make your factories run, only you are capable of production. Without you General Electric is nothing.

Workers of Quebec, start today to take back what is yours: take for yourselves what belongs to you. Only you know your factories, your machines, your hotels, your universities, your unions. Don't wait for an organization miracle.

Make your own revolution in your area, in your places of work. And if you do not make it yourselves, other usurpers, technocrats and others will replace the iron fist of the cigar smokers which we know now, and all will be the same again. Only you are able to build a free society.

We must fight, not one by one, but together. We must fight until victory is ours with all the means at our disposal as did the patriots of 1837-38 (those whom your sacred church excommunicated to sell out to the British interests).

From the four corners of Quebec, those who have been treated with disdain, the lousy French, and the alcoholics will vigorously undertake combat against the destroyers of liberty and justice. We will banish from our state all the professional robbers, the bankers, the businessmen, the judges and the sold-out politicians.

We are the workers of Quebec and we will go to the end. We want to replace the slave society with a free society, functioning by itself and for itself. A society open to the world.

Our struggle can only be victorious. You cannot hold back an awakening people. Long live free Quebec.

Long live our comrades who are political prisoners.

Long live the Quebec revolution.

Long live the Front de Libération du Québec.

Appendix B

Proclamation of The War Measures Act

Proclamation declaring that apprehended insurrection exists and has existed as and from the 15th October, 1970
ROLAND MICHENER
Canada
ELIZABETH THE SECOND, by the Grace of God of the United
    Kingdom, Canada and Her other Realms and Territories
    QUEEN, Head of the Commonwealth, Defender of the Faith.
To All to Whom these Presents shall come or whom the same may
    in anyway concern,   *Greeting:*

DONALD S. MAXWELL
Deputy Attorney General

A Proclamation

Whereas the War Measures Act provides that the issue of a proclamation under the authority of the Governor in Council shall be conclusive evidence that insurrection, real or apprehended, exists and has existed for any period of time therein stated and of its continuance, until by the issue of a further proclamation it is declared that the insurrection no longer exists.

And Whereas there is in contemporary Canadian society an element or group known as Le Front de Libération du Québec who advocate and resort to the use of force and the commission of criminal offences including murder, threat of murder and kidnapping as a means of or as an aid in accomplishing a governmental change within Canada and whose activities have given rise to a state of apprehended insurrection within the Province of Quebec.

Now Know Ye that We,, by and with the advice of Our Privy Council for Canada, do by this Our Proclamation proclaim and declare that apprehended insurrection exists and has existed as and from the fifteenth day of October, one thousand nine hundred and seventy.

Of All Which Our Loving Subjects and all others whom these Presents may concern are hereby required to take notice and to govern themselves accordingly.

In Testimony Whereof, We have caused these Our Letters to be made Patent and the Great Seal of Canada to be hereunto affixed. Witness: Our Right Trusty and Well-beloved Counsellor Roland Michener, Chancellor and Principal Companion of Our Order of Canada upon whom We have conferred Our Canadian Forces' Decoration, Governor General and Commander-in-Chief of Canada.

At Our Government House, in Our City of Ottawa, this sixteenth day of October in the year of Our Lord one thousand nine hundred and seventy and in the nineteenth year of Our Reign.

By Command
J. R. GRANDY
Deputy Registrar General of Canada

Appendix C

WAR MEASURES ACT
Public Order Regulations, 1970
Oct. 16, 1970

Whereas it continues to be recognized in Canada that men and institutions remain free only when freedom is founded upon respect for moral and spiritual values and the rule of law;

And whereas there is in contemporary Canadian society an element or group known as Le Front de Libération du Québec who advocate the use of force or the commission of crime as a means of or as an aid in accomplishing a governmental change within Canada and who have resorted to the commission of serious crimes including murder, threat of murder and kidnapping;

And whereas the Government of Canada desires to ensure that lawful and effective measures can be taken against those who thus seek to destroy the basis of our democratic governmental system, on which the enjoyment of our human rights and fundamental freedoms is founded, and to ensure the continued protection of those rights and freedoms in Canada;

Therefore, His Excellency the Governor General in Council, on the recommendation of the Prime Minister, pursuant to the War Measures Act, is pleased hereby to make the annexed Regulations to provide emergency powers for the preservation of public order in Canada.

REGULATIONS TO PROVIDE EMERGENCY POWERS
FOR THE PRESERVATION OF PUBLIC ORDER IN CANADA

Short title.

1. These Regulations may be cited as the Public Order Regulations, 1970.

Interpretation

2. In these Regulations,

(a) "communicate" includes the act of communicating by telephone, broadcasting or other audible or visible means;

(b) "peace officer" means a peace officer as defined in the Criminal Code and includes a member of the Canadian Armed Forces;

(c) "statements" includes words spoken or written or recorded electronically or electromagnetically or otherwise, and gestures, signs or other visible representations; and

(d) "the unlawful association" means the group of persons or association declared by these regulations to be an unlawful association.

3. The group of persons or association known as Le Front de Libération du Québec and any successor group or successor association of the said Le Front de Libération du Québec or any group of persons or association that advocates the use of force or the commission of crime as a means of or as an aid in accomplishing governmental change within Canada is declared to be an unlawful association.

4. A person who

(a) is or professes to be a member of the unlawful association,

(b) acts or professes to act as an officer of the unlawful association,

(c) communicates statements on behalf of or as a representative or professed representative of the unlawful association,

(d) advocates or promotes the unlawful acts, aims, principles or policies of the unlawful association,

(e) contributes anything as dues or otherwise to the unlawful association or to anyone for the benefit of the unlawful association,

(f) solicits subscriptions or contributions for the unlawful association, or

(g) advocates, promotes or engages in the use of force or the commission of criminal offenses as a means of accomplishing a governmental change within Canada

is guilty of an indictable offence and liable to imprisonment for a term not exceeding five years.

5. A person, who, knowing or having reasonable cause to believe that another person is guilty of an offense under these Regulations, gives that other person any assistance with intent thereby to prevent, hinder or interfere with the apprehension, trial or punishment of that person for that offense is guilty of an indictable offense and liable to imprisonment for a term not exceeding five years.

6. An owner, lessee, agent or superintendent of any building, room, premises or other place who knowingly permits therein any meeting of the unlawful association or any branch, committee or members thereof, or any assemblage of persons who promote the acts, aims, principles or policies of the unlawful association is guilty of an indictable offense and liable to a fine of not more than five thousand dollars or to imprisonment for a term not exceeding five years or to both.

7. (1) A person arrested for an offense under section 4 shall be detained in custody without bail pending trial unless the Attorney-General of the province in which the person is being detained consent to the release of that person on bail.

(2) Where an accused has been arrested for an offense under these Regulations and is detained in custody for the purpose only of ensuring his attendance at the trial of the charge under these Regulations in respect of which he is in custody and the trial has not commenced within 90 days from the time he was first detained, the person having the custody of the accused shall, forthwith upon the expiration of such 90 days, apply to a judge of the superior court of criminal jurisdiction in the province in which the accused is being detained to fix a date for the trial and the judge may fix a date for the beginning of the trial or give such directions as he thinks necessary for expediting the trial of the accused.

8. In any prosecution for an offense under these Regulations, evidence that any person

(a) attended any meeting of the unlawful association,

(b) spoke publicly in advocacy for the unlawful association, or

(c) communicated statements of the unlawful association as a representative or professed representative of the unlawful association

is, in the absence of evidence to the contrary, proof that he is a member of the unlawful association.

9. (1) A peace officer may arrest without warrant

(a) a person who he has reason to suspect is a member of the unlawful association; or

(b) a person who professes to be a member of the unlawful association, or

(c) a person who he has reason to suspect has committed, is committing or is about to commit an act described in paragraphs (b) to (g) of section 4.

(2) A person arrested pursuant to subsection (1) shall be taken before a justice having jurisdiction and charged with an

offense described in section 4 not later than seven days after his arrest, unless the Attorney-General of the province in which the person is being detained has, before the expiry of those seven days, issued an order that the accused be further detained until the expiry of a period not exceeding 21 days after his arrest, at the end of which period the person arrested shall be taken before a justice having jurisdiction and charged with an offense described in section 4 or released from custody.

10. A peace officer may enter and search without warrant any premises, place, vehicle, vessel or aircraft in which he has reason to suspect

(a) Anything is kept or used for the purpose of promoting the unlawful acts, aims, principles or policies of the unlawful association;

(b) there is anything that may be evidence of an offense under these regulations;

(c) any member of the unlawful association is present; or

(d) any person is being detained by the unlawful association.

11. Any property that a peace officer has reason to suspect may be evidence of an offense under these regulations may, without warrant, be seized by a peace officer and held for 90 days from the date of seizure or until the final disposition of any proceedings in relation to an offense under these regulations in which such property may be required, whichever is the later.

12. These regulations shall be enforced in such manner and by such courts, officers and authorities as enforce indictable offenses created by the Criminal Code.

Appendix D

Public Order (Temporary Measures) Act, 1970.

Third Session, Twenty-Eighth Parliament,
19 Elizabeth II, 1970

THE HOUSE OF COMMONS OF CANADA
BILL C-181

An Act to provide temporary emergency powers for
the preservation of public order in Canada

As passed by The House Of Commons,
the 1st December, 1970

Given Royal Assent the 3rd December 1970.

Whereas the Parliament of Canada continues to affirm that men and institutions remain free only when freedom is founded upon respect for moral and spiritual values and the rule of law;

And whereas the public order in Canada continues to be endangered by elements of the group of persons or association known as Le Front de Libération du Québec who advocate the use of force or the commission of crime as a means of or as an aid in accomplishing governmental change within Canada with respect to the Province of Quebec or its relationship to Canada, and who have resorted to murder, threat of murder and kidnapping as well as the commission of other acts involving actual or threatened coercion, intimidation and violence;

And whereas the Parliament of Canada, following approval by the House of Commons of Canada of the measures taken by His Excellency the Governor General in Council pursuant to the *War Measures Act* to deal with the state of apprehended insurrection in the Province of Quebec on the clear understanding that the authority for such measures should remain in force for a temporary period only, desires to ensure that lawful and effective measures can and will continue to be taken against those who thus seek to destroy our democratic governmental system, and agrees that all such measures as are hereafter determined to be necessary by reason of the present emergency be taken under the authority of and in accordance with the provisions of a law of Canada expressly enacted for that purpose, the terms of which provide for its continuation in force for a temporary period only;

Now therefore, Her Majesty, by and with the advice and consent of the Senate and House of Commons of Canada, enacts as follows:

SHORT TITLE

1. This Act may be cited as the *Public Order (Temporary Measures) Act, 1970.*

INTERPRETATION

2. In this Act,

(a) "communicate" includes the act of communicating by telephone, broadcasting or other audible or visible means;

(b) "peace officer" means a peace officer as defined in the Criminal Code, and includes a member of the Canadian Forces when assigned to perform the duties of a peace officer by authority of the Governor in Council;

(c) "statements" includes words spoken or written or recorded electronically or electromagnetically or otherwise, and gestures, signs or other visible representations; and

(d) "the unlawful association" means the group of persons or association declared by this Act to be an unlawful association.

288

GENERAL

3. The group of persons or association known as Le Front de Libération du Québec and any successor group or successor association of the said Le Front de Libération du Québec, or any group of persons or association that advocates the use of force or the commission of crime as a means of or as an aid in accomplishing the same or substantially the same governmental change within Canada with respect to the Province of Quebec or its relationship to Canada as that advocated by the said Le Front de Libération du Québec, is declared to be an unlawful association.

4. A person who

(a) is or professes to be a member of the unlawful association,

(b) acts or professes to act as an officer of the unlawful association,

(c) communicates statements on behalf of or as a representative or professed representative of the unlawful association,

(d) advocates or promotes the unlawful acts of, or the use of the unlawful means advocated by, the unlawful association for accomplishing its aims, principles or policies,

(e) contributes anything as dues or otherwise to the unlawful association or to anyone for the benefit of the unlawful association,

(f) solicits subscriptions or contributions for the unlawful association, or

(g) advocates, promotes or engages in the use of force or the commission of crime as a means of or as an aid in accomplishing the same or substantially the same governmental change within Canada with respect to the Province of Quebec or its relationship to Canada as that advocated by the unlawful association,

is guilty of an indictable offence and liable to imprisonment for a term not exceeding five years.

5. A person who, knowing or having reasonable cause to believe that another person is guilty of an offence under this Act, gives that other person any assistance with intent thereby to prevent, hinder or interfere with the apprehension, trial or punishment of that person for that offence is guilty of an indictable offence and liable to imprisonment for a term not exceeding five years.

6. An owner, lessee, agent or superintendent of any building, room, premises or other place who knowingly permits therein any meeting of the unlawful association or thereof, or any assemblage of persons who advocate or promote the unlawful acts of, or the use of the unlawful means advocated by, the unlawful association for accomplishing its aims, principles or policies, is guilty of an indictable offence and liable to a fine of not more than five thousand dollars or to imprisonment for a term not exceeding five years or to both.

7. (1) Subject to subsection (2), a person charged with an offence under section 4 shall be detained in custody without bail pending his trial.

(2) No person shall' be detained in custody pursuant to subsection (1)

(a) after seven days from the later of the time when he was arrested or the coming into force of this Act, unless before the expiry of those seven days the Attorney General of the province in which the person is in custody has filed with the clerk of the superior court of criminal jurisdiction in the province a certificate under this section stating that just cause

exists for the detention of that person pending his trial, or

(b) after any certificate issued under this section in respect of that person has been revoked, or the Attorney General of the province in which that person is in custody has otherwise consented to the release of that person on bail.

(3) Where a person who has been charged with an offence under this Act is being detained in custody pending his trial, and the trial has not commenced within ninety days from the time when he was first detained, the person having the custody of the person charged shall, forthwith upon the expiry of those ninety days, apply to a judge of the superior court of criminal jurisdiction in the province in which the date for the trial, and the judge may fix a date for the beginning of the trial or give such directions as he thinks necessary for expediting the trial.

8. In any prosecution for an offence under this Act, evidence that any person, either before or after the coming into force of this Act,

(a) participated in or was present at a number of meetings of the unlawful association or of any branch, committee or members thereof,

(b) spoke publicly in advocacy for the unlawful association, or

(c) communicated statements on behalf of or as a representative or professed representative of the unlawful association,

is, in the absence of evidence to the contrary, proof that he is a member of the unlawful association.

9. (1) A peace officer may arrest without warrant

(a) a person who he has reason to suspect is a member of the unlawful association;

(b) a person who professes to be a member of the unlawful association; or

(c) a person who he has reason to suspect has committed, is committing or is about to commit an act described in any of paragraphs *(b)* to *(g)* of section 4.

(2) Subject to subsection (3), a person arrested under subsection (1) may be detained in custody by a peace officer but

shall be taken before a justice, magistrate or judge having jurisdiction and charged with an offence under section 4, or shall be released from custody, not later than three days after his arrest, unless the Attorney General of the province in which the person is being detained has, before the expiry of those three days, issued an order that he be further detained until the expiry of a period not exceeding seven days after his arrest, in which case the person arrested shall, forthwith upon the expiry of that period unless he has sooner been released, be taken before such a justice, magistrate or judge and charged with an offence under section 4, or be released from custody.

(3) In its application to a person who, immediately before the coming into force of this Act, was being detained in custody without his having been charged with an offence under section 4 of the *Public Order Regulations, 1970* made pursuant to the *War Measures Act*, subsection (2) shall be read and construed as though for the reference therein to "three days" there were substituted a reference to "seven days" and for the reference therein to "seven days" there were substituted a reference to "twenty-one days", except that nothing in this subsection shall be construed to authorize the detention of any such person in custody, without his having been charged with an offence under section 4 of this Act, for any longer period than the Attorney General of the province in which he is being detained deems warranted having regard to the exigencies of the situation.

10. A peace officer may enter and search without warrant any premises, place, vehicle, vessel or aircraft in which he has reason to suspect

(a) anything is kept or used for the purpose of promoting the unlawful acts of, or the use of the unlawful means advocated by, the unlawful association for accomplishing its aims, principles or policies;

(b) there is anything that may be evidence of an offence under this Act;

(c) any member of the unlawful association is present; or

(d) any person is being detained by the unlawful association.

11. Anything that a peace officer has reason to suspect may be evidence of an offence under this Act may, without warrant, be seized by a peace officer and detained for not more than ninety days from the date of such seizure, unless before the expiry of those ninety days a justice, magistrate or judge is satisfied upon application that, having regard to all the circumstances, its further detention for a specified period is warranted and he so order, or proceedings in respect of an offence under this Act are instituted in which such thing may be required.

12. (1) It is hereby declared that this Act shall operate notwithstanding the *Canadian Bill of Rights.*

(2) Notwithstanding the declaration contained in subsection (1), nothing in subsection (1) shall be construed or applied so as to prevent the application of paragraphs *(a)* to *(g)* of section 2 of the *Canadian Bill of Rights* to this Act, in all respects as provided in those paragraphs subject only to the exceptions hereinafter expressly provided, namely:

(a) nothing in this Act shall be held to be a law of Canada that authorizes, or shall be held to operate so as to authorize, the arbitrary detention or imprisonment of any person; and

(b) for the purposes of that portion of paragraph *(f)* of section 2 of the *Canadian Bill of Rights* that relates to the right of a person charged with an offence not to be deprived of reasonable bail without just cause, just cause shall be presumed to exist where, under this Act, the Attorney General of the province in which the person in is custody has filed with the clerk of the superior court of criminal jurisdiction in the province a certificate stating that just cause exists for the detention of that person pending his trial and the certificate has not been revoked.

13. Notwithstanding the proclamation issued on October 16, 1970 pursuant to the *War Measures Act,* sections 3, 4 and 5 of that Act shall, on, from and after the day this Act is assented to, cease to be in force in consequence of the issue of that proclamation, and that proclamation shall be deemed to have been revoked.

14. On, from and after the day this Act is assented to, any offence committed under section 4, 5 or 6, respectively, of the

Public Order Regulations, 1970 made pursuant to the *War Measures Act* shall be deemed to be an offence committed under section 4, 5 or 6, as the case may be, of this Act, and any investigation, proceeding or other act or thing instituted, commenced or done under the authority or purported authority of those Regulations shall be deemed to have been instituted, commenced or done under the authority or purported authority of this Act and as though this Act had come into force on October 16, 1970.

15. This Act expires on the 30th day of April, 1971 or on such earlier day as may be fixed by proclamation, unless before the 30th day of April, 1971 or before any earlier day fixed by proclamation, both Houses of Parliament, by joint resolution, direct that this Act shall continue in force until a day specified in the resolution, in which case this Act expires either on that specified day or on such earlier day as may be fixed by proclamation.

Appendix E

(Letter sent on November 13, 1970, from jail by Robert Lemieux to the Bâtonnier of the Quebec bar, Marcel Cinq-Mars, Q.C.)

Mr. President, dear confrère,

In Germany when Hitler came to power, JUDICIAL DEMOCRACY disintegrated. What is particularly striking about the story is how slowly this disintegration came about. Some judges and lawyers first accepted small encroachments, and later the more horrible ones, which the Nuremburg Trials revealed. Since my dismissal (with a half hour's notice) in January 1968 from the law firm of O'Brien, Home, Hall, Nolan, Sanders, O'Brien & Smyth (for being involved in the cases of Robert Lévesque, Pierre Vallières and Charles Gagnon—I had been formally appointed by the Legal Aid Bureau of the Montreal Bar; this appointment, by the way, was retracted in July 1969 for the dubious pretext that a supporting committee already existed), my work has been mainly concerned with a particular type of criminal law. Indeed, I have defended a great number of disputants, demonstrators, workers, students, "hippies", revolutionaries and poor people before the courts of many of the judicial districts of Quebec, from the districts of Gaspé to Abitibi, in civil as well as criminal cases.

I will not go into the details of the difficulties which I have encountered: threats, difficulties and intimidations on the part of police officers, colleagues, administrators and judges. Financial and personal difficulties. I have had at most 10 days holiday in 3½ years. I quickly understood that all this was part of the "job".

Filled with the realistic theories of Oliver Wendell Holmes, inspired by masters such as Clarence Darrow and Frank Scott (my ex-professor), I set to work with passion.

I should emphasize however some of the occurrences which I believe are to the honour of our profession and of the "adversary system".

In July 1968, after a three week trial at the Montreal Assizes, Robert Lévesque of the Front de Libération du Québec (1966) was acquitted by a jury of having conspired to commit an armed robbery in a military armoury, after Lévesque had clamoured in detention simply to be tried for 24 months and 11 days!—a fact I have often deprecated, correctly so, I think. The Crown appealed from the verdict mentioned above. The Quebec Court of Appeal rejected the appeal.

On April 2, 1969, Charles Gagnon was acquitted by a jury of the involuntary homicide of Jean Corbo after a trial which lasted 7 weeks. I argued before the jury, without notes, for more than 2 days . . . On August 17, 1969, another jury remained divided on the verdict (9 out of 12 were in favour of acquittal) in the LaGrenade affair, after 10 weeks of trial and 67 hours of deliberation. I argued for more than 3 days without notes. Gagnon was finally acquitted in the LaGrenade affair on December 10, 1969 (after having undergone two hunger strikes— one lasting 20 days and the other lasting 15 days. His hunger strikes were solely for the purpose of obtaining his trial on this matter, the most important against him).

Between these two trials, after extremely long preparation, I argued before the Quebec Court of Appeal against the first conviction (manslaughter) against Vallières (LaGrenade). At the end of my oral argument, Hon. Mr. Justice George H. Montgomery congratulated me from the bench. The verdict was quashed. The Hon. Mr. Justice Jean Turgeon declaring in his judgment, "I believe that it is possible that Vallières was convicted for his writings and his ideas rather than for his participation in L'affaire LaGrenade!" Vallières was convicted a second time of this same charge after an incredible trial presided over by Hon. Justice Paul Miquelon from which I was expelled for a few hours after having made a completely normal and respectful but "embarrassing" objection. After the presentation of a 125-page brief, in support of a request for bail which we were making, the Chief Justice of Quebec, the Hon. Mr. Justice Lucien Tremblay granted Vallières bail (LaGrenade) stating, "I believe that the grounds for appeal are serious."

In the Sir George Williams affair, after a trial which lasted 8 weeks, I obtained 14 acquittals on 15 counts. Two of my three clients (five counts per indictment), are the only ones who have been completely cleared at trial of this matter up to now.

At Percé during the summer of 1970, three out of three of my clients were freed from political accusations which were both stupid and vexatious. Later, on August 31 (on the occasion of my third trip during the same month), at the end of the preliminary inquiry of 25 occupants of an American hunting and fishing club, Hon. Judge Jean-Marc Roy called me to his chambers to congratulate and thank me for having contributed to the serene and orderly proceedings during the inquiry. Two young people were freed at the end of the inquiry.

In 1969 I represented Michel Chartrand and Christian Lamontagne in sedition charges brought against the two. Mr. Chartrand was freed at preliminary inquiry by Hon. Judge Maurice Fauteux. Mr. Lamontagne was acquitted by a jury at the Quebec Assizes after a 6-day trial.

This fall, the Hon. Judge Henri Masson-Loranger acquitted a client, Yannick Chuit, of harbouring and of robbery in relation to the "police-spies affair". The police had been discovered in a projection booth at the Montreal Institute of Technology, before "Operation McGill". A stupid accusation instigated by Montreal chief lawyer Michel Côté. During the inquiry the policemen testified they were grateful to Chuit and his companions for having escorted them without harm outside the building. The youths had asked them to leave their equipment behind to avoid brawls under the understanding of picking it up later, and had even taken measures to ensure it would not disappear. Lawyer Michel Côté had decided to bring these charges to "save appearances" (policemen had been thrown out!), for the same reasons Jérôme Choquette, Q.C., has just decided to bring charges against Michel Chartrand, Gagnon, Vallières, Larue-Langlois, myself and many of the others in order to "save appearances". (Pierre Laporte is dead, no one or almost no one has been captured. It was necessary to pounce on someone. A scapegoat must be found.)

It is this same Michel Côté who sponsored the undemocratic Montreal Anti-demonstration By-law which has just been declared illegal and unconstitutional by the Hon. Justice Paul Trépanier. The grounds of this judgment are the same I had put forward in an opinion given to the Montreal-Central Council of the Confederation of National Trade Unions, an opinion which was published at the time in two Montreal dailies.

Lawyers Côté and Rémi Paul have repulsed an incalculable number of young people from legal or para-legal political action into clandestine action, either as a matter of fact or potentially, by systematically crushing movements which "came out of the street", such as a dozen citizens' and workers' committees in Montreal, the Mouvement d'integration Scolaire (M.I.S.), the Mouvement Syndical Politique (M.S.P.), the F.L.P., etc., by unfounded "political" accusations and by authorizing incredible police harassment (detention without warrants or without charges, brutalities, seizures without warrants . . .). Lawyer Côté even boasted at the Ottawa parliamentary enquiry into the C.Y.C. of having seized many "tons" of documents! Ninety per cent of these seizures were totally illegal because the documents seized were legal, no charges ever having been laid.

Let us come back to the September '70 term of the Montreal Assizes. I then protested against a manoeuvre by the office of Mr. Choquette to separate at the last minute the Roy-Morency-Lanctôt trials. On August 21 the Department of Justice had served the three men with identical written notices of trial for the 9th of September in first Division of Assizes. A common defence had been prepared! It fell through!

At the Morency trial I objected and even lost my temper (for the first time but I think Hon. Justice Claude Bisson has since forgiven me, our relationship having been very cordial since), when the judge ended my questioning of a prospective juror. I went directly to the Court of Appeal with a request for Habeas Corpus which was denied by Chief Justice Lucien Tremblay, but the Chief Justice declared that the grounds relied on could constitute sufficient grounds for appeal. I was no longer interrupted. I questioned the prospective jurors at length (a procedure which is rare here but usual in the U.S.A. in serious trials; Morency is accused of 20 counts many of which could get him life imprisonment). The result: 28 of the 60 candidates interrogated were declared biased by the examiners (46.6%). Many of these towards the defence! Prevention at the first instance level can avoid an appeal. I had learned that at my own expense.

These cases constitute approximately one quarter of my practice although they take up more than half my time. The rest of my practice is general (commercial law, contract law, domestic relations, etc.). In this area I think also that I have been a credit to the legal profession. Recently I won a case involving a humble shoe worker in a matter of "rats in his house" before Hon. Judge Léonce Côté (*Tomy vs. Quintan*). I have asked Quintan for $25 to cover disbursements.

This fall Hon. Judge Jean Tellier released a client (*R. vs. Georges Raçicot*) on a charge of being an "habitual criminal". I have been representing another client (*R. vs. Jacques Lévesque*) for a long time in a similar case. One knows the dozens of sittings and all the preparation these cases require. Some of our colleagues simply decline them. I have received from Raçicot less than a quarter of what our colleagues insist upon, from Lévesque I cannot receive a penny because he is completely destitute.

I have also made numerous suggestions for reform. For example, that Quebec amend its jury law to allow women to be jurors, that the required age be brought down from 21 to 18 years and that the requirement of having a residence (rented or owned—one name per residence) be abolished by creating a universal enumeration. I also suggested that Ottawa abolish from the Criminal Code the "stand aside rule" which gives the Crown 52 challenges against 12 for the Defence, which permits the Crown to "choose" the 12 jurors (which to my knowledge has only been used in cases involving the FLQ!).

This rather long narration, Mr. President, is simply to show that I love my work, that I think I do it well and that I intend to remain in practice. I am writing to tell you that some are trying unjustly to get me out, and to bring to your attention and to the attention of all members of the Bar some of the more serious and troublesome attacks by the Department of Justice on Judicial Democracy in Quebec of which my case is but one example of a long series.

As a preliminary, I would like to point out that in the 3½ years prior to the Cross-Laporte affair I was not a member of any group, movement or political party. Intentionally, I have not given a single political speech despite the hundreds of solicitations. I have given a few speeches in relation to the administration of justice where I have stated facts (for example, the refusal to Gagnon of his trial in regard to the LaGrenade Affair, the preventive detention for 29 months of Robert Lévesque, the judgment of the Court of Appeal in the Vallières case, the systematic denial of bail to the fellows of the FLQ, etc.). These speeches were limited solely to the following occasions: (1) various talks before a demonstration supporting Vallières-Gagnon on November 6, 1969 (in which I did not participate), (2) a talk to law students of Laval University, and (3) another to law students of McGill University (where the students attempted for a long time but in vain to shift the discussion to politics). I emphasize that section 61(b)(iii) of the Criminal Code says: "No one is deemed to have a seditious intention by reason only that he intends out of good faith to point out errors or defects in the administration of justice in Canada."

When I learned of the kidnapping of Mr. J. R. Cross, I decided like many Quebeckers, including Marcel Pépin, President of the C.N.T.U. (250,000 members), Louis Laberge, President, and Fernand Daoust, Secretary General of the Q.F.L. (250,000 members), Yvon Charbonneau, President of the C.E.Q. (65,000 members), Paul Alain, President of the U.C.C. (52,000 members), Mathias Rioux, President of the Alliance des Professeurs de Montréal, Alfred Rouleau, President of L'Assurance-vie Desjardins (one of the most respected persons in business), René Lévesque and Jacques Parizeau of the P.Q., Claude Ryan (Editor of *Le Devoir*), etc., to do EVERYTHING I could to avoid what I considered and still consider a catastrophe. Like all these well-known persons, I believed that it would be better, faced with two solutions, for the good of the people of Quebec, to liberate the 23 political prisoners, etc. . Like these gentlemen I intended to use my position to convince citizens, groups, associations, and the Government of my point of view. Like these people, I intended to do this through the persuasion of language and not through that of dynamite (a choice which the Government seems to want me to regret at all costs as for many others).

The government launched its extremist McCarthy-like aggression against me on October 11, 1970, by arresting me by means of warrant at the beginning of a long week-end for having supposedly impeded the work of the police by statements (S.110(a) Criminal Code). (Choquette had proceeded some 10 days before by means of a summons against Ernest Crépault in a matter which was much more serious). I have never been able to find out which statements among the hundreds are reprehensible
(there is no preliminary inquiry!). I was held incommunicado in isolation for 48 hours, without paper, newspapers . . .

While I was being held all of my professional files, notes, documents were seized and taken from my office and my residence. Could the search not have been carried out on the spot rather than create a total mess? My secretary tells me that a great number of files, agendas, . . . are missing, but the authorities claim that everything was returned to me except two wills!

Finally I was called from my cell at 8 o'clock on Monday evening by lawyer Robert Demers who invited me to negotiate with him after the receipt of a communique from the FLQ designating me as their negotiator. Lawyer Demers then showed me a copy of the communique issued by lawyer Robert Bourassa declaring that lawyer Demers had been designated to negotiate with me. I accepted after studying this document. It was agreed that I would be released on my own recognizance at the request of the government.

I presumed the good faith of our colleague Demers, until he told me later that the "negotiations" were only a pretext to gain time. Lawyer Demers said to me that he had agreed to deceive me in order to save the life of Pierre Laporte. It was not the first time that a colleague had deceived me in 3½ years. Lawyer Louis Paradis, then Chief Prosecutor, had purposely distorted my arguments at the time of the simultaneous trials which were imposed upon Vallières and Gagnon in the fall of 1969. Another sinister joke!

This first charge little concerned me, but the second charge of the Government against me and many others is grotesque and will be a catastrophe for Judicial Democracy if it proceeds. We may well be shocked at what is going on in Brazil, in Greece. We are in it, Mr. President, up to our necks! But when it is in our own backyard it takes a little more guts to recognize it, to intervene, and denounce it.

Indeed, after having kept us for 21 days, illegally deprived of the rights of visits, of telephone, of lawyer, of fresh air, of walks, of correspondence, of "canteen," of paper, of certain lawful reading material, of all hygenic necessities, of clothes, of legal texts. (These deprivations lasted between 7 and 21 days): charge C.B.R.M. no. 70-6700 was laid on November 5, 1970, by Jérôme Choquette, Q.C., (by "preferred indictment" which deprives us of a preliminary inquiry! What concern for Justice!). This absurd charge should startle and shock all those who are concerned with the administration of Justice, the Bar above all.

The charge reads as follows:

"In the City of Montreal, district of Montreal and elsewhere in the Province of Quebec, between January 1, 1968, and October 16, 1970 inclusively, Pierre Vallières, Charles Gagnon, Robert Lemieux, Jacques Larue-Langois and Michel Chartrand illegally and without colour of right took part in a seditious conspiracy aimed at changing the Canadian government and more particularly in the Province of Quebec, by advocating the use of force, without the authority of the law, contrary to the provisions of section 62, paragraph (c) of the Criminal Code."

Firstly, taken at face value the document is absurd: it says we conspired "by" advocating! One conspires "to" advocate or achieve an end. The charge covers a period of two years, ten months and eleven days! This is laughable! It's a mockery!

My comments will be limited to an analogy. I have followed closely the famous "conspiracy" matter of the "Chicago Seven" tried by a judge and jury at Chicago in 1969. Let us remember that Attorney-General Ramsay Clark under the Johnson Administration had formally vetoed this trial. Let us remember that the trial provoked the indignation of tens of thousands of American jurists, of the most respected newspapers . . . In the end, a very large majority of informed opinion thought that Justice had been undermined by the trial. The Appeal Court intervened immediately after the trial to release the accused on bail. They had all the benefit of bail until the end of the trial. Also sentences of many years of jail had been imposed upon all of the accused for contempt of court.

I do not wish to go into a lengthy debate, Mr. President; suffice it to say that I believe the Chicago Trial was really quite insignificant as compared to the monumental farce that this proposed trial would be. The Chicago matter was based on a special law which had been voted in a year earlier to deal with these "situations", which is not the case in the macabre farce which the government wants to "produce" here! The Chicago trial lasted 5½ months, the charges covered only a very short period of time, the actions of the accused were relatively homogeneous . . . The "theatrical production" that our colleague Choquette proposes to bring about covers a period of 34 months, the occupations of the five accused are quite diversified . . . We expect (we talk about it a lot) the trial to last at least 18 months—if in fact it should ever be held!

But yet more ridiculous and more odious, all five, and others (we are all, with the exception of Larue-Langlois, isolated from the other prisoners, I do not have sufficient information . . .) are also charged, to wit:

"On October 16, 1970, was or had been declared to be a member of an illegal organization: contrary to the provisions of Section 4(a) of the 1970 Public Order Regulations."

One wants to laugh. The law was promulgated on October 16th at 4:00 a.m. I am sleeping. I am awakened. I turn on the radio and CKAC gives me the essential details. I am thrown in jail where I still remain.

Let us hypothesize that I am a "member" at 4:00 a.m. The regulation not being retroactive and it being presumed that one knows and observes the law (if it is constitutional?!), I must have the opportunity to desist from the actions and activities that have just been declared illegal. I must have the opportunity to commit or not to commit an offence.

There was a time in Quebec, Mr. President, when one could

(as the honourable Judge Jean Turgeon stated, along with two international societies devoted to defending human rights, the International Association of Democratic Jurists and the International Federation of Civil Liberties Unions) institute murder proceedings against people because of their ideas and writings, but there was some concern for outward appearances. But here we have "closed down shop" as Mr. Trudeau would say! But what a clever little ploy to keep us in jail! The Minister who is the opposite party decides if we are to be granted bail! Oops! A little stroke of the pen in "Cité libre" style, and we destroy an institution acquired in 1215, the role of judges, etc. The first time it is somewhat harsh. Later it becomes easy! And then easier and easier as in Hitler's Germany. History does not lie.

302   I think we should all ponder a little before scuttling Democracy and the Judicial System. Especially, Mr. President, I think the Bar *must* concern itself in this matter and *intervene*. Objectively, this matter concerns the Bar. Subjectively also, because the rights of one of its accredited members (also a member of the Junior Bar and of the Canadian Bar) are being usurped (fortunately, my fellow-prisoners tell me!). Furthermore this member represents the interests dear to hundreds of people in your jurisdiction who are hurt by these acts (see above; also, for example, a case before the Hon. Justice Mitchell, involving more than $10,000 (Seaway Landscape and Nursery Limited vs. Sera Inc.) which might be lost because key documents seem to have been lost during the police seizure and, what is more, I cannot complete a verbal agreement which has already been begun with our colleague Lawyer Lawrence Glazer concerning the details of notes to be submitted before final judgment. It involves many hundreds of documents in a complicated accounting matter).

Very humbly, Mr. President, I am asking you as well as all members of the Bar:

1. To demand, upon receipt of this letter (this is a matter of great importance), that I be allowed to receive at once certain files in order to write memoranda, urgent letters . . . and that I be permitted to communicate on this subject with a colleague and my secretary . . . These demands strictly concern my practice.

2. To demand immediate bail from the Minister (the presumption of innocence always exists and bail is its corollary) on this

ridiculous charge laid pursuant to the public order regulation. As for the other charge (the accused in the "Tunnel" matter are out on bail!), there is not a case in our judicial history where bail has been denied in a matter of sedition.

3. To demand immediate *nolle prosequi* respecting the three ludicrous charges brought against me, *solely to get rid of a vigorous adversary in a system which is said to be an "adversary system"*—as well as in other cases after examination. I can assure you that the charges are just as ludicrous (if not more so) in the cases of Chartrand, Vallières, Larue-Langlois and Gagnon. Once again, I do not know the condition of the others, but I have heard that in certain cases it is even more loathsome; the Government might have even prosecuted some of its own supporters!

4. To intervene vigorously in regards to the gradual erosion and debasement of the Administration of Justice in Quebec these last years, in these political affairs said to be ordinary "Common Law" cases which are in many instances only UTILIZATIONS BY THE EXECUTIVE POWER OF THE JUDICIAL POWER IN ORDER TO ANNOY AND CRUSH SOME CITIZENS. The counts of sedition against Michel Chartrand, Raymond Lemieux, Reginald Chartrand, Laurier Gravel, Vallières, Gagnon, Lamontagne and myself, the various proceedings instituted against Daniel Waterlot, Y. Chuit, Mario Bachand are only some flagrant examples. What is even more revolting is that an ever growing number of our colleagues (furthermore they make fabulous money at it) and judges are complacent about the situation.

303

5. To designate a colleague or a committee to make sure that this matter proceeds properly and to intervene . . . he, or it, will account to you and to the council.

From Hitler's Germany comes this story. The first time they came to pick up a certain person he was an anarchist Jew. A Jew! An Anarchist! I did not "protest". The second time they picked up a German, but he was a Communist. I found this a little curious, but I did not "protest". The third time they came to get me. There was no longer anybody to "protest". Let this be a warning to everybody!

Yours most faithfully, M. le Bâtonnier Cinq-Mars,

ROBERT LEMIEUX
Avocat au Barreau de Montréal

(Authors' Note: This letter was sent in French. Its translation was undertaken at our request by Mr. Lemieux.)

Appendix F

Correspondence tabled in the House of Commons on October 16, 1970 by Prime Minister Trudeau.

[Translation]

GOVERNMENT OF QUEBEC
THE PRIME MINISTER

Quebec City, October 16, 1970.

Mr. Prime Minister,

During the last few days the people of Quebec have been greatly shocked by the kidnapping of Mr. James R. Cross, representative of the British Government in Montreal, and the Hon. Pierre Laporte, Minister of Labour and Manpower and Minister of Immigration of Quebec, as well as by the threats to the security of the state and individuals expressed in communiqués issued by the Front de Libération du Québec or on its behalf, and finally by all the circumstances surrounding these events.

After consultation with authorities directly responsible for the administration of justice in Quebec, the Quebec Government is convinced that the law, as it stands now, is inadequate to meet this situation satisfactorily.

Under the circumstances, on behalf of the Government of Quebec, I request that emergency powers be provided as soon as possible so that more effective steps may be taken. I request particularly that such powers encompass the authority to apprehend and keep in custody individuals who, the Attorney General of Quebec has valid reasons to believe, are determined to overthrow the government through violence and illegal means. According to the information we have and which is available to you, we are facing a concerted effort to intimidate and overthrow the government and the democratic institutions of this province through planned and systematic illegal action, including insurrection. It is obvious that those participating in this concerted effort completely reject the principle of freedom under the rule of law.

The Quebec Government is convinced that such powers are necessary to meet the present emergency. Not only are two completely innocent men threatened with death, but we are also faced with an attempt by a minority to destroy social order through criminal action; it is for those reasons that our government is making the present request.

The government is confident that, through such powers, it will be able to put an immediate stop to intimidation and terror and to ensure peace and security for all citizens.

Please accept, Mr. Prime Minister, my very best regards.

Robert Bourassa

The Right Honourable Pierre Elliott Trudeau,
Prime Minister of Canada,
House of Commons,
Ottawa

305

[Translation]

CITY OF MONTREAL
CANADA

Office of the Chairman
of the Executive Committee
15 October 1970

City Hall
The Right Honourable Pierre Elliott Trudeau, P.C., Q.C.,
Prime Minister of Canada,
Parliament Buildings,
Ottawa, Canada

Mr. Prime Minister,

The chief of the Montreal Police Service has informed us that the means available to him are proving inadequate and that the assistance of higher levels of government has become essential for the protection of society against the seditious plot and the apprehended insurrection in which the recent kidnappings were the first step.

We are forwarding as a matter of the utmost urgency the report describing the scope of the threat and the urgent need to reinforce the machinery to cope with it.

We ask for every measure of assistance the federal government may deem useful and desirable in order to carry out the task of protecting society and the life of citizens in this difficult period.

Lucien Saulnier   Jean Drapeau
Chairman of   Mayor of Montreal
the Executive Committee

Police Department   City of Montreal
Office of the Director   City Hall Annex
                                                   October 15, 1970

306 His Lordship Mayor Jean Drapeau
    Mr. Lucien Saulnier
    Chairman of the Executive Committee

Gentlemen:

An extremely dangerous subversive organization has gradually developed in Quebec over the last several years with a view to preparing the overthrow of the legitimate government by seditious means and eventually armed insurrection.

The recent kidnappings of a foreign diplomat and of a minister of the Crown of the province of Quebec by this organization are the first stage of its seditious plan and of activities leading directly to insurrection and the overthrow of the State.

Under the circumstances, the investigation which must be carried out by police authorities must necessarily include all the activities of the various cells of this seditious organization and should not be restricted, if it is not to be doomed to failure to a mere search for the individuals who have perpetrated the heinous kidnapping of the two (2) persons who are still being held.

The threat to our society from this seditious conspiracy that has swung into action in the last eleven (11) days, the investigation problems created by the internal structure of this organization divided into many small autonomous cells and the incredible amount of checking and searching imposed upon us have taxed and are taxing to the utmost the resources available to our Police Department.

The extreme urgency of obtaining concrete results in

uncovering all the ramifications of this organization and its seditious activities, the volume and complexity of evidence to be gathered and filed, finally the enormous task that we must carry out without resorting to unhealthy and undesirable repression, make it essential for higher levels of governments to come to our assistance if we are to succeed.

The slow pace of procedures and the restrictions resulting from the legal machinery and means at our disposal do not allow us to meet the situation.

Consequently, I recommend to the Executive Committee of the City to ask the higher levels of government to give us the means which in their estimation are suitable and useful to enable us to gather and submit the evidence necessary to protect society against the seditious and insurrectionary activities triggered by the kidnappings.

307

Very truly yours,
M. St-Pierre,
Director.

From Hansard, October 16, 1970

SOURCES

Tape-recorded interviews with the participants in the events provided a major source of material, as is apparent from the text. Contemporary newspaper accounts were relied on chiefly for Government statements, FLQ communiques, and for a general sense of reaction to events. These newspapers were The Toronto Star, The Globe and Mail, La Presse, Le Devoir, The Montreal Star, The Gazette, Le Petit Journal and Quebec Presse as well as the radio news and public affairs service of the Canadian Broadcasting Corp. The transcript of evidence presented to the Coroner's Court was used for details of the Laporte crime.

Chapter One *A Birthday Present for Mr. Cross*
Debates of the House of Commons, October 6, 1970. et seq.
The Blaster's Handbook

Chapter Two *Mon Cher Robert*
Evidence, Rugene Rossides, assistant secretary, Treasury Depart-

ment, before Committee on Government Operations, United States Senate.

Chapter Three *The Debate in Parliament: Non-Facts and Non-Decisions*
Debates of the House of Commons, October 5, 1970 to December 3, 1970.
From Sea Unto Sea, W. G. Hardy; Doubleday, 1959.

Chapter Four *Get Your Clothes On, You're Coming With Us.*
The Journal of a Prisoner of War; Gérald Godin, Quebec Presse, Nov. 1, 1970.

Chapter Five *The Law in Mothballs*
Ordeal by Fire, Canada 1910-1945, Ralph Allen, Doubleday Canada Limited, 1961.

308

Mr. Prime Minister, 1867-1964, Bruce Hutchison, Longmans Canada Limited, 1964.
Debates of the House of Commons, Special War Session, 1914
Debates of the House of Commons, 1919
Debates of the House of Commons, Special War Session, 1939
Debates of the House of Commons, 1945, 1946
War Measures Act, Revised Statutes of Canada, 1952, Chapter 288 as amended by The Canadian Bill of Rights, Statutes of Canada, 1960, Chapter 44. (Originally Statutes of Canada 1914 (5 George V) Chapter 2.)
Debates of the House of Commons, 1960
Proclamation of September 1, 1939, Canada Gazette (Extra) September 1, 1939.
The National Emergency Transitional Powers Act, 1945, Statutes of Canada, 1945, (9-10 George VI) Chapter 25, amended by Statutes of Canada, 1946, (10 George VI) Chapter 60.
Halsbury's Laws of England, 3rd Edition, Constitutional Law, War and Emergency.
Debates of the House of Commons, United Kingdom, August, 1939.
Attorney-General of Canada v. Alexander Brown Milling and Elevator Company, (1923) 4 Dominion Law Reports 443.
Re Price Brothers and the Board of Commerce of Canada, (1920) 60 Supreme Court Reports 265.
Reference Re Validity of Orders in Council respecting Japanese Canadians, (1947) 1 Dominion Law Reports 577 (Privy Council), affirming 1946 Supreme Court Reports 248, (Supreme Court of Canada).
Attorney-General of Canada v. Wheeler, (1944) 1 Dominion Law Reports 784.

Rex. v. Duquette 76 Canadian Criminal Cases 304.

R. V. Stewart 1940 Ontario Reports 178, (1940) 1 Dominion Law Reports 689.

In Re Beraneck (1915) 25 Dominion Law Reports 564, per Meredith C.J.C.P. at page 565.

Schenk v. United States, Baer v. United States 249 U.S. 47

Chapter Six *Big Fish Little Fish*
Debates of the House of Commons, October 26, 1970

Chapter Seven *Philosopher of the Revolution*
Negrès blancs d'Amerique; Pierre Vallières. Copyright, Ottawa, 1968 by Editions Parti Pris. English translation copyright 1970 by Monthly Review Press Inc. and McClelland and Stewart, Toronto.

Regina v. Vallières, Quebec Court of Appeal. September 23, 1969; Canadian Criminal Cases, 1970, Vol. 4, pg. 69

Chapter Eight *The Outlaw Organization*
Mr. Prime Minister 1867-1964, Bruce Hutchison, Longmans Canada Limited, 1964.

The Challenge to American Freedoms, Donald Johnson, University of Kentucky Press, 1963.

Bill Haywood's Book, The Autobiography of William D. Haywood, International Publishers, New York, 1929.

R. v. Felton, 25 Canadian Criminal Cases 207, 28 Dominion Law Reports 372

R. v. Trainor (1917) 1 Western Weekly Reports 415

The Trade Union Movement of Canada 1827-1959, Charles Lipton, Canadian Social Publications Limited, Montreal, 1966.

Debates of the House of Commons, 1919.

An Act to Amend the Criminal Code, Statutes of Canada 1919 (9-10 George V) Chapter 46.

Repealed Statutes of Canada 1936 (1 Edward VIII) Chapter 29.

Ordeal by Fire, Canada 1910-1945, Ralph Allen, Doubleday Canada Limited, 1961.

R. v. Russell (1920) 51 Dominion Law Reports 1

Winnipeg Free Press, March and April 1920.

Article "Section 98 Was Surely a Bad Law But We Might Draw a Better One" by B. K. Sandwell, Saturday Night, August 16, 1947.

R. v. Burk et. al. 57 Canadian Criminal Cases 290

R. v. Evans 62 Canadian Criminal Cases 29.

Debates of the House of Commons, 1936.

Defence of Canada Regulations, Consolidated 1942 as amended

thereafter by Orders in Council collected and indexed annually as Canada War Orders and Regulations, published by the Statutory Orders and Regulations Division of the Privy Council Office under the authority of P.C. 10793, Nov. 26, 1942.

Boucher v. The King, 1951 Supreme Court Reports 265.

Chapter Nine *The Four-Point Plan*
Zeckendorf: The autobiography of William Zeckendorf; with Edward McCreary; Holt, Rinehart and Winston, 1970.

Minutes of Proceedings and Evidence, Standing Committee on Broadcasting, Films and Assistance to the Arts, No. 14, November 27, 1969 et seq; Queen's Printer, Ottawa.

Chapter Ten *The Provisional Government Plot*
Debates of the House of Commons, October, 1970

310

Chapter Eleven *The Unjudicial Process*
R. V. Hicks, 1945 3 Western Weekly Reports 674

The Canadian Bill of Rights, Statutes of Canada, 1960, Ch. 44.

The Report of the Royal Commission Appointed under Order in Council, P.C. 411 of February 4, 1946 To Investigate the Facts Relating to and the Circumstances Surrounding the Communication, by Public Officials and Other Persons in positions of Trust of Secret and Confidential Information to Agents of a Foreign Power, June 27, 1946.

Report of Hon. Mr. Justice W. Roach "In the Matter of an Investigation under Section 46 of the Police Act R.S.O. 1950, Chapter 279, as to the arrest and detention of Robert Wright and Michael Griffin, 1954."

Detention Before Trial, Martin L. Friedland, University of Toronto Press, 1965.

Coroners Act, Statutes of Quebec 1967.

The Canada Evidence Act, Revised Statutes of Canada, 1952, Chapter 307.

R. V. Barnes, 36 Canadian Criminal Cases 40, and (1921) 61 Dominion Law Reports, 623.

Batary v. The Attorney General for Saskatchewan et. al. 1965 Supreme Court Reports, 465.

The Canadian Bill of Rights, Walter S. Tarnoposky, The Carswell Company Company Limited, 1966.

Chapter Twelve *The Cause is Always Noble*
Laurier, Joseph Schull, MacMillan of Canada, 1965.

Torazo Iwasaki v. The Queen, (1969) 1 Exchequer Court Reports 281, affirmed in Supreme Court of Canada at 1970, Supreme Court Reports 437.

The Japanese-Canadians, F. E. LaViolette, The Canadian Institute of International Affairs, 1945.

Debates of the House of Commons, 1942, 1943, 1945 and 1946.

Reference re Validity of Orders in Council respecting Japanese-Canadians (see Chapter five)

Canada War Orders and Regulations, 1942-1946.

Defense of Canada Regulations, 1941 and 1942.

Debates of the House of Commons, 1940.

R. v. Clarke (1941) 4 Dominion Law Reports 299.

Donald v. Hamilton Board of Education, 1945 Ontario Reports 518.

Re Fiegehen 1942 Ontario Weekly Notes 575.

The Canadian Forum, Monthly Column, "Civil Liberties" from December 1939 to December 1940 inclusive.

R. v. Burt 1941 Ontario Reports 35, (1941) 1 Dominion Law Reports 598

Re Sullivan 1941 Ontario Reports 417

The Canadian Forum, January 1941, Those Defence Regulations, G.M.A. Grube, Page 304.

Memorandum for the Members of the House of Commons on Democracy in Wartime and particularly on the Defence of Canada and Censorship Regulations, May 1940, The Civil Liberties Association of Toronto.

Report of the Committee on Civil Liberties, presented to the annual meeting of the Canadian Bar Association at Toronto, August 30, 1944. Vol. 22, 1944 Canadian Bar Review, page 598.

The Canadian Forum, November 1941, The Story of Samuel Levine, by Leopold Infeld, page 245.